TRANSNATIONAL CANADAS

TRANSNATIONAL CANADAS

Anglo-Canadian Literature and Globalization

KIT DOBSON

Wilfrid Laurier University Press

This book has been published with the help of a grant from the Canadian Federation for the Humanities and Social Sciences, through the Aid to Scholarly Publications Programme, using funds provided by the Social Sciences and Humanities Research Council of Canada. We acknowledge the support of the Canada Council for the Arts for our publishing program. We acknowledge the financial support of the Government of Canada through the Book Publishing Industry Development Program for our publishing activities.

 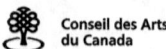 

Library and Archives Canada Cataloguing in Publication

Dobson, Kit, 1979–
    Transnational Canadas : Anglo-Canadian literature and globalization / Kit Dobson.

(TransCanada series)
Includes bibliographical references and index.
ISBN 978-1-55458-063-7 (paper)
ISBN 978-1-55458-165-8 (pdf)   ISBN 978-1-55458-668-4 (epub)

    1. Canadian literature (English)—20th century—History and criticism. 2. Canadian literature (English)—21st century—History and criticism. 3. Literature and globalization—Canada. 4. Transnationalism in literature. 5. Canadian literature (English)—Minority authors—History and criticism. I. Title. II. Series: TransCanada series

PS8071.D62 2009   C810.9'0054   C2009-900709-6

© 2009 Wilfrid Laurier University Press
Waterloo, Ontario, Canada
www.wlupress.wlu.ca

Cover photograph by Kit Dobson. Cover design by David Drummond. Text design by Daiva Villa, Chris Rowat Design.

No part of this publication may be reproduced, stored in a retrieval system or transmitted, in any form or by any means, without the prior written consent of the publisher or a licence from The Canadian Copyright Licensing Agency (Access Copyright). For an Access Copyright licence, visit www.accesscopyright.ca or call toll free to 1-800-893-5777.

CONTENTS

ACKNOWLEDGEMENTS vii

INTRODUCTION
Globalization and Canadian Literature ix

PART ONE
RECONSTRUCTING THE POLITICS OF CANADIAN NATIONALISM 1

INTRODUCTION TO PART ONE 3

CHAPTER ONE
Spectres of Derrida and Theory's Legacy 9

CHAPTER TWO
Ambiguous Resistance in Margaret Atwood's *Surfacing* 27

CHAPTER THREE
Nationalism and the Void in Dennis Lee's *Civil Elegies* 41

CHAPTER FOUR
Leonard Cohen's *Beautiful Losers* and the Crisis of Canadian Modernity 55

CONCLUSION TO PART ONE 67

PART TWO
INDIGENEITY AND THE RISE OF CANADIAN MULTICULTURALISM 69

INTRODUCTION TO PART TWO 71

CHAPTER FIVE
Critique of Spivakian Reason and Canadian Postcolonialisms 79

CHAPTER SIX
Multiculturalism and Reconciliation in Joy Kogawa's *Obasan*   91

CHAPTER SEVEN
Multicultural Postmodernities in Michael Ondaatje's *In the Skin of a Lion*   105

CHAPTER EIGHT
Dismissing Canada in Jeannette Armstrong's *Slash*   113

CONCLUSION TO PART TWO   135

PART THREE
CANADA IN THE WORLD   137

INTRODUCTION TO PART THREE   139

CHAPTER NINE
Transnational Multitudes   143

CHAPTER TEN
Mainstreaming Multiculturalism? The Giller Prize   157

CHAPTER ELEVEN
Global Subjectivities in Roy Miki's *Surrender*   169

CHAPTER TWELVE
Writing Past Belonging in Dionne Brand's *What We All Long For*   179

CONCLUSION TO PART THREE   201

CONCLUSION
Transnational Canadas   203

BIBLIOGRAPHY   211

INDEX   225

ACKNOWLEDGEMENTS

A book is a collaborative, even communal effort. This book would not exist without the communities that have contributed to it. Thanks are due to everyone who read all or part of this project since its humble beginnings in my doctoral work, my supervisor, Linda Hutcheon, and committee members Heather Murray and Daniel Heath Justice foremost among them. My gratitude goes out to those who have helped me work with this material in other ways: Len Findlay served as the external examiner of the original dissertation, and Smaro Kamboureli continues to be a hugely important supporter. They gave me invaluable feedback on aspects of my thinking and writing, as did (alphabetically speaking) David Chariandy, Chantal Fiola, Manina Jones, Maia Joseph, Lindy Ledohowski, Jody Mason, Ashok Mathur, Katherine McKittrick, Andrea Medovarski, Roy Miki, Caroline Rueckert, Jessica Schagerl, Rinaldo Walcott, and Kristen Warder. I am grateful, moreover, for the communities in which I have lived and worked while completing this project, and have nothing but gratitude for Melina Baum Singer, Allison Burgess, Sean Carrie, Anthony Collins, Rohanna Green, Em Harding, Krysta Harding, Anna Lidstone, Eli MacLaren, Elysha Mawji, Arti Mehta, and Archana Rampure. All of these people have helped my thinking and writing in one way or another, although any flaws that remain here are necessarily mine.

Earlier versions of portions of Part Three appeared in two installments in *Studies for Canadian Literature*; many thanks are due to the editors and readers of the journal. I am further indebted to my colleagues and mentors past and present in the Department of English at the University of Toronto, in the School of English and Theatre Studies at the University of Guelph, and in the Department of English at Dalhousie University, as well as to the Social Sciences and Humanities Research Council of Canada and the Killam Trusts. Wilfrid Laurier University Press deserves a great deal of gratitude for taking me on as a first-time, upstart author, Lisa Quinn in particular, and the feedback from my two anonymous readers at the press was invaluable.

Thanks are also very much due to my ever-supportive parents, Debbie and Keith, my sister, Beth, and my daughters, Alexandra and Clementine, both of whom arrived during the writing of this book. This book is dedicated to my indefatigable partner, Aubrey Hanson, who remains my most thorough and thoughtful critic, and a constant source of inspiration and conspiration.

INTRODUCTION

Globalization and Canadian Literature

In David Chariandy's 2007 novel, *Soucouyant*, the protagonist silences his black Caribbean mother's conversation with her own memories by insisting that "there are no ghosts" in the Scarborough, Ontario, neighbourhood in which they live.[1] In a sense, he is right: there have not been any ghosts in that mostly white society that they can recognize for themselves. The ghosts there are those of the white families and the Indigenous people who came before them. At the same time, the protagonist's mother, Adele, in her creeping dementia, is letting ghosts from her past in both Canada and Trinidad take on a life of their own. Trinidadian spirits like the vampiric soucouyant of the book's title are becoming, in Chariandy's narrative, part of the Canadian psychosocial landscape.

Chariandy's protagonist's words are a direct echo of ones spoken by the character Mr. D— in Susanna Moodie's 1852 *Roughing It in the Bush*. Mr. D—states famously that "there are no ghosts in Canada" because "the country is too new for ghosts."[2] Mr. D— means, of course, white ghosts, those of the settler community that is beginning to clear the lands through which Moodie travels. In a dialogue that David Chariandy was generous enough to conduct with me about his novel, he acknowledged the reference, suggesting that the line in his book "might cast considerable irony on the idea that the spaces now named Canada have no ghosts of their own."[3] Having ghosts to call one's own profoundly affects one's relationship to space in Canada. In SKY Lee's 1990 novel, *Disappearing Moon Café*, the characters who populate Vancouver's Chinatown call the whites that surround them "devils" and "ghosts."[4] These ghosts, belonging firmly in another world, remind the novel's Chinese and Chinese Canadian characters of their outsider status.

Canada's settlers spent a long time before these recent works populating the country with ghosts of their own. These ghosts, to borrow a concept for which Daniel Coleman has recently and intelligently argued, contributed to the construction of Canada as a country of "white civility."[5] This process intensified after 1951, when the Massey Commission found that despite a lengthy literary history including Moodie and other authors, "neither in French nor in English have we yet a truly national literature."[6] The subsequent years witnessed an intensification of the development of precisely such literatures, with the support of a growing series of institutions and bodies. It is at the point of such growth that this book begins its inquiry.

At the heart of *Transnational Canadas* lies the argument that, from a literary perspective, the nationalism of Canada in the 1960s and '70s that worked to consolidate this literature, and the multiculturalisms of the '80s, '90s, and new millennium that have sought to reformulate it through dismantling its ethnocentrism, have become conjoined with the world of globalization. While it was formerly popular to celebrate the nation as a bastion against globalization on the left, today it seems that the national and the global are, instead, interlocking scales of capital. The existing arguments that seek to read Canadian literature in relation to globalization or transnational studies have made inroads in discussions of Canadian literature but have not yet been articulated in depth. This study began, at least in part, over a feeling of dissatisfaction with statements such as the following by Stephen Henighan that

> the collective idea of Canada was demolished on November 21, 1988, when Canadians voted to subordinate our national project to the requirements of continental free-trade.... A nation-state erodes in a neo-liberal, free trade environment: dismantle the state and the nation washes away. Deprived of the abstract ideals of a nation, people return to the *Gemeinschaft*: their horizons

ever narrower, they vote for the Reform Party or the Bloc Québécois, or define themselves according to ethnicity rather than citizenship.[7]

Henighan's rhetoric simplifies many of the arguments of transnational studies, although I do want to emphasize that his writing is important and will be discussed further below. Yet there are several assumptions in the above passage: that his ideal of a collective Canada has ceased to exist (an assumption that evokes the spectre of George Grant, who made this argument a generation earlier), that "we" share a national project, that this national project is of necessity good — or better than a free trade environment — and that ethnic understandings of the self are necessarily static and bad. Henighan's logic is, moreover, imperfect: the Reform Party that has been subsumed into the currently governing Conservative Party was intensely neo-liberal in its economic policies, while the Bloc Québécois is intensely nationalistic — albeit with a different nationalism than that which Henighan appears to promote here.

This book therefore tries to fill the need to rescale Canadian literature in a global era. Canadians are experts at creating maps of the national landscape — Noah Richler's enthusiastic *This Is My Country, What's Yours: A Literary Atlas of Canada* is a recent good example — but there is an increasing need to map Canada's relationship to the discourses of globalization. Considering the question of a national literary community is fraught in an age in which corporations champion the erosion of state borders as a means of facilitating production and resource extraction. At the same time, the so-called war on terror is erecting new, racialized barriers that keep people from crossing these same state borders. Within Canada, recent debates about "reasonable accommodation" and difference parallel and are symptomatic of such global barriers. Accepting notions of national belonging for the sake of resisting capitalism, as Henighan seems to do, might mean not only an erasure of the historical divides between peoples, but also an erasure of how the nation intervenes in cultural production in this country. There is a need to think carefully about questions of belonging and subjectivity in the world of global capitalism.

Working with the theoretical terrain of the transnational, *Transnational Canadas* recontextualizes literature written in Canada since the period of cultural nationalism surrounding the 1967 centennial and examines its relationship to global politics as a means of unpacking problems of belonging and subjectivity. This book is not interested in rehashing the question of what it means to be a Canadian, but is interested instead in seeing what Canada's dominant modes of thinking mean for the possibilities for writing in this country. As such, it moves from its point of departure to consider the politics of writing in Canada that interrogates the transnational directly. It keeps in play discourses of the broad term "globalization," as well as "transnationalism," the latter of which is taken to highlight the ways in which national entities are criss-crossed by the global order. This book, as such, conducts an examination of the disruption and reinscription of Canadian nationalism that accompanied the rise of multicultural cultural productions in the '80s, '90s, and noughts. It examines Canada's contemporary, institutionalized form of literature and is interested in finding a way to look beyond the concept of solitudes while not buying into an easy concept of Canadian universality. It is interested in thinking about how writers are dealing with the problems that Canadians face as increasingly global citizens, and, conversely, in looking at how writing has been appropriated to a national project. In sum, *Transnational Canadas* examines the intellectual and creative conditions that have led to where Canada is today.

Margaret Atwood's *Survival*, as read by Roy Miki, afforded a second line of entry into these materials. *Survival*, published in 1972, is one of the key books of the period of cultural nationalism, one that continues to affect the popular reception of Canadian literature. Towards the end of that book, Atwood asserts that

> the tendency in English Canada has been to connect one's social protest not with the Canadian predicament specifically but with some other group or movement: the workers in the thirties, persecuted minority groups such as the Japanese uprooted during the war. English Canadians have identified themselves with Ban the Bombers, Communists, the F.L.Q., and so forth, but not often with each other—after all, the point of identifying with those other groups was at least partly to distinguish oneself from all the grey WASP Canadians you were afraid you might turn into.[8]

Miki criticizes Atwood's blanket statement for privileging what he calls "the normalizing power of English-Canadian nationalism" as she assumes that the self is a WASP.[9] Miki's diagnosis is apt, and yet the confidence with which Atwood asserts her idea that WASPishness is not a protest-worthy position seemed to be worth deeper investigation. Her generalization is a far cry from the Canadian literature and culture that is familiar today. In the years since *Survival* and dissident texts such as Leonard Cohen's *Beautiful Losers* (1966) and Atwood's earlier works, attempts to connect social protest with particular groups seem to have shifted with the valorization of texts written by writers of colour and with the increasing circulation of concepts of globalization or transnationalism.

With the proliferation of what has been called "minority" writing, the margins are used not only to identify an "other" to the nation, an other to "the Canadian predicament specifically" as Atwood puts it, but also to change the nation itself. This writing, while disrupting norms, recognizes that racial privilege persists and even proliferates, although the function of this writing may be changing anew in today's Canada. As global capitalism reconfigures the composition and demographics of Canada and the world, especially in the wake of the social and economic upheavals of 1989 and thereafter — the collapse of the Berlin Wall and the coming into effect of the original Canada–U.S. Free Trade Agreement and everything since — more people are able to articulate their own, distinct visions. These, in turn, present their own questions, as this book discusses in examining such discourses' relationship to the nation.

The disruption of the older, more centred nationalism that Atwood advocates in her thematic model — her confident identification of a national "we" — is key to the emergence of Canadian literature in the context of transnational studies. *Transnational Canadas* may begin by asking questions that derive from Atwood's analysis, but it moves towards tracing how the patterns that she identifies have shifted, leaving behind the texts of the centennial period and working towards the contemporary moment, one in which "we" become more complex. These shifts are neatly evoked by bpNichol's simple concrete poem engraved on the lane named for him in Toronto, "A / LAKE / A / LANE / A / LINE / A / LONE," pictured on the cover of this book. The development of the survival thesis, or Northrop Frye's well-known "garrison mentality," relies upon a naturalistic perspective on Canada, one that is embodied in the opening "lake" of Nichol's poem. Such a lake appears often in Canadian writing, taking on frightening dimensions in, for example, Atwood's own *Surfacing*, which is discussed below. The lake, however, shifts in Canadian writing to an increasingly urban perspective, evoked in the image of the "lane." Writing moves from the rural to the urban and in this process comes into contact with Canadian diversity, forcing a recognition of difference, recorded from the small towns of books like Fred Wah's biotext *Diamond Grill* to the forbidding Toronto of Dionne Brand's *In Another Place, Not Here*. These ideas are commonplace enough, and have been recounted in analyses of Canadian writing.

But this should not be seen as a simple lineage, and the relationship is not one always of literary parentage or an anxiety of influence. While Canadian writing passes from rural narratives of settlement and the outdoors to an increasingly privileged urban perspective, this movement is not a straight line. This is an expectation that Nichol simultaneously evokes and ruptures at the end of his poem. After evoking the "line" that flows from the lake to the lane, the final two lines, "A / LONE," conjure an image of solitude at the same time as they break the word "alone" in two. This break leaves the viewer with the word "lone," a word that also adjectivally connotes the lone pine that one might expect to see in the context of the solitary lake that begins the poem. The poem also comes back to the idea of solitude. The movement of writing in Canada from survival against nature and the other to the disruption of the garrison mentality in urban writing is not clear-cut. Canadian writing can still, however, be understood in a less linear manner through these common narratives as writers question the spaces in which they find themselves.

This tracery connects not only to the literature that *Transnational Canadas* studies, but also to changes in political and social thought. Intimately connected to the developments of a politically conscious transnational Canadian literature are changes in cultural theory since the 1960s, changes that shift towards an increasing focus on the transnational. This book develops a model for transnational studies that derives from the interconnections, overlaps, and debates between Marxism, poststructuralism, and postcolonial studies. These fields provide a theorized and politically engaged ground for transnational studies in Canada, particularly when refracted through the North American lens of indigeneity—following Len Findlay's call to "always indigenize" and the work of Taiaiake Alfred and Craig Womack on questions of sovereignty. *Transnational Canadas*, working through Marxist models of value and the capitalist drive towards colonization, rejects the reduction of cultural debates to an economic base. At the same time, it calls for a self-critical and responsible deconstructive politics, taking its cue from Jacques Derrida's later and now posthumous writings about Marx, sovereignty, and ethics. These are put to work in developments in transnational feminisms, especially

Gayatri Spivak's ongoing revisions of her stance on the subaltern, which are discussed in order to see shifts in her thinking since the publication of her most famous piece over twenty years ago.

Transnational studies itself, however, has emerged as a cultural field of its own most forcefully since Michael Hardt and Antonio Negri's controversial book *Empire*, published in 2000. Responses to that book and to its 2004 sequel, *Multitude*, have generated a broad discussion of transnational studies as a field. Hardt and Negri's perspective comes out of a more Deleuzian than Derridean postmodernity and European communism rather than the Anglo-German Marxism on which this book focuses in its early stages. Although useful, the manner in which Hardt and Negri hearken to an ultimately limited multitude in resistance to global capitalism is unsatisfactory upon close reading. While they attempt to respect the deconstructive disruption of metaphysics, they fall into a negotiation between the metaphysical and the decentred by calling for a politics of immanence. This is a politics in which the potential of human effort leads to breaking past the narrow politics of national or statist jurisdictions, but its articulation is unstable. While remaining an excellent perspective for debating what is to be done, their politics becomes one of universalism, and the growing critiques of their work as Eurocentric and neglectful of anti-sexist and anti-racist debates suggest limits to their work.

This book turns to aspects of transnational feminist theory, which, when working with Spivak's writing, has adopted a deconstructive approach. While the totalizing elements of Hardt and Negri's multitude is a tempting clarion call to arms, transnational feminism advocates, as Rey Chow puts it, "responsibly engaged rather than facilely dismissive judgments."[10] It is in this light that Canadian writing is read on a transnational scale. This writing is influenced by the nation and the state, but it also disrupts these structures when confronted with questions of the global. The nation is ambiguous. In this book's readings of, among other texts, Jeannette Armstrong's discussion of the Indigenous need to resist falling prey to Canada and the "slave markets of the corporations" in *Slash*,[11] and Roy Miki's *Surrender*, the ambivalence that governs cultural production is foregrounded, as is these texts' open-endedness towards difference.

Methodologically, this book develops its theoretical perspective in tandem with its analyses of literary works produced in Canada. It is, therefore, concerned not only with reading the later Derrida, Spivak, Hardt and Negri, and others. Rather, while reading their thinking helps to focus this book's consideration of the legacy of postmodernism and poststructuralism from a Marxist perspective in mainstream Canada in Part One, it also begins to articulate questions about the function of the nation and the nation-state in the contemporary world of postcolonialism and neo-imperialism. These become the questions that are examined in reading texts from the period of cultural nationalism in the 1960s and '70s in Part One, focusing upon Margaret Atwood's *Surfacing*, Dennis Lee's *Civil Elegies*, and Leonard Cohen's *Beautiful Losers*. These texts feed this book's reading of the postcolonial intervention into Marxist and poststructural theories in Part Two. This part is concerned with how these fields have provided the terrain for theorists of autonomy and agency such as Spivak to begin their work. Spivak's work on subaltern women is shifted towards North America in *Transnational Canadas*' readings of Indigenous theories about the concepts of sovereignty and nationhood. These seek agency for specifically situated peoples, but on a more collective scale than in Spivak's writing.

These postcolonial and Indigenous challenges connect with literary interventions into the nationalist mythos of Canada in Part Two. These undermine and rewrite the narratives of the nation formulated by the earlier generation. The rise and impact of Canadian multiculturalism is looked at critically, particularly in terms of how its discourses relate to Joy Kogawa's oft-taught book *Obasan*, Michael Ondaatje's *In the Skin of a Lion*, and Jeannette Armstrong's *Slash*. These interventions propel writing in Canada into confrontation with global flows, prompting this book's readings of Hardt and Negri's writing in Part Three in order to appraise how political and cultural theorists might conceptualize resistance to capitalism and the need for change. While this book is sympathetic to much of Hardt and Negri's analysis, their conclusions and methods offer grounds for concern. *Transnational Canadas* unpacks these problematics as a means of turning to the writings of transnational feminist thinkers. These debates, in turn, prompt the discussion in Part Three of the Giller Prize and Vincent Lam's *Bloodletting and Miraculous Cures*, Roy Miki's *Surrender*, and Dionne Brand's *What We All Long For*. These texts offer complementary and competing takes on what it means to maintain one's being under global capitalism, and they are turned to for their takes on the problems of understanding subjectivity and social change in the transnational world. This book, then, evolves as it goes, picking up theoretical tools in order to perform its work of untangling what it means to read writing produced in Canada in the global era.

The analyses of this book should be read as only one way of reading the shifts taking place in literary writing in Canada. *Transnational Canadas* makes an effort to connect its focal texts with others, both within a single writer's oeuvre and within broader literary communities. In so doing, it focuses upon both Canadian and non-Canadian sources, enacting in its criticism the very sorts of things it sees happening in literature in Canada today. Its drive towards texts coming from both home and abroad comes from a desire to create links between writers, books, and intellectual strains. This linking work seems precarious in an environment that segregates people from one another through the drive towards individualist consumption. Literature in the contemporary era is absolutely marked as a cultural product for such consumption, a fact that makes each work part of that individualizing process; recovering the connections and communities that underlie writing is important in this context.

This book also sees itself as furthering some of the earlier projects in Canadian literary criticism such as Frank Davey's *Post-National Arguments*, a book that ultimately relies on the nation to provide a political defence against capitalist globalization at a moment when the Canadian nation-state is adopting a globalist mentality. *Post-National Arguments* is, indeed, the most obvious precursor to this present work. Davey's well-known discomfort with both the national and the global side of the free trade debate signals a dawning awareness of the interpenetration of the two terms. Davey opts to support the nation in that book, but one wonders if he would do so in the same terms today. Instead of relying on the national as the grounds for discussion, *Transnational Canadas* is interested in seeing what happens when the transnational is taken to be the ground from which we begin discussions about literary production within a geopolitical space like Canada. This approach is a means of recognizing and coping with the global world system into which people are increasingly interpolated as citizens, refugees, undocumented migrants, or otherwise.

The central thesis of this book is, at its most reduced, that writing in Canada has become transnational. It is transnational in terms of its interests and its politics, and in terms of the publishing industry that supports it. Writing in Canada is concerned with crossing national borders thematically, just as it is concerned with marketing on a global scale. This transnational mindset can be seen in the writing, in Canada's cultural industries and cultural institutions, and in our methods of reading. It is important to look beyond the nation (without forgetting that it's still there) in order to rethink, rework, and resist what global capitalism has meant for those excluded from the dominant within nation-states, since the nation-state and neo-liberal models of globalization are ever more similar. A transnational mindset, however vexed, might play a role in resisting, for example, cynical deployments of difference as marketing tools in this country. In order to continue to conduct its political and cultural experiment, Canada needs the transnational, in all of its configurations, as a means of looking to different scales in confronting political and social problems.

Notes to Introduction

1. David Chariandy, *Soucouyant* (Vancouver: Arsenal Pulp, 2007), 113.
2. Susanna Moodie, *Roughing It in the Bush*, ed. Michael A. Peterman (New York: Norton, 2007), 178.
3. David Chariandy and Kit Dobson, "Spirits of Elsewhere Past: A Dialogue on *Soucouyant*," *Callaloo* 30.3 (2007): 816.
4. SKY Lee, *Disappearing Moon Café* (Vancouver: Douglas and McIntyre, 1990).
5. Daniel Coleman, *White Civility: The Literary Project of English Canada* (Toronto: U of Toronto P, 2006).
6. Government of Canada, *Royal Commission on National Development in the Arts, Letters, and Sciences: Report* (Ottawa: King's Printer, 1951), 223.
7. Stephen Henighan, *When Words Deny the World: The Reshaping of Canadian Writing* (Erin Mills, ON: Porcupine's Quill, 2002), 99.
8. Margaret Atwood, *Survival: A Thematic Guide to Canadian Literature* (Toronto: Anansi, 1972), 242.
9. Roy Miki, *Broken Entries: Race, Subjectivity, Writing* (Toronto: Mercury, 1998), 102.
10. Rey Chow, *Ethics After Idealism* (Bloomington: Indiana UP, 1998), 13.
11. Jeannette Armstrong, *Slash* (Penticton, BC: Theytus, 1985), 248.

PART ONE

RECONSTRUCTING THE POLITICS OF CANADIAN NATIONALISM

INTRODUCTION TO PART ONE

Madhava Prasad suggests in a study of postcolonial / Third World literature that

> literature, or a national culture in general, is one of the representational machineries that serve to consolidate the nation-state. Its historical emergence in Europe is tied to the rise of the primary capitalist nation-states, and in this sense literature is "national." Of course this claim is of little value in itself, but a Marxist theory of literature cannot begin anywhere else.[1]

This argument about the functioning of the nation-state holds true in important ways for Canadian literature around the centennial period. Since the Royal Commission on National Arts, Letters and Sciences released its report in 1951, the federal government of Canada has undertaken massive and long-term projects of fostering Canadian nationalism through policy and infrastructural mechanisms related to culture. Literature itself has become one of the important mechanisms of fostering national identity. The 1951 report, often referred to as the Massey Commission for its chair, Vincent Massey (who was later governor general of Canada) led to the implementation of a host of national projects whose wide-ranging effects continue to this day. Foremost from a cultural standpoint were the creation of the National Library of Canada in 1953, the founding of the Canada Council for the Arts in 1957, and the establishment of national television broadcasting in 1952. Other national projects were already afoot: the CBC had been established as a radio broadcaster by 1936, and the report bridged the transformation of the earlier Social Sciences Federation and the Federation of the Humanities into the Social Sciences and Humanities Research Council of Canada in 1978. These developments followed the recommendations of the commission's report, which, in turn, derived from the finding that the arts in Canada could be usefully promoted in order to develop national cohesion. Private ventures were developed in this environment, such as McClelland and Stewart's creation of the New Canadian Library series in the late '50s. This series continues to provide an affordable canon of Canadian writing for instructors and consumers of literature. The programs implemented as a result of the Massey Commission have contributed to Canadian literature's growth in the '60s and thereafter.

Part One of *Transnational Canadas* establishes preliminary aspects of transnational theory by examining tensions between Marxism and poststructuralism/postmodernism. It then examines three literary works that reflect both these issues and those of the Massey Commission and the surrounding cultural environment. It looks not only at ways in which texts work through questions of cultural nationalism, but also pays attention to how the readers of these texts have viewed such questions over time. These readerly shifts reflect Marxist and poststructural questions about the function of the sovereign state and the role of nationalism: Is the nation-state merely a part of a colonizing capitalist force, a part of the expansion of international markets that is necessitated by capitalism and, in the case of Canada, tied to fear of a loss of power to the United States? Can a national culture be used in order to secure stable markets at home? What role might literature play? If the world became an increasingly disjunctive world in the postmodern era, as Fredric Jameson argues, then what role does cognitive mapping within a national framework play in terms of creating a sense of belonging, no matter how impermanent or fleeting? What ends do these processes serve?

The phrasing above points to the directions that this book will pursue in subsequent chapters. It sees the national construction of selfhood that is encouraged by the federal government as one of consciously creating categories of identity that have the potential to be exclusive. This creation is mobilized in an effort to define Canada against its European forebears in England and France, as well as against the United States—and, also, against Canada's internally displaced First Nations. These acts of self-definition serve politically resistant purposes in the face of an ascendant postwar United States. At the same time, self-definition has not entailed definition by all Canadians and, moreover, has at times served to limit what the label of "Canadian" might mean. Its imposition on people who do not match the developing self-image of the nation can be tied to either assimilationist or exclusionary attitudes, in spite of the state's benevolent discourses of inclusion. For the present, however, *Transnational Canadas* is interested in how a cultural nationalist stance emerged as an important one for political resistance around Canada's centennial. Nationalism exists across the political spectrum in Canada today, but it is no longer a particularly radical or dissident position. Examining how discourses of nationalism shift in Canadian literature written around the centennial provides a means of reading how discourses of dissidence have shifted into an era defined by transnational concerns.

We might think about transnationalism or globalization in a wide variety of ways, of course, from Luddite rejection to an unquestioning celebration. The task of Part One is to establish a set of theoretical and political hypotheses against which to read Canadian writing from the period of the centennial celebrations of 1967. While this task is potentially an infinitely broad one, this book will focus upon a limited number of key texts. Specifically, this first part details and analyzes conflicts between Marxism and poststructuralism (and postmodernism) in relation to incipient globality as a means of approaching Canadian literary nationalism as an act of political resistance. This discussion sets up the chapters of Part One, but also the book's subsequent theoretical discussions.

Part One, then, works by setting Marxism and poststructuralism in opposition in order to uncover some of their potential commonalities. This juxtaposition illuminates the political struggles involved in questioning globalization from the left, particularly since the two fields have often been hostile to one another during the rise of globalization as a popular concept. Setting the fields into dialogue is intended to clarify discussions that have been strained, even though the project of reconciling the poststructural and Marxism has been underway since at least Michael Ryan's 1982 book *Marxism and Deconstruction*. The situation today, in which this debate has become less heated, might allow for these two fields to interact meaningfully. It is too easy to conclude, as Thomas Docherty did in 1990, that "the current postmodern condition is inimical to Marxism."[2] Chapter One begins with a consideration of Jacques Derrida's

Specters of Marx: The State of the Debt, The Work of Mourning, and the New International before moving on to Marxist critiques of the postmodern/poststructural nexus, especially those of Fredric Jameson and Terry Eagleton. The clashes between competing strains of theory ask vital questions about how best to deal with politics and culture at a time of rapid corporatization and media concentration, coming to different but not entirely incommensurate conclusions.

Chapter Two then addresses these concerns by examining the reception history of Margaret Atwood's *Surfacing*, one of her most popular and often-read novels — within Canada. The function of this reading is, in part, to examine in greater depth Atwood's arguments in *Survival*, which was published in the same year as *Surfacing*, 1972. Her creation of the dissenting Canadian as a grey WASP suggests the implicit racialization of the national subject in Canada. This construct connects also to this subject's link to American culture, which is a prime focus in *Surfacing*. The novel's readership, in turn, displays a shifting and sometimes uneasy relationship with these threads of the text.

Dennis Lee's 1972 *Civil Elegies*, which is discussed in Chapter Three, allows the uncovering of some of the poststructural workings that underpin the Canadian—American dialectic in *Surfacing*. *Civil Elegies* focuses upon similar issues to Atwood's book, but works them through with a rhetoric that is heavily imbued with the concepts of George Grant's *Lament for a Nation*. Grant's 1965 work is a key text, one that underlies the nationalism of both Lee's and Atwood's writing. Lee reworks Grant's nationalist rhetoric with a metaphysical vocabulary that brings the tensions of Canadian modernity to the fore.

If *Surfacing* and *Civil Elegies* offer relatively coherent images of a nationalist longing or nostalgia, Leonard Cohen's 1966 proto-postmodern novel, *Beautiful Losers*, upsets the narratives of the nation being constructed around the centennial even while it works closely with them. Here the record of critical readings demonstrates substantial shifts in reception over time. This reading, which looks at ways in which the text shatters the nationalist mythos and displays the risks of nationalist longing through its unnamed narrator and the controversial F., is filtered by previous ones, which suggest the vitality and complexity of debates surrounding the politics and policies of cultural nationalism in Canada around the centennial period.

Notes to Introduction to Part One

1 Madhava Prasad, "On the Question of a Theory of (Third) World Literature," *Dangerous Liaisons: Gender, Nation, and Postcolonial Perspectives*, ed. A. McClintock et al. (Minneapolis: Minnesota UP, 1997), 153.
2 Thomas Docherty, *After Theory: Postmodernism/Postmarxism* (London: Routledge, 1990), 205.

CHAPTER ONE

Spectres of Derrida and Theory's Legacy

The goal of this chapter is to begin to develop a genealogy for transnational studies from its legacies in Marxism and postmodernism. Postmodernism has been declared by Linda Hutcheon to be "a thing of the past,"[1] one that can now start to be historicized. The most apparent theoretical successor to postmodernity is the era of globalization, transnationalism, Empire, or neo-imperialism, terms that compete and depend upon one's reading of the competing strains of theory. The competition between the strains, however, ensures that no single, clear, successive movement can easily establish a hegemonic relation over the rest. These are all perhaps more rightly considered to be aspects of geopolitics than capital-T Theory, and the future has to be determined. What seems clear is that questions of the global predominate. These turn on questions of time and space, reconfigured to new, larger scales. How, politically, we are to assess this moment of war, environmental destruction, and economic change is ambivalent at best. The most prudent critic will judge at present that there is "in the current globalization both a threat and an opportunity,"[2] though where these threats and opportunities lie remains unsolved.

This examination of the transnational begins with a focus upon the Marxist legacy. Marxism's demise has long been prophesied, as Jacques Derrida recalls in *Specters of Marx*. At the same time, Marxism returns, again and again, haunting the present and creating openings into the future. Marxism is a crucial opening point not merely because of its politics and its continued spectral presence, but also because it has, since its inception, been directly interested in the transnational. *The Communist Manifesto* theorized the overthrow of the nation-state in the rise of the class-free global communist society. Karl Marx and Friedrich Engels write in *The Communist Manifesto* that "the bourgeoisie has through its exploitation of the world market given a cosmopolitan character to production and consumption in every country."[3] The imbalance in capitalist economics, with its increasing concentration of wealth in the hands of few capitalists whose exploits spread across the globe, creates for Marx and Engels the conditions for global communism to ensue through the unification of the proletarian working classes. The overthrow of the bourgeois classes and the rise of communism, contend Marx and Engels, have the following results: "the exploitation of one individual by another is put an end to" just as "the exploitation of one nation by another will also be put an end to."[4] That is, the elimination of the nation-state as a political model under communism, for them, ends antagonisms on a global scale, just as the demise of the bourgeois classes ends individual oppressions.

Marxism has, then, been since its inception a utopian theory of globalization. This utopian space has an imagined cultural reality for Marx and Engels, one that they see emerging through the rise of a genuine "world literature." This literature first emerges via the spread of bourgeois exploitation, in its elimination of national barriers through the spread of industrial capitalism.[5] The determination of culture by economics in Marxist theory, summed up in the famous dictum that material conditions determine consciousness, is reflected in the adoption of an international or postnational cultural stance in literature. This literary and cultural state of affairs is concurrent for them with the rise of transnational capitalism.[6] This cultural postnationality becomes, in turn, one goal of the communist project. The exploitations of transnational capitalism, via colonialism, become the incipient means of the achievement of communism.

This is one aspect of Marxist theory that Derrida notes in *Specters of Marx*, the most explicitly anti-capitalist of his works and his most thorough engagement with Marxism. "Communism was essentially distinguished from other labor movements by its *international* character," he notes, going on to state that "no organized political movement in the history of humanity has ever presented itself as *geo-political*, thereby inaugurating the space that is now ours and that today is reaching its limits, the limits of the earth and the limits of the political."[7] The intersection of Derrida and Marx in the former's reading of the latter thus becomes one possible starting point for theorizing transnational studies.

This intersection may be useful in the face of state socialisms that have failed to live up to Marx and Engels's theories, as well as in light of the repression of communist movements in much of the world. The dialectical and inevitable processes that were said to lead to communism have been seriously challenged by the shortcomings of socialist experiments, leading to widespread rejection of communism itself. But the collapse of communist and socialist states at the end of the twentieth century did not necessarily signal inevitable cultural progressions, although the history of the end of the century has required a rethinking of Marxist thought. One influential rethinking has posited capitalism as the teleological endpoint of human development. In the 1991 book *The End of History and the Last Man*, Francis Fukuyama declared that (hu)mankind had reached its highest achievement in liberal democratic capitalism. Fukuyama positioned himself as an heir to Marx's method of analysis—which asserted that the internal contradictions of capitalism would lead to its eventual and inevitable demise and the rise of communism—while refuting Marx's political goals. Fukuyama, a Republican adviser and one-time member of the conservative RAND think-tank, read the fall of the Berlin Wall as evidence that Marx's theories were not simply wrong, but, rather, that history was unfolding to its end with the triumph of capitalism. For Fukuyama, the American triumph over its Cold War adversaries suggested that dialectical history finds its end in global capitalism and democratic liberalism. The only remaining details are those of the universal implementation of this system. Fukuyama granted that inequities persist on a global scale, but he reduced these to simple detractions from the fact that global equity is arriving specifically through capitalist liberalism. In doing so, Fukuyama revived Hegel's conception of history as a process that finds its conclusion in perfectability, a framework that returns to an idealist model rather than the materialist framework upon which Marx built his work.[8]

Fukuyama's premise and somewhat odd claim to a Marxist inheritance come under fire in *Specters of Marx*. Derrida grants that the end of the Cold War and contemporary events may, indeed, signal the terminus of a "*certain* concept of history" rather than history itself.[9] That is, "where history is finished," *pace* Fukuyama, Derrida finds that "the historicity of history begins," and this new historicization, which looks beyond Fukuyama's (and Hegel's and Marx's) "determined concept of man," with endpoints and goals, can finally promise an emancipation, one that is conceived "as *promise* and not as onto-theological or teleo-eschatological program or design."[10] Instead of a history that looks for a specific endpoint or perfection, Derrida advocates one founded on process, on the ongoing work of a time to come. For Derrida this historicity and emancipatory potential "is the condition of a re-politicization" that is necessary during the rise of transnational capitalism and continued incursions of power into ever-new reaches of global and individual autonomy.[11] Fukuyama becomes Derrida's target in his discourse against the death knells sounded over the corpus of Marxist thought, and he calls Fukuyama's writing simply the most successful "new gospel...on the subject of the death of Marxism as the end of history."[12] Accusing Fukuyama of elaborate "philosophical naïveté" and sheer crudeness in discounting the range of contemporary and ongoing global iniquities from his calculus of neoliberal perfection,[13] Derrida discusses the drive towards what he sees as Fukuyama's Christian eschatology as a reiteration of the desire to reach an historical goal, be it apocalyptic, utopian, communist, or liberal capitalist.

As much as Fukuyama's premise is misguided, some possibility seems to remain therein for Derrida: the end of the Cold War does signal a shift. For one, the end of the Cold War has come to signal the end to any effective notion of an "outside" to capitalism. The system becomes total, and alternatives are readily discounted. There is no longer, in a Derridean sense, anything outside of the text of capitalist thinking. Romantic notions of literature or culture as being located outside of the system of economic exchange need to be shattered in this environment. But this need not signal the end of the possibility of change or, indeed, of transforming capitalism and social relations. For Derrida, the end of the Cold War could come instead to signal an end to any centred or dialectical conceptualization of history, with all of the teleological certainties attached to such models. The potential for reformulating history is then opened up: the end of this "*certain* concept of history" allows for the theorization of history to move beyond diachronic analyses of cause and effect, permitting events instead to unfold and proceed without strict reference to origins and goals. This perspective creates the possibility for opening the present up to change beyond that which the ravages of history might otherwise make available. Goals and endpoints are always contestable, and rethinking what history might mean—and how, indeed, it might mean—becomes an important task, as we are asked to consider ways in which we might create futures that can change the logic of that which has preceded us.

At the same time as *Specters of Marx* rejects a Marxist dialectic in its conceptualization of history, it becomes a key work for its discussion of the necessity of Marxism in the contemporary world. Derrida's frequent identification in popular academic thought and Marxist theory as an apolitical theorist makes him seem at first to be an unlikely defender of Marx. But the unlikeliness of Derrida's intervention makes it noteworthy. Derrida suggests that the Marxist inheritance in his other work should be seen as implicitly and deliberately avoided because, for him, Marxist thought has for too long "been welded to an orthodoxy" with which he found himself unable to agree.[14] Nevertheless, *Specters of Marx* is a significant departure from Derrida's earlier writing, and it can be seen as the keystone to the political turn in Derrida's later thought. It is noteworthy as a gesture of solidarity, coming at a time when, Derrida states, theorists and pundits in the West have been particularly keen to declare that Marx's ideas are dead. But "after the end of history," Derrida notes, Marx's "spirit comes by *coming back* [revenant], it figures both a dead man who comes back and a ghost whose expected return repeats itself, again and again."[15] That is, the anxious desire to expel Marx in light of contemporary political changes figures precisely his continued influence, the anxiety that he and his political project might return, again and again. Derrida suggests that "at a time when a new world disorder is attempting to instill its neo-capitalism and neo-liberalism, no disavowal has managed to rid itself of all of Marx's ghosts. Hegemony still organizes the repression and thus the confirmation of a haunting."[16] The organized repression, which Derrida identifies with Freud's triumphant phase of mourning, is a sign of the continued importance of Marx's ideas, and Derrida seeks to uncover their utility to a deconstructive politics in the context of global capitalism.

For Derrida, the spectre, both that of Marx and in general, becomes an image of undecidability between presence and absence. We might think of the "absences" of ghosts in Moodie and Chariandy that signal very important presences. The spectre is both a physical entity and one that is dead or absent, one whose effect is undoing, Derrida states, the opposition "between actual, effective presence and its other."[17] Marx, despite his literal demise and the collapse of state communisms, remains a potent figure, one whose presence is undeniable. Rather than being ontologically present or absent, Marx exists somewhere in between, and Derrida playfully introduces the concept of "hauntology" to deal with the persistence of this spectral Marx whose death is everywhere celebrated. Given his continued presence, Derrida states that "it will be more and more a fault, a failing of theoretical, philosophical, political responsibility" not to read Marx, especially because "no text in the tradition seems as lucid [as the *Communist Manifesto*] concerning the way in which the political is becoming worldwide, concerning the irreducibility of the technical and the media in the current of the most thinking thought."[18] Retaining a "certain spirit" of Marx is thus a means of ensuring continued political responsibility in the present and into the future, a future in which not only will the ghost of Marx persist, but now Derrida's own ghost will haunt metaphysics.

Attending to the Marxist legacy is therefore central to constructing a field of transnational studies and will inflect considerations of Canada's national productions around the centennial. The spirit of Marx that Derrida promotes is important for what is rejected from earlier Marxist orthodoxies, especially the dialectical materialism that Fukuyama transforms into a conservative neo-Hegelianism. Building on Maurice Blanchot's identification of three strains of Marxism in the Marxist inheritance, Derrida stresses the "radical and necessary *heterogeneity*" of that inheritance.[19] This reading permits Derrida to formulate a spirit of Marx that dispenses with aspects of the Marxist tradition(s) while retaining others. It is specifically the clash between traditions that can allow for a new spirit of Marx, one that remains open to the future and its alterity. For Derrida, "heterogeneity opens things up, it lets itself be opened up by the very effraction of that which unfurls, comes, and remains to come—singularly from the other."[20] Derrida's spirit of Marx is always plural and disunified, even as he identifies what are for him the most useful aspects of Marx's theory for dealing with globalization.

Derrida's heterogeneous Marx has certain desirable traits. For Derrida, "Marxism remains at once indispensable and structurally insufficient" because

> it is still necessary *but* provided it be transformed and adapted to new conditions and to a new thinking of the ideological, provided it be made to analyze the new articulation of techno-economic causalities and of religious ghosts, the dependent condition of the juridical at the service of socio-economic powers or States that are themselves never totally independent with regard to capital.[21]

This is a Marxism refracted through the critical theory of the later twentieth century, a Marx combined not only with transnational scholarship on economics, but also with the conceptualization of the disciplinary society of biopolitics derived from Foucault's work and more recently discussed by critics such as Giorgio Agamben, Achile Mbembe, and Michael Hardt and Antonio Negri. For Agamben, the politicization of what he terms "bare life," life reduced to its basic elements, "constitutes the decisive event of modernity and signals a radical transformation of political philosophical categories of classical thought," without which "the development and triumph of capitalism would not have been possible."[22] Derrida's "techno-economics" is tied in Agamben's thought to new ideologies of being, as the socio-economically determined juridical realm is expanded to incorporate all aspects of physical being into the category of the political. These aspects of life are in turn implicated in capitalism as part of its own process of expansion. The colonization of ever-new markets within the physical body comes as a response to the diminishing of external markets, given the nearly exhausted possibility for capitalist exploitation to occur at the margins of today's largely colonized globe. For Derrida, Marxist thought remains vital because it responds to the struggles of technological change. The impact of technology on capital and the social being of biopoliticized humans are now interpolated into the Marxist mix. This opening up of Marx's thought, Derrida states, requires a voiding of Marxist science, specifically its "messianic eschatology."[23] That is, while Derrida seeks to retain Marxism by adding an analysis of contemporary biopolitics, he seeks to rid it of any totalizing, ideological, and underpinning attempt to discover the ideal, transhistorical communist state.

This Marxism leads to a strategy in which deconstruction emerges as an insufficient project. Derrida seeks to distinguish his spectre of Marx from what could be called...a deconstruction, there where the latter is no longer simply a *critique* and where the questions it poses to any critique and even to any question have never been in a position either to identify with or especially to oppose symmetrically something like Marxism, the Marxist ontology, or the Marxist critique.[24]

That is, deconstruction without critique or positioning, a deconstruction void of responsibility towards politics, can be distinguished from the spirit of Marx that Derrida follows. In this respect, Derrida answers some of the legion of critics who have seen his work as politically lacking because deconstruction has been considered a merely disruptive analytic tool.[25] A specific line of inquiry, an openness to the future and to the possibility for emancipation along the lines conceived of by Marx, becomes crucial to the thinking of a deconstructive politics of responsibility. Deconstruction reveals flaws in existing structures, but it does not, or even cannot, in and of itself offer a political alternative in the manner of Marxism. Adopting a "spirit of Marx" in one's deconstructive endeavours, Derrida posits, offers a possible corrective.

Derrida's insistence on the category of the undeconstructible becomes, as a result of the emphasis that he places on the politics of deconstruction, a crucial juncture. Derrida seeks to distinguish what he sees as undeconstructible messianism, a messianism of open-ended hope, from any eschatological meanings that it might contain, be they scientific or religious. "What remains irreducible to any deconstruction," Derrida argues, is "a certain experience of the emancipatory promise; it is perhaps even the formality of a structural messianism, a messianism without religion, even a messianic without messianism, an idea of justice."[26] He claims that this messianic promise is one that he "will never be ready to renounce," especially the Marxist "emancipatory and *messianic* affirmation," a promise of a justice to come at some undetermined future time.[27] Derrida argues that the future, since it has not yet arrived, is undeconstructible, and that we can, therefore, place our hopes for emancipation in a justice that is yet to come. This justice is, Marx and Engels argue in *The Communist Manifesto*, inevitable, but the forms that it will take and the time of its arrival necessarily remain deferred into the future. This is a messianism that does not await the Messiah, since the Messiah would be unrecognizable in this context. What remains universal, if anything, is the concept of Marxist emancipation, but this remains an open formulation.

The direction that this open, messianic future might take is that of what Derrida terms a "new International," one that steers away from the party lines of earlier socialist Internationals. This portion of *Specters of Marx* constitutes its most overt political program. Derrida notes that the international is already an aspect of contemporary society, as the law shifts to an increasingly international stage. He is, however, cautious about the direction of this law, and therefore suggests that "international law should...include...the *worldwide* economic and social field, beyond the sovereignty of States,"[28] rather than dealing with interactions between nation-states. Derrida's own International looks towards such non-statist political interventions, and requires a lengthy quotation. For Derrida, the new International is

> a link of affinity, suffering, and hope, a still discreet, almost secret link, as it was around 1848, but more and more visible, we have more than one sign of it. It is an untimely link, without status, without title, and without name, barely public even if it is not clandestine, without contract, "out of joint," without coordination, without party, without country, without national community (International before, across, and beyond any national determination), without co-citizenship, without common belonging to a class. The name of the new International is given here to what calls to the friendship of an alliance without institution among those who, even if they no longer believe or never believed in the socialist-Marxist International, in the dictatorship of the proletariat, in the messiano-eschato-logical role of the universal union of the proletarians of all lands, continue to be inspired by at least one of the spirits of Marx or of Marxism...and in order to ally themselves, in a new, concrete, and real way, even if this alliance no longer takes the form of a party or of a workers' international, but rather of a kind of counter-conjuration, in the (theoretical and practical) critique of the state of international law, the concepts of the State and nation, and so forth: in order to renew this critique, and especially to radicalize it.[29]

This passage offers a non-totalizing form of political universalism, one that lacks a reliance upon a single ideology, or even upon any strict Marxism as such—but that seems to Derrida to be present in globalization. He does not envisage emancipation in this climate through, for example, totalizing national struggles: "like those of the blood," he states, "nationalisms of native soil not only sow hatred, not only commit crimes, they have no future, they promise nothing even if, like stupidity or the unconscious, they hold fast to life."[30] While critics have alleged that such a rejection of nationalism is too simple, Derrida's model does not allow for regional insistences upon difference that would separate instead of welcome the other.[31] Difference is to be recognized, but that recognition involves an open reception of change and its possibility, which Derrida does not see as viable within national constructs. Instead, Derrida's spirit of Marx enables politics to coalesce around a desire for change, one that hovers about the old Marxist concerns, but that does not rely upon Marx himself. For Derrida, the key to his International as a politics is the retention of openness towards the future. Openness towards this temporal other enables a politics of hospitality or a politics of friendship, and a continued possibility, for example, for an anti-racist future in which the other can be embraced. Difference will persist, even under erasure, and any universalism can be deconstructed; the possibility for the future lies for Derrida instead in the opportunity to recognize difference and incorporate it into political alliances. This openness constitutes, for Derrida, the possibility of politics itself.

Derrida's Marx is, then, as Marx himself claimed to be, not a Marxist at all. Derrida cites the famous Marxist joke in *Specters of Marx*:

> what is certain is that I am not a Marxist, as someone [Marx] said a long time ago, let us recall, in a witticism reported by Engels. Must we still cite Marx as an authority in order to say "I am not a Marxist"? What is the distinguishing trait of a Marxist statement? And who can still say "I am a Marxist"?[32]

The claim for a prominent, central relationship with Marxism does not necessitate, Derrida points out, that he identify himself as a Marxist. *Specters of Marx* is thereby evidence of a deconstruction that is engaged at a level of politics that Marxists have often denied Derrida. Most important, perhaps, is that this deconstruction posits a world stage on which politics increasingly takes place, but does not seek to efface difference in a politics of vague inclusivity. As this book's reading of transnationally oriented Canadian literatures emerges, it will be important to retain a simultaneous perspective of recognizing difference while welcoming it, including it but neither reducing it to a one-dimensional human sameness (as, this book contends, popular notions of multiculturalism in Canada sometimes do), nor excluding it through a dogmatic insistence upon its irreducibility. *Transnational Canadas* will be, increasingly, concerned with concepts of subjectivity and belonging in Canada, and this twin process of open-ended inclusion and active disruption will remain key for reading difference in ways that are neither exoticizing nor universalizing. In the undecidability between human presence and absence, and in the unerasable, irreducible difference between human subjects, contemporary politics can emerge as a field in which global exchanges need not be administered through doctrinarian capitalist imperialisms. Derrida makes this claim at some length in *The Other Heading*:

> if it is necessary to make sure that a centralizing hegemony (the capital) not be reconstituted, it is also necessary, for all that, not to multiply the borders, i.e., the movements [*marches*] and margins [*marges*]. It is necessary not to cultivate for their own sake minority differences, untranslatable idiolects, national antagonisms, or the chauvinisms of idiom. Responsibility seems to consist today in renouncing neither of these two contradictory imperatives. One must therefore try to *invent* gestures, discourses, politico-institutional practices that inscribe the alliance of these two imperatives, of these two promises or contracts: the capital and the a-capital, the other of the capital.[33]

That is, politics need to be conducted, at least in Derridean thought, through an exchange between the capital and the a-capital, an exchange that might modify each (perhaps beyond the centre-margin model upon which Derrida relies) but that would not deny their difference. The undermining of the centred Western subject is key to this concept of the political, and the recognition of the decentred nature of human society that follows from that undermining. This recognition will enable a depiction of the contemporary moment of writing in Canada, as well as those that led up to it.

Derrida's Marxism, not surprisingly, has had a number of detractors. Derrida notes that "it is easy to imagine why we will not please the Marxists" in *Specters of Marx*,[34] and there are real difficulties. For a number of Marxist critics, Derrida's revision of Marx — and deconstruction in general — is an impediment to political agency or revolution. Marxist reactions to deconstruction range from cautious optimism to downright hostility, perhaps best exemplified by Terry Eagleton, who decries *Specters of Marx* as "the ultimate post-structuralist fantasy" in its discussion of what he characterizes as "a promise which would betray itself in the act of fulfillment, a perpetual openness to the Messiah who had better not let us

19

down by doing anything as determinate as coming."[35] Eagleton's skepticism arises for a number of reasons, one of which derives from a conflation of several Derridean categories. In particular, poststructuralism appears to have shifted in some Marxist readings from a set of methodologies for analysis to being how the world itself is thought to be. This latter point is, however, more rightly aligned with the postmodernism of theorists such as Jean Baudrillard. That is, while poststructural deconstruction is a means of opening up layers of sedimented cultural meanings for reinvestigation, society has begun to seem increasingly deconstructed *avant la lettre*, as the deterritorializations and decentrings of contemporary capitalism have changed how critics perceive the (post-) postmodern world. Rather than providing tools of analysis, then, Derrida's thought, in readings such as Eagleton's, provides an impetus towards the nihilistic apoliticism of contemporary capitalism.[36] This appearance is questionable, but the overlap between poststructuralism and postmodernism has become an historical accretion from which we probably cannot escape.

Fredric Jameson's now-classic *Postmodernism, or, The Cultural Logic of Late Capitalism* is a Marxist analysis that can more usefully be read as a counterpoint to *Specters of Marx*.[37] Jameson asserts that a "weakening of historicity" is one of the "constitutive features of the postmodern," a concern that is similar to Derrida's reading of Fukuyama.[38] Jameson goes on to describe what he sees as the "search-and-destroy mission of poststructuralism that finds traces and contaminations of the diachronic" in order to deconstruct or reject them.[39] That is, for Jameson, history itself is jettisoned by the postmodern and poststructural, leaving the present to grapple with the means of situating itself in spatial terms. This grappling, Jameson suggests, should be conducted through projects of cognitive mapping. While Jameson highlights the late twentieth-century reconsiderations of historical meaning and narrative—from Foucault's genealogical searches to Hayden White's recognition of the narrative aspects of Western history—this reconsideration does not necessarily lead to an outright rejection of the term "history" itself. Linda Hutcheon has suggested, in contrast, that "history is not made obsolete; it is, however, to be rethought—as a human construct."[40] A rejection of history characterizes some portions of the postmodern and poststructural, but this need not necessarily be the case. Foucault, Derrida, and others are intensely, even anxiously involved with questions of history, proposing more nuanced concepts than earlier teleologies. While history and historicism become fragmented in late twentieth-century thought, it need not follow that historical thinking itself has been jettisoned—except, perhaps, for the more totalizing form upon which Jameson focuses. Derrida's "*certain* concept of history" in *Specters of Marx* is perhaps that which Jameson is observing the disruption of—an historical way of thinking modelled on dialectics, with the formal linearity advocated in earlier Marxist thought that theorized its way to an inevitable revolution.

Jameson is concerned with these questions of history. One of his primary concerns is that because "personal identity is itself the effect of a certain temporal unification of past and future with one's present," the dissolution of linear or totalized versions of history leads to a breakdown of "biographical experience or psychic life."[41] Jameson's insistence upon the unified subject with a stable identity has, however, been seen as a potential limit to agency for theorists who emphasize, for example, the hybrid postcolonial subject that will turn up again in Part Two of this book, or subjectivities that cannot be reduced to such positions. That said, his concern over the psychic life of the postmodern world is certainly appropriate. In particular, he worries that "we do not yet possess the perceptual equipment to match [the] new hyperspace" of technologized late capitalism, and sets out the goal of cognitively mapping the present as a means of maintaining a foothold for politics.[42] This project of mapping, in turn, reflects Jameson's earlier and well-known exhortation in *The Political Unconscious* to "always historicize."[43] Mapping the present is also a means of connecting it to the past.

Jameson's take on the collapse of history requires him to rethink the Marxist insistence upon the revolution in a manner that runs parallel to Derrida's thinking about the new International. Discussing Marx's legacy, Jameson notes that

> Marx powerfully urges us to do the impossible, namely, to think this development [the rise of capitalism] positively *and* negatively all at once; to achieve, in other words, a type of thinking that would be capable of grasping the demonstrably baleful features of capitalism along with its extraordinary and liberating dynamism simultaneously within a single thought.[44]

Capitalism, in other words, is both a beneficial development and a harmful shift based upon relations of exploitation. But Marx never advocates a return to a feudal past in response. An intelligent response to capitalism involves theorizing a way through its structures. The same holds true in the era of transnational capitalism. The challenge is to think *through* capitalism rather than simply *against* it. Such theorization, in turn, runs up against the problem of the new in postmodern thought, as Jameson notes, granting that "the very category of the new...loses its meaning and becomes itself something of a modernist survival" in the light of postmodern disruptions of ideas of change.[45] That is, while the postmodern may itself have been seen as new, the deconstruction of oppositions that accompanies it disrupts that very idea of newness. The new is founded in the old; our now well-worn practices of bricolage resurrect the past in the present at every turn. This failure of the concept of the new, Jameson goes on to state, challenges "Revolution itself, in the sense in which its concept once embodied the ultimate vision of the Novum become absolute."[46] Under what Jameson characterizes as the postmodern—and accepting the challenge to teleological thinking as irreparably bound to an ideology of "progress"—the revolution as a concept itself needs to be rethought, since change no longer inaugurates the utterly new. The revolutionary impulse to create change needs to be rethought; what, exactly, does revolution mean in the current era? In its place, it may be more appropriate to think about transformative changes that respond to the material confusion of the postmodern era, Jameson suggests, creating linkages that foster a leftist politics.

A deconstructive Marxism, then, or one that responds to late capitalism, may be one that relies upon a questioning of history and historicity. These are processes that have been at work in Canadian literature, especially in works that display what Linda Hutcheon has termed historiographic metafiction—that is, texts that display an overt self-consciousness in telling historically derived stories. Hutcheon sees such patterns as constitutive of Canadian postmodernism and arising in the period around the centennial that I will be discussing in the next chapters. It is, however, important to note that at political, theoretical, and literary levels, deconstructive historical thinking is being challenged anew. Jameson has revised his position on the ahistoricism of the present moment, discussing in 2002's *A Singular Modernity* the manner in which Western society has been regressing into modernity. Its understanding of history is one important aspect thereof. Similarly, Slavoj Žižek has noted that the events of September 11, 2001, have revealed that "America's 'holiday' from history was a fake."⁴⁷ By this he indicates the "end of history" narrative, but this critique extends to postmodern and poststructural thinking on historicism. If indeed this is the case, and the West has returned into history after a decades-long absence, deconstruction still plays a role in determining how the politics of globalization will play out. Deconstructive concerns remain a useful means of understanding the failure of mass leftist party politics—those founded upon unanimity and doctrinal adherence—opening up alternative possibilities for being. These alternatives will become key as I read shifting deployments of subjectivity in writing in English in Canada.

Questions remain about how the narratives of Marxism and deconstruction, both ultimately political, might create a space in which the transnational can emerge as a ground for study. Both demonstrate an impatience with nationalism—classical Marxism in its desire to achieve world liberation through the workers' struggle, poststructuralism in its distrust of totalizing structures—thereby suggesting one terrain upon which transnational studies might be built. Questions about the nation are at the fore, however, in the next chapters, as I read the works of a generation for whom national struggles were defined in opposition to the monolith of the United States. The question of Canada—its existence, what being Canadian means in the first instance—emerges with great force in literary debates, and is a question that continues to interest many Canadians. In the remaining chapters in Part One, literary production in Canada around the 1967 centennial is examined. This is the period that coincides with the rise of deconstruction. The rest of Part One will be concerned with the limits that Canadian nationalism presents, examining ways in which an oppositional Canadian mentality struggles to account for the world in writing by Margaret Atwood and Dennis Lee. Their constructs of Canada grapple in many ways with the possible void that underwrites it. The contestation of dualistic oppositions in Leonard Cohen's writing will, in turn, suggest some of the possibilities of the deconstructive mindset discussed in this chapter, although there, too, it will be necessary to account for the limitations of Cohen's (proto-)postmodern discourse. The period of high cultural nationalism occurred in Canada around the centennial year for a variety of reasons, many material and historical, but at least some of them intellectual. These links will be my immediate concern.

Notes to Chapter One

1 Linda Hutcheon, *The Politics of Postmodernism*, 2nd ed. (London: Routledge, 2002), 165.
2 Paik Nak-Chung, "Nations and Literatures in the Age of Globalization," *The Cultures of Globalization*, ed. F. Jameson and M. Miyoshi (Durham, NC: Duke UP, 1998), 227.
3 Karl Marx and Friedrich Engels, *The Communist Manifesto* (London: Penguin, 1967), 83.
4 Marx and Engels, *The Communist Manifesto*, 102.
5 Marx and Engels, *The Communist Manifesto*, 84.
6 The determination of consciousness by material conditions is one of the key points to the Marxist understanding of materialism, and is put as follows in Marx's 1844 *German Ideology*: "what individuals are depends on the material conditions of their production" (Amherst, MA: Prometheus, 1998), 37. This is a point to which Marx and Engels continually return.
7 Jacques Derrida, *Specters of Marx: The State of the Debt, the Work of Mourning, and the New International*, trans. Peggy Kamuf (New York: Routledge, 1994), 38.
8 It is important to note that Fukuyama became a prominent apologist for neo-conservative liberalism during the second Gulf War, largely rejecting these earlier claims. They nevertheless have had important cultural ramifications.
9 Derrida, *Specters of Marx*, 15.
10 Derrida, *Specters of Marx*, 74–75.
11 Derrida, *Specters of Marx*, 75.
12 Derrida, *Specters of Marx*, 56.
13 Derrida, *Specters of Marx*, 68.
14 Derrida, *Specters of Marx*, 92.
15 Derrida, *Specters of Marx*, 10.
16 Derrida, *Specters of Marx*, 37.
17 Derrida, *Specters of Marx*, 40.
18 Derrida, *Specters of Marx*, 13.
19 Derrida, *Specters of Marx*, 16.
20 Derrida, *Specters of Marx*, 33.
21 Derrida, *Specters of Marx*, 58–59.
22 Giorgio Agamben, *Homo Sacer: Sovereign Power and Bare Life*, trans. D. Heller-Roazen (Stanford: Stanford UP, 1998), 3–4.
23 Derrida, *Specters of Marx*, 59.
24 Derrida, *Specters of Marx*, 68.
25 There are innumerable unsympathetic criticisms of deconstruction along these lines, which bleed over into criticisms of poststructuralism and postmodernism. But from a more sensitive perspective, Ernesto Laclau sums it up well when he states that "from the fact that there is the impossibility of ultimate closure and presence, it does not follow that there is an ethical imperative to 'cultivate' that openness or even less to be necessarily committed to a democratic society" in "The Time Is Out of Joint," *Diacritics* 25.2 (1995): 93. Michael Ryan complained earlier, and similarly, that "deconstruction lacks a social theory" to follow up on its practices of disruption in *Marxism and Deconstruction: A Critical Articulation* (Baltimore: Johns Hopkins UP, 1982), 35.

26 Derrida, *Specters of Marx*, 59. The undeconstructible is key in the writings of a thinker whose project is the deconstruction of Western metaphysics. Derrida encounters the field of undeconstructibility again in his essay "Force of Law," which offers insights into the field of the undeconstructible in *Specters of Marx*. In "Force of Law," the undeconstructible is the field of justice. "Justice itself," Derrida states, "outside or beyond the law, is not deconstructible," and "deconstruction is justice," in *Deconstruction and the Possibility of Justice*, ed. D. Cornell et al. (New York: Routledge, 1992), 14–15. Derrida distinguishes justice from the law, invoking the promise of a justice to come as an undecidable space of possibility in which a politics of openness towards the other might ensue. Deconstruction occurs, Derrida argues, in the gap between justice (as an abstract) and the law (as justice applied). Justice is yet to come, while the law attempts to achieve this ever-elusive and shifting justice; the seeming stability of the law stands in contrast to a concept of justice that does not operate through the violence of moral determinations of value.

27 Derrida, *Specters of Marx*, 89.

28 Derrida, *Specters of Marx*, 84.

29 Derrida, *Specters of Marx*, 85–86.

30 Derrida, *Specters of Marx*, 169.

31 Pheng Cheah, for instance, argues that Derrida is too "hasty" to reject the nation and notes that "Derrida inherits the treatment of nationalism as a subcase of religion and mysticism that has been rendered *effete* by globalization even though he is critical of the Marxist ontology that opposes rational work to mystical belief" in "Spectral Nationality: The Living On [*sur-vie*] of the Postcolonial Nation in Neocolonial Globalization," *Boundary 2* 26.3 (1999): 249.

32 Derrida, *Specters of Marx*, 88.

33 Jacques Derrida, *The Other Heading: Reflections on Today's Europe*, trans. P. Brault and M. Naas (Bloomington: Indiana UP, 1992), 44.

34 Derrida, *Specters of Marx*, 87.

35 Terry Eagleton, "Marxism Without Marxism: Jacques Derrida and *Specters of Marx*," *The Eagleton Reader* (Oxford: Blackwell, 1998), 264. Eagleton's review essay and others are collected in *Ghostly Demarcations: A Symposium on Jacques Derrida's Specters of Marx*, ed. Michael Sprinker (London: Verso, 1999), as well as Derrida's spirited, argumentative response to them.

36 Eagleton is an interesting case. Since his influential book *Literary Theory: An Introduction*, published in 1983, he has distanced himself from theoretical discourse, reaching a renunciation of his understanding of "theory" in his 2003 book *After Theory*. Eagleton suggests that while Marxism can provide a grounded means of engaging with the world, what he sums up as "deconstructionism" can "do little more than reproduce some of the most commonplace topics of bourgeois liberalism" in its embrace of diversity and non-totalizing gestures in *Walter Benjamin, or, Towards a Revolutionary Criticism* (London: NLB, 1981), 137. Eagleton reads the disavowal of master narratives as a symptom "of political defeat for the left" in *The Illusions of Postmodernism*, subsuming the concerns of poststructural thought into a complicity with late capitalism by claiming that "not looking for totality is just code for not looking at capitalism" (Oxford: Blackwell, 1996), 10–11. There are several rebuttals to be made to Eagleton's claims, from the argument that looking for totality is complicit with the methods of capitalism, to the point that one of the things that deconstruction *might* do is to disrupt capitalist totalitarianism through

the dismantling of totalizing structures. Eagleton is at times correct in accusing the postmodern of depoliticized complicity, but his out-of-hand dismissal of "theory" *tout court* is brash.

37 Jameson's review essay of *Specters of Marx*, "Marx's Purloined Letter," is less useful because Jameson seems to be genuinely undecided about Derrida's offering "to coordinate Marxism with deconstruction," in *New Left Review* 209 (1995): 84. Jameson is also interested in the aesthetic and the utopian there. The essay is reprinted in *Ghostly Demarcations* and is one with which Derrida strongly disagrees in his response, arguing that *Specters of Marx* is distinctly anti-utopian and that his oeuvre is far from concerned with the aesthetic. See Jacques Derrida, "Marx and Sons," in *Ghostly Demarcations: A Symposium on Jacques Derrida's* Specters of Marx, ed. Michael Sprinker (London: Verso, 1999), 213–69.

38 Fredric Jameson, *Postmodernism, or, The Cultural Logic of Late Capitalism* (Durham, NC: Duke UP, 1991), 6.

39 Jameson, *Postmodernism, or, The Cultural Logic of Late Capitalism*, 218.

40 Linda Hutcheon, *A Poetics of Postmodernism: History, Theory, Fiction* (New York: Routledge, 1988), 16.

41 Jameson, *Postmodernism, or, The Cultural Logic of Late Capitalism*, 26–27.

42 Jameson, *Postmodernism, or, The Cultural Logic of Late Capitalism*, 38.

43 Jameson, *Postmodernism, or, The Cultural Logic of Late Capitalism*, 9.

44 Jameson, *Postmodernism, or, The Cultural Logic of Late Capitalism*, 47.

45 Jameson, *Postmodernism, or, The Cultural Logic of Late Capitalism*, 311.

46 Jameson, *Postmodernism, or, The Cultural Logic of Late Capitalism*, 311.

47 Slavoj Žižek, *Welcome to the Desert of the Real! Five Essays on September 11 and Related Dates* (London: Verso, 2002), 56.

CHAPTER TWO

Ambiguous Resistance in Margaret Atwood's *Surfacing*

It seems to be almost as difficult to not talk about *Surfacing* as it is to talk about it. Much has been said about the book, and Margaret Atwood looms very large in the field of Canadian literature: her writing is constantly taught and much discussed, and it has won pretty much every literary prize for which it is eligible, short of the Nobel (to date). Her books circulate widely, with *Surfacing* being ubiquitous in its cheap, convenient New Canadian Library edition. *Transnational Canadas* could hardly neglect Atwood's relationship to Canada, the United States, and broader social trends, as they are important for the formation of a globally inflected CanLit. Atwood is a big part of how Canadian literature got to where it is today and how it markets itself on the world stage. Her twin 1972 publications, *Surfacing* and *Survival*, helped to cement her reputation on this score, given their wide reception in Canada (the books are read outside Canada, of course, but the reception is different there; criticism in the United States, for instance, is more likely to focus on works such as *The Handmaid's Tale*). *Surfacing* and *Survival* contribute to national discussions in Canada in a couple of well-known ways: from the integral link between Atwood's and Northrop Frye's writing to the ambiguous relationship between Canadians and Americans in *Surfacing*, these books have proven to be important to debates about Canadian identity and belonging. Perhaps equally interesting are ways in which the critical reception of *Surfacing* has shifted over time and geographies; recently, this novel has diminished in importance. Assessing how readings of *Surfacing* have changed helps to understand how the text has come to play a role in informing the CanLit of our global era. These shifts demonstrate some of the overall patterns in Canadian literature since 1967, but they also show how these patterns are conditioned by the critical readership of Canadian writing. In other words, the patterns that *Transnational Canadas* identifies in Canadian literature may be as much a product of shifting critical foci as of shifting creative work; the two cannot be separated.

Briefly, a recap: *Surfacing* is a deeply ambiguous and ambivalent book that centres on four characters: an unnamed female narrator; her partner, Joe; and another couple, Anna and David. They drive into rural Quebec to the narrator's parents' home, which has been abandoned since her father went missing (although she is less than forthcoming to her friends about the details). As the narrative progresses, readers are given insights into the narrator's past, and learn that she has not been with Joe long and that she has a difficult relationship with her body, in part relating to the traumatic loss of a child that was aborted. As the holiday begins to degenerate under the sexist attitudes of the men, David in particular, and as a result of the narrator's own inward search, the narrative begins to fracture. The characters venture further into the wilderness, and the narrator begins to disassociate herself both from them and from the elements of what can be categorized as civilization, which she identifies with "the Americans." After having sex with Joe and telling readers that she has become pregnant, she retreats into the bush, where she plans to raise her child without language or civilization, free from taint. The narrative concludes, however, on a highly ambiguous note: her friends come searching for her, and she realizes that she will be able to return to the city in order to confront the American menace. Whether she returns or not, however, remains unsaid.

While the initial reviews and essays on *Surfacing*—in particular those produced in Canada[1]—were quick to recognize its connections to a national discourse of (anti-American) resistance, later discussions move towards discussing the novel's unnamed protagonist's mental state, grounding the novel in psychoanalytic and feminist debates. In part, this shift can be accounted for by the academic and popular Zeitgeist: the national context is explicit in *Surfacing*, and its publication coincides with the nationalist consolidation of Canadian literature as a field in Canadian universities. It is little surprise that the early Canadian appraisals of the book take up its national themes. Later criticisms, looking at the novel through different lenses, move towards readings of the unresolvable tensions in the narrator's mind. This shift is consonant with trends in literary criticism, and in particular the focus in the 1980s and '90s upon highly theorized identity politics. This focus was supported by the increased attention paid to the postmodern elements of deconstructive contingency that permeate the book. Most recently, a number of critics have been reassessing the national debates in the novel, looking to integrate national and bodily focused readings. These readings, in turn, reflect the direction in which this book reads Canadian literature: while paying attention to the intricate histories of literary methodologies, it seems that examinations of literature today require that readers look at the impacts of transnational debates upon cultural production. *Surfacing* provides a (deliberately misleadingly) straightforward image of cross-border tensions and slippages between Canada and the United States as the divisions between the two disintegrate in the text. This disintegration occurs at the same time as the novel reveals a number of trans- and intranational tensions, especially those between the French and English in Quebec and between Canadians and Indigenous people. This chapter of *Transnational Canadas*, as a result, reads the shifts in the readings of *Surfacing* while providing its own reading in the context of national and transnational debates. This reading, which focuses on the novel's production of hopeful indeterminacy and contingency, will begin to suggest how deconstructive and Marxist projects might provide a productive vision of openness that relates to thinking across national and physical boundaries. This is a vision that might recuperate some of *Surfacing*'s tensions, looking towards a cognitive mapping of a transnational world that remains a potential threat, as the narrator of the novel suggests, but that might nevertheless become navigable.

The question of how to navigate Canadian national space is a focus of the initial readings of the text, especially in Canada. The novel invites such an assessment as its four primary characters head into Quebec. The narrator's search for her father prompts her to decode her father's sketches of Indigenous rock drawings and his maps of the nearby lakes.

At the same time, the taints of her life in the city—especially her repressed abortion—lead her further and further into nature. This rapprochement with the natural world is tied to her movement away from the other three characters, as she comes to see them as marred by a creeping Americanness, one that she associates with technology, violence, and destruction. Nature becomes her refuge, leading to her ambivalent rejection of and likely return to society in the novel's later stages as her tidy divisions between purity and contamination break down. The novel is careful in this disruption of absolute differences, illustrating the contingency of all ethical and political categorizations: while initially positioning all that is negative as American, in contrast to a seeming Canadian purity, elements of "American" corruption enter the Canadian sphere, both literally and figuratively. The novel opens by mentioning how a "disease is spreading up from the south,"[2] one that is killing the birch trees, and David exclaims against the "fascist pig Yanks,"[3] but distinctions between Canada and the United States become untenable. The narrator is approached by a hunter named Bill Malmstrom, who wishes to buy her property for a group of Detroit-based outdoorsmen, the "Wildlife Protection Association of America," whose desire to kill animals confirms her anti-American biases.[4] Later, however, a pair of fishermen who kill a heron for no apparent reason turn out to be Canadian, from Sarnia and Toronto, despite the narrator's initial confidence that "it must have been the Americans" who perpetrated the deed.[5] The novel emerges as one about mapping, taking place, as the narrator notes, in "border country,"[6] illustrating the difficulty with which any absolute lines can be drawn between geographical spaces. The Canadian heron-killers become, for the narrator, Americans, regardless of their national affiliation: she states that "it doesn't matter what country they're from ... they're still Americans, they're what's in store for us, what we are turning into."[7] Polarized differentiations between Canadians and Americans continue to be hazarded, but these are divisions that the narrator can uphold only with great difficulty. The cultural map does not conform to the geographical one.

The difficulties of national mapping were apparent to early Canadian readers of the text. George Woodcock, writing in 1973, characterizes both *Surfacing* and *Survival* as "propaganda for Canadian literature"; Atwood's writing is, for him, "an index to the development of our literary tradition."[8] Sandra Djwa approvingly notes that, retrospectively, "Atwood was the first of her generation to acknowledge that she was writing from within a continuum of Canadian" poetry and writing.[9] Writers reviewed *Surfacing* in terms of Hugh MacLennan's concept of the two solitudes of the French and the English, discussing the separations and gaps between characters throughout the text in this respect, gaps that were also seen in terms of Canadian literary patterns of national sado-masochism.[10] Most early critics treat *Surfacing* and *Survival* as twin works, which is not surprising, given their near-simultaneous publication and the similarities between them. Survival is a dominant theme in *Surfacing*. Surviving against nature, against the Americans, and against oneself—all themes of *Surfacing*—are issues that Atwood foregrounds in her discussion in *Survival*. In *Survival*, Atwood forwards her thematic thesis of survival as the defining trope of Canadian writing. This recognition is, ultimately, one means of fulfilling the lack reported by the Massey Commission in 1951: Atwood's stated goal was to write "something that would make Canadian literature, as *Canadian* literature...accessible," as well as recognizable as such, by way of a "political manifesto."[11] Atwood's writing Canada into coherence, then, is thought of as a political project in which nationalism creates an affirming community. Whatever reservations Atwood may have had about seeing her fiction in this light, both *Survival* and *Surfacing* were read as part of broader Canadian processes, seen as examples of the intense nationalism of the centennial period.[12] Understanding the Canadian cultural map was a central concern during the period in which Atwood came to prominence, and she was suited to that circumstance, promoting a politics of national identification. However complex and unstable this vision, it has played a role in assuring Canadian audiences that, even if protagonists die or fail within the cultural mythos, a tenacity of spirit permeates the national body, one that continues to exist in a recognizable form despite colonial threats from without.

At the core of *Survival* is a focus upon tropes of victimhood in Canadian literature. Atwood suggests that "Canada as a whole is a victim, or an 'oppressed minority.'"[13] This status is dependent upon Canada's historical and present status as a colony, and leads Atwood to postulate four of what she terms "victim positions," which move towards an emancipation from colonization. These are well known, but worth stating, because *Surfacing* can also be read as a halting progression from Atwood's position one ("to deny the fact that you are a victim") to position four ("to be a creative non-victim"). The narrator of the novel is in the process of gaining an appreciation for her victimhood, and her rejection of the

Americans is a part of moving beyond her feelings of being dominated. But her moves are far from straightforward, as she proceeds through position two. Position two is, Atwood states,

> to acknowledge the fact that you are a victim, but to explain this as an act of Fate, the Will of God, the dictates of Biology (in the case of women, for instance), the necessity decreed by History, or Economics, or the Unconscious, or any other large general powerful idea.

The narrator of *Surfacing* contends with all of these "large general powerful ideas," particularly the dictates of biology. The men in the novel assume these ideas and she is learning to question them. Her rejection of Joe, for instance, allows her to move towards position three, "to acknowledge the fact that you are a victim but to refuse to accept the assumption that the role is inevitable." Indeed, the narrator's taking her fate and that of her child-to-be into her own hands is an act of refusing the inevitability of victimhood at the hands of civilization — although it does, in turn, challenge her ability to survive in a very real and physical sense. The final chapter of the novel suggests that she will transcend this position, as it opens with the following sentences: "this above all, to refuse to be a victim. Unless I can do that I can do nothing."[14] Whether she reaches this point, however, remains unknown, a promise that she cannot realize within the confines of the text. Her mapping of the American-free margins of society allows her to begin to trace her way out of victimhood, but it leaves many hanging questions and conditional statements.

Ongoing processes of questioning and issues of mapping are highlighted in the novel's connection to the work of Northrop Frye. The Frygian context leaps out once one learns that early drafts of the novel (the first and third, specifically) were entitled "Where Is Here."[15] The question "Where is here?" is famously posed by Northrop Frye in his 1965 conclusion to the *Literary History of Canada* and discussed by Atwood in *Survival*.[16] Frye suggests that this question is the central one in any inquiry into Canadian identity, one that foregrounds the geographical dimension of being Canadian. Frye argues that "Canadian sensibility has been profoundly disturbed, not so much by our famous problem of identity, important as it is, as by a series of paradoxes in what confronts that identity." Frye suggests that this Canadian sensibility is, ultimately, "less perplexed by the question 'Who am I?' than by some such riddle as

'Where is here?'"[17] Frye reiterates the importance of space to Canadian identity, and this particular formulation stuck (it is eye-rollingly familiar to many critics of CanLit). He suggests that the metaphorical locus of Canada is unclear, and that being Canadian involves an ongoing search for the location of the self. This search might be paralleled to the argument that postmodernity entails an ongoing process of cognitive mapping. The Frygian phrasing of the search implies a strong sense of confusion, a sense that the search is a constant one. It has a direct impact upon Atwood's thinking, as her palimpsestic allusions to Frye's question and his notion of the "garrison mentality" demonstrate. Allusions to Frye's question abound in *Surfacing*, appearing again and again in the statements made by its characters, for example on the final page of the book, when Joe calls out to the narrator, asking "Are you here?" and is trailed by an echo of the word "here."[18] Frye's writing, moreover, deeply informs Atwood's *Survival*. The question of surviving against nature or the other in Canada relates to the open-ended sense of Frye's question, since survival does not constitute an end in itself, but is, rather, an ongoing process. Atwood makes direct use of Frye's writing in both texts, binding it to thematic Canadian debates about identity. George Woodcock suggests that the primary difference between Frye and Atwood is that while Frye is "descriptive" in his mapping of the Canadian scene, Atwood is instead "tactical," creating "charts to help us repel a cultural invasion."[19]

There are further national contexts to the novel: not only is the Canada–U.S. split prominent, but the relationship between Anglo-Canadian and Quebecois cultures is present in the narrator's references to a childhood of being excluded from Catholicism and her local community because of her status as one of the "*maudits anglais.*"[20] Moreover, Indigenous cultures form a backdrop to the novel, prompting an awareness of ways in which Canada, while under colonial threat from the United States, in turn remains a colonizing nation. That which is identified with Indigenous life appears in the novel to be historical, not part of the present-day world. The narrator describes the rock drawing that her father is investigating at the time of his disappearance as "prehistoric,"[21] coming from a time before Western history can record. This idea is reiterated when the narrator considers her parents' era, which she sees as "prehistoric... remote as Eskimoes or mastodons."[22] She equates both her parents and the Inuit with an extinct species from the ice age, and accepts a vision of Indigenous peoples as having vanished from the landscape, even though material evidence of them remains. Critics have suggested that the novel permits an ossified depiction of indigeneity, one that presents "Indianness as merely a phase that the white narrator must pass through on her route to self-realization."[23] In seeking to include occluded Indigenous perspectives, in other words, *Surfacing* re-creates stereotypical images, although these are, by and large, a representational mirroring of the worldview that the protagonist has inherited. However, while the American tensions are more clearly articulated, and deliberately stereotyped in order to foster the narrator's resolve, the novel's Indigenous context is not as developed, leaving its readers with possible concerns. Although the narrator is reminded of her position on occupied land, the downplaying of English colonialism augments her victimization by the United States, bolstering her claims to resistance. But no one in *Surfacing* is ever a pure victim, and the layers of disenfranchisement and oppression complicate the narrator's claims to suffering. And her ultimate refusal of victimhood suggests that any functional national vision of Canada needs to account for its deficiencies as well as its positive potential. Both inter- and intranational tensions thereby enter the novel, and their unresolvable nature leaves critics reading for the uneasy liberation grounded in natural spaces that the narrator associates with being Canadian.

While the narrator's tidy division between the "American" and the "Canadian" breaks down in the novel the more the distinction is scrutinized, this breakdown is not only the result of the artificiality of these divisions. The novel projects a series of American values that are connected to industry, militarism, and a disrespect for nature, and decries them. But that these are found in Canada, and among Canadians, does not necessarily indicate that the division is a false one that should be disregarded—at least not in the terms of the novel. Instead, the failure of these distinctions can function as a call for stronger resistance to destructive "American" values. The narrator of *Surfacing*, at the same time as she posits radical instability for all categories of being, suggests a desire to root out not only Americans, but "American" values as well. David's anti-Americanism, on this note, is shown to be hypocritical: while he bemoans the creeping Americanness that he outwardly loathes, he is also a baseball fan, one who is irritated that he cannot receive a radio transmission of "the scores" from the bush,[24] and he has lived in New York, where he acquired his political views. He symbolically desires the penetration of American values into Canada, but only those of his choosing. The narrator, however, is searching for a sort of symbiosis with nature, equating Canada with the rural spaces of her childhood, which have been contaminated by the encroachments of "civilization." Her values include the solitude of living at long distances from other people, the virtue of survival, and the desire to maintain a Frygian "garrison mentality," a defensive mindset that Frye suggests derives from the "small and isolated communities" of the Canadian frontier era.[25] There is something deeply historical about the narrator's consciousness, a desire to connect with the past. But it is also of a piece with the nationalism of the '60s and '70s, with a consciously problematic Canadian/American distinction being maintained despite its flaws.[26] The narrator advocates a search for a failed, naturalistic, yet pure Canadian identity. This purity is acknowledged to be impossible or at least untenable, but such impossibility does not preclude hope.

Atwood's perspective on Canadian–American relations suggests that even while she points out the hypocrisies of popular Canadian anti-Americanism through characters like David, political resistance might still take the form of national struggle. Although there are far more similarities than differences between Canadians and Americans, this fact does not negate the argument for a strong national body as a means of collective empowerment in *Surfacing* and elsewhere. Being interviewed by a House of Commons committee on the issue of free trade in the lead-up to the 1988 Free Trade Agreement between Canada and the United States, Atwood stated, in discussing the relationship between Canada and the United States, that "the only position they have ever adopted towards us, country to country, has been the missionary position and we're not on top."[27] The result, for Atwood, is a need to defend Canada's borders against sexualized exploitation by the United States. Canada, as a country with a complex colonial heritage, becomes a site in which liberation is envisioned through a project of nation-building, one in which it might be possible to identify dominant themes as a means of creating a collective identity. As with any collective identity (with the implications of limiting sameness that the term "identity" contains), this position entails a degree of erasure, as with the erasure of French and Indigenous perspectives in *Surfacing*. These are recorded, sometimes only in passing, as a part of noting the instability of Canadian identity. But these are to be read optimistically with the narrator's suggestions, perhaps erased only in a Canada contaminated by "the Americans"; one free of American or civilizational taint would provide a strong grounds for resistance for the narrator. She sympathizes both with Indigenous people and the rural French, as opposed to the outsiders who maintain that they are "not civilized,"[28] and she projects a desire for solidarity against the foreboding city to which she projects her return. As much as being American is not an exclusive category, and as much as the novel equates being a part of urban society with Americanization, the ideal of a unified Canadian community in resistance to American imperialism, both mental and geographical, is a driving force in *Surfacing* and a strong link to achieving the sort of creative non-victimization that Atwood suggests Canadians need in *Survival*.

How are we to read *Surfacing* in a global era? Atwood's 2003 novel *Oryx and Crake* presents a dystopic look at where global corporatism may take the world, replete with postnational privatized compounds modelled on today's gated communities, and the endpoint of genetic modification in ChickieNobs, a post-chicken organism that grows either a dozen breasts or drumsticks for human consumption. In this world, the internet governs the lives of characters Jimmy and Crake, particularly its endless streams of pornography, which they watch in tandem with live executions.[29] This is a world away from the stark naturalism of *Surfacing*—although perhaps only on first glance. David and Joe, in *Surfacing*, propose an early vision of what becomes the internet's rampant pornography in the film that they set out to produce while they are on holiday, which they call *Random Samples*. Their plan is to capture bits and pieces of things, to string them together, and produce an art film from this thin premise. Working with a rented camera, they film the things that they come across, including statues of moose, the dead heron, and so on. The film becomes menacing to the women when David proposes to turn the camera on Anna. David tells her that he and Joe "need a naked lady with big tits and a big ass" for their film,[30] and then forces Anna to expose herself for the film, despite Joe's weak protests. Technology is turned on women to capture them, as in *Oryx and Crake*, to fragment their bodies through images thereof. The narrator in *Surfacing* expresses feelings of bodily separation and detachment, stating, for instance, that she feels as though she is "nothing but a head, or no, something minor like a severed thumb."[31] The patriarchal visions of David and Joe render women in such fragments, and it is, similarly, not coincidental that Jimmy and Crake learn about women and sex through pornography that they watch alongside decapitations and other killings. David and Joe's sexism is sent underground, into porn studios, rampantly decorporealizing and fragmenting women's bodies into the futures that Atwood imagines in her later writing.

In *Surfacing*, the men's hold on their power is shown to be unstable, and what remains of society in *Oryx and Crake* is crumbling. David and Joe's act of recording Anna is consonant with Laura Mulvey's later and now-classic theorization of the patriarchal aspect of the narrative cinema, in which, she argues, the gaze of the camera lens is masculine, pushing women to identify against themselves and with patriarchy.[32] David and Joe's *Random Samples* upholds Mulvey's analysis of the gaze and extends its symbolic violence against women through the very real violence that David inflicts on Anna in order to trap her on celluloid. This filmic violence is, moreover, also the violence of language, as the narrator notes, stating that language, like film, "divides us into fragments, I wanted to be whole."[33] While her revolt against language is mixed in its results, the capturing and fragmentation on film is fleeting: the men's rented camera— an example of the technology that the narrator associates with the American taint—is not their property, and the narrator rebels against their domination by releasing the film, unfurling their "hundreds of tiny naked Annas" into the lake, Annas that are "no longer bottled and shelved" like her vision of her unborn fetus.[34] This act of freeing Anna's image precedes the narrator's disappearance into the wilderness, and suggests that the technological codes that are used to dominate women, and by extension Canada, can be undermined.

If Atwood's vision of Canadian resistance in *Surfacing* requires untangling, however, it is in part because her protagonist's openness to difference is limited to that which is already within Canada. If the transnational now informs how literature in Canada conceptualizes itself, then cross-border influences may need to be thought differently. The problems that *Surfacing* has in maintaining its divisions between Canada and the United States illustrate the very conscious limitations of its vision, at the same time as it projects an ideal, imagined community. In *Surfacing*, the cognitive map necessary to navigate the world of 1970s Canada contains many exclusions and divisions, and the disjunctive failure of this mapping process leads at least in part to the narrator's breakdown. This breakdown does not mean, however, that such maps would not prove handy. The popularity of *Surfacing* and *Survival* suggests a broad desire for whatever provisional maps might be available.

Notes to Chapter Two

1 Linda Hutcheon notes this geographical dimension to the early appraisals in *The Canadian Postmodern* (Toronto: Oxford UP, 1988), 145.
2 Margaret Atwood, *Surfacing* (Toronto: McClelland and Stewart, 1972), 7.
3 Atwood, *Surfacing*, 39.
4 Atwood, *Surfacing*, 94–95.
5 Atwood, *Surfacing*, 117.
6 Atwood, *Surfacing*, 26.
7 Atwood, *Surfacing*, 129.
8 George Woodcock, "Surfacing to Survive: Notes on the Recent Atwood," *Ariel* 4.3 (1973): 18–19.
9 Sandra Djwa, "The Where of Here: Margaret Atwood and a Canadian Tradition," *The Art of Margaret Atwood: Essays in Criticism*, ed. A. Davidson and C. Davidson (Toronto: Anansi, 1981), 16.
10 James Harrison, "The 20,000,000 Solitudes of *Surfacing*," *Dalhousie Review* 59 (1979): 74–81, and Gloria Onley, "Margaret Atwood: Surfacing in the Interests of Survival," *West Coast Review* 7.3 (1973): 51–54.
11 Margaret Atwood, *Survival: A Thematic Guide to Canadian Literature* (Toronto: Anansi, 1972), 13.
12 For example in Frank Davey's *Margaret Atwood: A Feminist Poetics* (Vancouver: Talonbooks, 1984), 153.
13 This and the following quotes are all from Atwood, *Survival*, 35–39.
14 Atwood, *Surfacing*, 191.
15 Sandra Djwa, "'Here I am': Atwood, Paper Houses, and a Parodic Tradition," *Essays on Canadian Writing* 71 (2000): 170.
16 Northrop Frye, Conclusion to *Literary History of Canada: Canadian Literature in English*, ed. Carl F. Klinck (Toronto: U of Toronto P, 1965), 826. Atwood cites it in *Survival*, 17.
17 Frye, Conclusion, 826.
18 Atwood, *Surfacing*, 192. See Djwa, "'Here I am,'" 170. Djwa notes Joe's question "Where is this?" upon waking (41), the narrator's exclaiming "Here I am...I'm here" to her dead parents (172), and her statement "I am a place" (181) and the novel's concluding page (192). To this list might be added several further minor references: the narrator's notion that "the truth is here" (170) and her statement that the twentieth century is "not here" (151).
19 Woodcock, "Surfacing to Survive," 20.
20 Atwood, *Surfacing*, 56.
21 Atwood, *Surfacing*, 114.
22 Atwood, *Surfacing*, 144.
23 Janice Fiamengo, "Postcolonial Guilt in Margaret Atwood's *Surfacing*," *American Review of Canadian Studies* 29 (1999): 157. See also Marie-Françoise Guédon, "*Surfacing*: Amerindian Themes and Shamanism," *Margaret Atwood: Language, Text, and System*, ed. S. Grace and L. Weir (Vancouver: U of British Columbia P, 1983), 91–111.
24 Atwood, *Surfacing*, 39.
25 Frye, Conclusion, 830.

26 See Fiamengo, "Postcolonial Guilt," 157. See also Guédon, "*Surfacing*: Amerindian Themes and Shamanism," 159.
27 Quoted in Peter Wilkins, "Defense of the Realm: Canada's Relationship to the United States in Margaret Atwood's *Surfacing*," *Yearbook of Research in English and American Literature* 14 (1998): 206.
28 Atwood, *Surfacing*, 26.
29 Margaret Atwood, *Oryx and Crake* (Toronto: McClelland and Stewart, 2003), 85–86, 201–203.
30 Atwood, *Surfacing*, 134.
31 Atwood, *Surfacing*, 108.
32 Laura Mulvey, "Visual Pleasure and Narrative Cinema," *Feminism and Film Theory*, ed. C. Penley (New York: Routledge, 1988), 57–79.
33 Atwood, *Surfacing*, 146.
34 Atwood, *Surfacing*, 166.

CHAPTER THREE

Nationalism and the Void in Dennis Lee's *Civil Elegies*

The desire for a mappable national imaginary, expressed by Margaret Atwood's protagonist in *Surfacing*, appears much more clearly in a contemporary book of poetry, Dennis Lee's *Civil Elegies*. If Atwood's inquiry into national resistance to imperialism is ambiguous in *Surfacing* because the differences between Canadians and Americans collapse, then Dennis Lee's *Civil Elegies* provides a simultaneously clearer and more muddied way of examining the nationalist politics of the centennial period. Lee moves away from the American colonization of rural spaces that we see in Atwood's narrative, and laments instead the urban space of Toronto, looking at the ways in which the Canadian nation has failed. Atwood sees Lee's poem as one that details "cultural castration and stunting of vision" at the hands of the American empire.[1] Rather than doubting the contrasts between Canada and the United States, *Civil Elegies* puzzles about what the Canadian nation might mean given its failure and its lost possibilities. Lee's writing is a representative timepiece of high cultural nationalism, but it's also an anomaly to a period that was celebrating Canada's arrival on the world stage. By seeing Canada as a failure rather than as a rising success, Lee looks like a doubter and naysayer, even while he upholds

Canada as a space of possibility. He sounds like Northrop Frye when the latter suggests in his preface to *The Bush Garden* that "the true north strong and free often looks more like a sham south weak and occupied."[2] Lee gives such sentiments literary utterance, working Frye's, and, more particularly, George Grant's ideas (in *Lament for a Nation* and elsewhere) into poetic form. Grant works from the premise that the Canadian nation has failed, and looks at the consequences of this failure in the context of a technological modernity. He ponders the value of a universal culture rooted in American values and makes scathing critiques of the submissive attitudes of the Liberal Party in accepting the terms and mores of the United States. But the central irresolution emerges as that of modernity itself in *Lament for a Nation*: Grant argues that

> if the best social order is the universal and homogenous state, then the disappearance of Canada can be understood as a step towards that order. If the universal and homogenous state would be a tyranny, then the disappearance of even this indigenous culture can be seen as the removal of a minor barrier on the road to that tyranny. As the central issue is left undecided, the propriety of lamenting must also be left unsettled.[3]

Grant remains (at least at the level of rhetoric) undecided about how culture should be formulated, and worries about the role of difference and, more specifically, nations in an increasingly global era. Lee's *Civil Elegies* brings readers to the brink of this debate and then similarly holds back, seeing the potential for a culture within Canada based upon difference rather than unanimity, but then shying away from embracing this position. This irresolution positions Lee on the brink of a poststructural ethos, one that he queries and from which he finally returns. Rather than seeing potential in a decentred chaos, as a more celebratory moment in postmodernity might, Lee sees only "void." This stance places Lee at a potential turning point in narratives of modernity in the West that coincides with his poem's moment at the height of cultural nationalism. Lee's speaker remains in a Yeatsian universe in which the centre remains a place of longing and nostalgia, even though it cannot hold and he knows it.

Civil Elegies is of interest primarily because of the ways in which it attempts to work out problems of nation and space within its poetic form. The speaker of the nine elegies that make up the poem—routinely identified with Lee in criticism—sits in Toronto's Nathan Phillips Square, which is used as a synecdoche for Canada. He casts his gaze over both the immediate setting—particularly Henry Moore's abstract sculpture, known as *The Archer*—and the broader country, lamenting its history of defeat. As the structures of the nation fail to coalesce, the speaker reaches a point of either despairing or resigning to the present. He decides to attempt "to honour the void" of present-day Canada in the absence of available alternatives.[4] But this void, which equates in part with a disrupted metaphysics that eschews the concept of presence itself, is a difficult one for him to accept, let alone work with. The speaker returns from his position of honouring the void towards the end of the poem, ending instead with hope and a prayer to the earth for wholeness and completion:

> Earth, you nearest, allow me.
> Green of the earth and civil grey:
> within me, without me and moment by
> moment allow me for to
> be here is enough and earth you
> strangest, you nearest, be home.[5]

The modernity within which the poem operates recognizes the fragmentation of Canadian social space—lamenting it by recalling historical details and evoking the present's poisonous atmosphere in Toronto—but takes this fragmentation as a contemplative point that leads to a nostalgia for presence. This is a presence that cannot exist, however, because of the failure of history to generate a stable nation. In an Eliotic manner, Toronto becomes a wasteland beneath a "noxious cloud" of smog and technologized colonization,[6] one for whose redemption the speaker hopes. But salvation remains off-stage, impossible in the contemporary, secular world.

Civil Elegies is equally interesting in terms of its critical reception, one that approaches the interpretation that *Transnational Canadas* gives the poem, although recent appraisals have not come to quite the same point. *Civil Elegies* has not received the substantial critical attention that Atwood's writing has, but a number of recent essays (and a monograph by Robert Lecker) suggest the text's retrospective importance. It is also a work that Lee has been writing about and discussing until the present. The poem was, however, read only occasionally after the period in which it was recognized as a significant Canadian work by being awarded the Governor General's Award for Poetry in 1972. It was, perhaps, the difficulty of its

43

two early editions—the first, in 1968, was substantially revised for republication in 1972—that slowed critical reception.[7] The poem is also frequently seen as imperfect or awkward, as raising questions without providing coherent answers. By the early '80s, however, critics began to recognize ways in which Lee's poem develops a trajectory of thought about the colonization of Canadian spaces, especially mental ones, by the United States. Dale Zieroth contended then that the speaker of the poem faces the problem of "the attempt of consciousness to become at home in its own body" despite having "a colonized consciousness," one that is connected to the colonization of national space. The resultant void with which the poem flirts becomes a potential place of promise in this landscape, but it is rejected in the end, Zieroth contends, because it is little more than "a neurotic vision of detachment."[8] This rejection leads to an uneasy compromise of living within the colonized nation. Stan Dragland supports this contention in arguing that the "the void is least ambiguous when it is identified with the evil done in the name of empire; it is both attractive and dangerous in its pervasive form as the context of being."[9] R.D. MacDonald, in an essay recognizing Lee's close ties to Grant's thinking, inquires similarly after the poem's quest for authenticity and being, a questing that links to the poem's concern with the void. The void represents, in part, the possibility that authenticity is false or illusory. MacDonald states that the concluding prayer of the elegies, quoted above, should be seen as a "turn to the promise of the here and now and future of the human city" and the grounds for possibility in opposition to the fear prompted by the void. The promise of the here and now emerges, after consideration and lamentation, as all that is possible for Lee, whom MacDonald identifies as "the modern liberal."[10] These critics wrestle with the poem, often finding it to be muddled, incomplete in its thought, and at times uncertain in its language. These findings, however, do not prevent them from drawing similar conclusions about the poem's ending, where truth, in whatever form it remains, emerges in the everyday, in the tentative reconciliation of Lee's dialectical vision. This reconciliation attempts to fill the void by seeking home within it, and therein the speaker discovers the world.[11] How we get to this conclusion is, however, rather more complex than the conclusion itself.

These readings, in recognizing the importance of "the void" to *Civil Elegies*, are complemented by recent criticisms. These recognize the poem's complexity, its concerns for ecology, and argue that the poem is one that cannot be resolved, despite the seeming closure of the conclusion. Instead, it is important to see how the speaker assumes responsibility for finding home in a world of disconnections between the city and the land, and between the nation and the body.[12] Isaías Naranjo is concise in his appraisal of what the poem's irresolution suggests, stating that "just as Derrida suggested that there inheres in Heidegger a certain nostalgia for Being, we could say that even in his disbelief, Lee still longs for a belief in transcendent things" in his search for home.[13] *Civil Elegies* supports this contention, as the speaker states that "there is / nothing [he] would not give to be made whole."[14] This desire, one that he knows he cannot fulfill, is one that maps closely to a desire for certainty and transcendence.[15] Jonathan Kertzer, mapping the poem along similarly Heideggerian lines, suggests that while the speaker's belief in Canada is shattered, leaving him forced to "use inauthentic language to report on an inauthentic place," the poem remains rooted in a modernity that does not question "the nation as a valid political form." Reading the void as a danger that threatens to undermine the poem-as-art, forcing the poem to recognize that it, in itself, cannot enact the justice that Lee seeks, Kertzer states that the speaker "refuses to enter the void because he is unwilling to relinquish justice."[16] This modern form of justice, based on an already-defined set of values, is indeed absent in the world of the void, in which definitions disappear. Most recently, Robert Lecker, in his monograph, suggests that the void is, ultimately, something "pedestrian," a negative space, a sort of cultural black hole, one that is simply to be overcome.[17] Whether this dismissal is a fair one in a contemporary world of moral relativism remains an important question.

Dennis Lee recognizes these limitations; the struggles of his prose mirror those of his poetry. The essay "Cadence, Country, Silence: Writing in Colonial Space," which attempts, in part, to provide an interpretation of *Civil Elegies*, is instructive. This essay, first published in 1974, and re-published with revisions in 1998's *Body Music*, came out of the experience of writing *Civil Elegies*. *Civil Elegies* was, for Lee, a breakthrough after his first volume of poetry, *Kingdom of Absence*. "Cadence, Country, Silence" explores what it means for Lee to write poetry in the Canada that he knows. Lee avers that he writes in order "to find out ... what it would be to write authentically."[18] But authenticity is difficult to achieve, he states, in a space that has been colonized by the United States. It involves a search for a particular voice, one that Lee discusses in terms of "cadence," a term

45

that he defines as a rhythmic authenticity used to convey a specific space. He uses the metaphor of sculpting, suggesting that cadence is the stone that a poet uses, and within which the poem is found. This stone varies from region to region, making the essay an apposite comparison to *Civil Elegies*, which is, in part, concerned with the extraction of Canada's natural resources. Cadence remains elusive, however, leading Lee to wonder if "perhaps our job was not to fake a space of our own and write it up, but rather to find words for our space-lessness."[19] This query parallels Lee's approach to the void in *Civil Elegies*, and the question remains, similarly, unresolved; the only answers possible are tentative, imperfect ones. The best that Lee can propose is the paradox that "to be authentic, the voice of being alive here and now must include the inauthenticity of our lives here and now" because it is not possible to uncover absolute truths in a colonized space.[20] This stance does not question the validity of absolute truths, but rather upholds the notion that the world's missing truths are not, at present, recoverable, and certainly not through the imperfect medium of (colonized) language. It is in this stance that Lee can be associated with a modern or modernist tradition. He elsewhere expounds "truth," "the certainty of moral limits," and "the recognition that evil is real,"[21] and he is far from a relativist, despite his recognition of the impossibility of determining what, exactly, truth, moral limits, or evil might always be. For Lee, "a poem enacts in words the presence of what we live among."[22] The absence of presence in the contemporary world leads him to lament.

Lee bases this theorization in the thinking of Grant, a writer whose ideas "felt like home," Lee states, when he first read them.[23] Lee later finds that Grant's thinking is "both exemplary and limited,"[24] but it is an important starting point for what became the final version of *Civil Elegies*. His thinking is exemplary for Lee in that it explores the inescapability of one's specific place in the world, paralleling Lee's own quest for an authentic sense of Canadian space. Grant is concerned in *Lament for a Nation* with how Canada has developed a "role as a branch-plant of American capitalism" in the twentieth century.[25] This development is, of course, part of a longer history, and Grant argues that Canada's "very existing has at all times been bound up with the interplay of various world empires."[26] Grant questions Canada's failure, but he leaves unresolved the final question as to whether the nation should persist as a political structure (he wrote this indecisive conclusion, however, in an intensely nationalistic environment, as he knew, which was ready to side with the argument that Canada's erasure would be part of a road towards tyranny). Grant identifies modernity with a "universal and homogenous state" and examines how Canada, situated next to the United States — which he sees as the exemplary modern state — is ineluctably drawn into this liberal modernity.[27] Modernity is multivalent, of course, but Grant links it with technologized society, following Heidegger and echoing Marshall McLuhan's then-recent concept of the global village. Lee's modernity is slightly different, but related: while he similarly questions the modern liberal state, he does not reject modern beliefs as such. Instead, he questions master narratives and concepts of truth along what can be seen as structurally modern lines of thought. He is able, as a result, to take Grant's dissection of Canada's relationship to technologized modernity personally, and to turn it into an emotional search for home in an environment that threatens to void that term's content.

So what, exactly, happens in *Civil Elegies*? While it is problematic to read the poem strictly in narrative terms, it is instructive to look for these competing versions of the modern within it. Throughout, the coherence of the speaker and the mania of his vision needs to be kept in mind; his is a mania that disrupts what might otherwise be a tidy poem.[28] It opens by establishing the speaker's position, "brooding over the city," and recounts the history of the many who "were born in Canada...living unlived lives."[29] For the speaker, Canada specializes in the "deprivation" of being a country that cannot create a sense of "home" for its citizens. The poem establishes its central questions, asking "whether Canada will be" in a context in which it "has no past" because it is made up of a nation of "Indian-swindlers, / stewards of unclaimed earth and rootless." The speaker longs "for men to complete / their origins," but finds that this rootlessness prevents completion.[30] Rather than looking only towards the European colonization of North America for the source of this rootlessness, the speaker instead laments the ways in which "the people accept a flawed inheritance" within the country, as well as the ways in which the country has been sold out to American interests.[31] Canada's innocence is ruined by American-style technological advance, as "empire permeates" Nathan Phillips Square and the nation-state.[32] Nathan Phillips Square is a site for finding elements of empire: *The Archer*, Henry Moore's sculpture in the square, can be seen, as Robert Lecker has argued, as "a symbol of the intrusion of foreign art."[33] The modern empire drives back the spiritual "Master and Lord" for whom the speaker searches in the second

47

elegy, declaring instead the "real absence" of certainty. As a result, everything appears to contain only "emptiness"; certainty, while longed for, has no place in the contemporary, colonized space that the speaker encounters in the city. The speaker insists that "there was a / measure once" and that there "was a time when men could say / my life, my job, my home / and still feel clean."[34] This nostalgic vision of masculinist certitude and ownership drives a contemporary desire to return to such a space, and underlies the poem.

This urban perspective about absence moves to an arterial look at the nation. Beginning from the premise that "we live on occupied soil," the speaker considers how the "despotic land" of the Canadian Shield is mined in order to serve the needs of the far-flung peoples of empire. This consideration focuses upon the vein-like systems of transport that connect the country:

> as [the settlers'] cars settled back to slag and now what
> races towards us on asphalt across the Shield —
> by truck, by TV minds and the ore-bearing flatcars —
> is torn from the land ...
> ... shipped and
> divvied abroad though wrested whole from the Shield.[35]

The technological society takes complete, whole elements and transforms them, breaking them and combining them such that they become impure, ensuring that what may once have been an authentic space becomes muddled and unclean. Beyond the environmental issues that readers have seen in the poem, this concern with mining is equally about imperial conquest, which operates internationally through extraction as well as occupation. This industrial landscape is contrasted to the naturalistic work of painter Tom Thomson, giving evidence of a "downward momentum" in Canada, in which genuine spaces, as Lee perceives them, disappear.[36]

But this disappearance prompts, in turn, the crux of the poem. This is the speaker's suggestion that, perhaps, "it is time to honour the void" in the face of this decline.[37] If, in other words, the authentic does not exist or cannot be recovered, it may be time to look at alternative ways of being in the world. This line, which ends the third elegy, is a turning point for the speaker as well, one that reorients the poem towards a discussion of the possibility of absence itself becoming an adequate structure for being.

The difficulty of reconciling the failure of authentic space and the promise of the void as a way of rethinking subjectivity comes to preoccupy the poem, and runs as a strong current alongside the speaker's recording of the difficulties of being Canadian.

The fourth elegy opens, as a result, by wondering whether the void might, in fact, be "our / vocation." But the enjambed line suggests a reluctance, a reticence. The speaker continues to lament the "many / lives gone down the drain in the service of empire," but wonders if "we [are] not meant to / relinquish it all, to begin at last / the one abundant psalm of letting be." This query is followed by a long series of statements in which the speaker bids "goodbye" to aspects of the country, from "the poisoned air" to "the grainy sense of place." In its place, the speaker holds out the possibility that "nothing / belongs to us, and / only that nothing is home." Embracing nothingness as plenitude provides the promise of finding oneself "in the midst of what abounds."[38] This emptiness resembles a deconstructive embrace of absence and the disavowal of certainties in favour of a recognition of the provisional nature of society. The poem thus moves towards a politics in which any position requires ethical articulation, based upon relative determinations of value rather than belief in transcendence or absolute truths. It seems at this moment that the speaker moves towards a position in which moral determinations become place- and time-specific as a means of defending Canada against threats from abroad. This is a position that might allow the speaker to acknowledge the manner in which the space that he wishes to inhabit is colonized not only by the United States, but also by his own, European-descended consciousness, and those contradictions may allow Canada, nevertheless, to remain a precariously livable space.

This open-endedness, with which the speaker flirts, is rejected in favour of a more materialist stance. The speaker wonders "what good" such an embrace of the void might do "in a nation / of losers and quislings." The immediate problems at hand include "watching the / ore and the oil and the shorelines gutted / for dollars by men from abroad, watching Canadians / peddle their birthright." This worrying vision (given the erasure of Indigenous people, who might also be entitled to this "birthright") brings Lee to a focus upon "the patsies of empire" and the concerns of living in Canadian space.[39] Although the speaker recognizes that "it is / hard to stay at the centre when you're losing it one more time," he suggests that it is "better ... to avoid the scandal of being" in favour of an examination of the country's evils, especially those of the Liberal Party, with Paul Martin, Sr., Secretary of External Affairs under Lester B. Pearson, bearing his contempt. Such politicians are, the speaker states, "the sellouts of history" who allowed Canada to be implicated in the American invasion of Vietnam by producing the napalm that was used to bomb the impoverished Vietnamese. The abdication of recognizable moral values, the speaker states, can be equated with the "void, to participate in an / abomination larger than yourself." He argues, further, that it is void "to fashion / other men's napalm and know it." It is this void that the speaker fears, worrying that "we will carry napalm for our side, proud of our clean hands."[40] More abstractly, he wonders "if there is no regenerative absence" — that is, if there is no benefit to the void — and questions whether "the void that compels us is only a mood gone absolute."[41] In other words, he wonders whether an apparently popular embrace of the void is little more than a fad. An acquiescence to moral relativism presents itself all around him, as "there are / few among us who are competent at being" and "we cannot command the courage outright to exist," leading to myriad poorly considered compromises.[42] The speaker himself, while wishing "to be made whole,"[43] recognizes his incompleteness and longs for plenitude through the nation, but it fails to materialize. The fact that, as he sees it, "we are a conquered nation" ensures that he will not become whole in this space.[44]

As the poem comes to its conclusion, he feels that it is "better however to try" to become whole, even if he "will not reach it where he longs to, in the / vacant spaces of his mind." His survey of the square, of Toronto, and of Canada comes home, comes back to the self. The void, he states, "is not a place, nor / a negation of place"; paradoxically, "we enter void when void no longer exists."[45] This void comes to represent a recognition of the constructed and relative nature of Western values, as well as of the speaker's unwillingness to relinquish what few certainties he maintains. The speaker sees that the deconstruction of certainties is possible and may not be logically avoidable, but a plunge into uncertainty is not desirable in the context of the Vietnam War and the American pillage of the resources of Canada. The speaker recounts a period of embracing the void, but then retracts:

... when the void became void I did
let go, though derelict for months

and I was easy, no longer held by its negative presence
as I was earlier disabused of many things in the world
including Canada, and came to know I still had access to them,
and I promised to honour each one of my country's failures of nerve and
its sellouts.[46]

The void seems relaxing, "easy," and no longer negative. It holds promise, but it is a position that the speaker can occupy only as long as things go well and the nation's failures remain in the past. When they intersect with the present, the speaker retreats, relying on the values in which he believes. These, while perhaps laudable—his objection to ecological destruction and war foremost among them—illustrate a reliance upon determined cultural values. These values also involve an erasure of Indigenous concerns and a gendered perspective that equates national strength with masculinity. The speaker is, finally, unable to let these things go, given the risks of moral relativism. He holds onto the fractured promise of the self and the nation as a defence against threats from without, from the international threat of the United States in particular.

Dennis Lee's *Civil Elegies* flirts, then, with open-ended concepts of belonging and subjectivity, but retreats from these when the poem equates them with the loss of the ability to distinguish right from wrong. Critics have suggested that the poem encapsulates a stilted, uneasy movement towards an incomplete self-knowledge for the speaker, one that is strongly alinear. This weaving motion is demonstrated in the poem's embrace and then rejection of the void. Instead of seeing a mobile form of subjectivity as containing open-ended potential for transforming space into a locus that can be inhabited despite difference, open-endedness becomes a threat to the possibility of coherence. It is equated with the technologized society about which Lee worries, one that homogenizes the globe through a capitalism that operates through destructive resource extraction and the endless spewing of toxins. Although Lee's worries about the environmental destruction wrought by the capitalist machinery are important, this final equation between the void and arbitrary, exploitative free play is uncertain and illustrates the gap between a modern and a postmodern vision of the world. *Civil Elegies* appears, moreover, to be an instance of deconstruction versus Marxism, Lee siding with the latter's seemingly more defined values to the exclusion of the former. Lee's struggle also illustrates something of how the politics of resistance in Canada have shifted: the absolute moral values that Lee finally upholds, once they have been challenged by intranational Canadian anti-racist work in literature and citizenship, come in turn to be seen as constructed and therefore malleable. Shifting values have allowed changes that welcome people who might have been previously excluded from inhabiting space-as-home at the same time as such open-endedness has become Canada's strength under neo-liberalism. Lee's equation of mobile subjectivities in the void with resource-based capitalism—important for an international defence of Canada to be mounted—is not an assured one, and later writers suggest that there is a broader debate to be had. Malleability need not be seen as the evacuation of all ethics, as Lee's speaker fears; instead, it might become a place in which mobile conceptualizations of subjectivity become ways of resisting empire. But this is a different interpretation than that which Lee offers.

Notes to Chapter Three

1. Atwood, *Survival*, 244.
2. Northrop Frye, *The Bush Garden: Essays on the Canadian Imagination*, 2nd ed. (Concord, ON: Anansi, 1995), xxx.
3. George Grant, *Lament for a Nation: The Defeat of Canadian Nationalism* (Toronto: McClelland and Stewart, 1965), 96.
4. Dennis Lee, *Civil Elegies and Other Poems* (Don Mills, ON: Anansi, 1972), 36.
5. Lee, *Civil Elegies*, 51.
6. Lee, *Civil Elegies*, 40.
7. Criticism of the poem relies upon the later, 1972 edition, as does this analysis (in this case, in its mid-'90s reprint).
8. Dale Zieroth, "Reclaiming the Body / Reclaiming the Nation: A Process of Surviving Colonization in Dennis Lee's 'Civil Elegies and Other Poems,'" *Canadian Literature* 98 (1983): 35–36, 42.
9. Stan Dragland, "On Civil Elegies," *Tasks of Passion: Dennis Lee at Mid-Career*, ed. Karen Mulhallen et al. (Toronto: Descant Editions, 1982), 176.
10. R.D. MacDonald, "Lee's 'Civil Elegies' in Relation to Grant's 'Lament for a Nation,'" *Canadian Literature* 98 (1983): 12–13.
11. These ideas are drawn from both Ann Munton, "Simultaneity in the Writings of Dennis Lee," *Tasks of Passion: Dennis Lee at Mid-Career*, ed. Karen Mulhallen et al. (Toronto: Descant Editions, 1982), 143–69, and Dennis Duffy, *Gardens, Covenants, Exiles: Loyalism in the Literature of Upper Canada / Ontario*, (Toronto: U of Toronto P, 1982), 122.
12. See, for example, Nicholas Bradley, "'Green of the Earth and Civil Grey': Nature and the City in Dennis Lee's *Civil Elegies*," *Canadian Poetry* 55 (2004): 15–33.
13. Isaías Naranjo, "Visions of Heidegger in Dennis Lee and Robert Kroetsch," *University of Toronto Quarterly* 70.4 (2001): 869–80.

14 Lee, *Civil Elegies*, 46.
15 E.D. Blodgett made a similar argument in suggesting that ontology "governs Lee's thought," and that the focus on absence in his writing shows, ultimately, his "metaphysics of presence" in "Reflections on the Prose of Dennis Lee," *Tasks of Passion: Dennis Lee at Mid-Career*, ed. Karen Mulhallen et al. (Toronto: Descant Editions, 1982), 111.
16 Jonathan Kertzer, *Worrying the Nation: Imagining a National Literature in English Canada* (Toronto: U of Toronto P, 1998), 92, 111.
17 Robert Lecker, *The Cadence of* Civil Elegies (Toronto: Cormorant, 2006), 18.
18 Dennis Lee, "Cadence, Country, Silence: Writing in Colonial Space," *Boundary 2* 3.1 (1974): 151.
19 Lee, "Cadence, Country, Silence," 163.
20 Lee, "Cadence, Country, Silence," 165.
21 Dennis Lee, "Grant's Impasse: Beholdenness and the Silence of Reason," *Body Music* (Toronto: Anansi, 1998), 158.
22 Lee, "Cadence, Country, Silence," 168.
23 Lee, "Cadence, Country, Silence," 159.
24 Lee, "Grant's Impasse," 151.
25 Grant, *Lament for a Nation*, 9.
26 George Grant, "Canadian Fate and Imperialism," *Technology and Empire: Perspectives on North America* (Toronto: Anansi, 1969), 63.
27 Grant, *Lament for a Nation*, 54.
28 Robert Lecker makes this point in *The Cadence of* Civil Elegies, 22.
29 Lee, *Civil Elegies*, 27.
30 Lee, *Civil Elegies*, 27–29.
31 Lee, *Civil Elegies*, 29.
32 Lee, *Civil Elegies*, 39.
33 Lecker, *The Cadence of* Civil Elegies, 11.
34 Lee, *Civil Elegies*, 31–32.
35 Lee, *Civil Elegies*, 34.
36 Lee, *Civil Elegies*, 35.
37 Lee, *Civil Elegies*, 36.
38 Lee, *Civil Elegies*, 37–38.
39 Lee, *Civil Elegies*, 38–39.
40 Lee, *Civil Elegies*, 40–43.
41 Lee, *Civil Elegies*, 49.
42 Lee, *Civil Elegies*, 44–45.
43 Lee, *Civil Elegies*, 46.
44 Lee, *Civil Elegies*, 50.
45 Lee, *Civil Elegies*, 50.
46 Lee, *Civil Elegies*, 49.

CHAPTER FOUR

Leonard Cohen's *Beautiful Losers* and the Crisis of Canadian Modernity

While Margaret Atwood and Dennis Lee voice desires for a national space in resistance to American imperialism in Chapters Two and Three, in Leonard Cohen's 1966 novel *Beautiful Losers*, such nationalism is exploded into a panoply of proto-postmodern opportunities that are threatening at the same time as they present a bizarre vision of the new, and that challenge ethics and morals to the core. In the 2005 film *I'm Your Man*, Leonard Cohen—thinking about this book and discussing his preface to the recent Chinese edition—describes it as more of a "sunstroke" than a novel, a product of his removal from its Canadian setting while he was living in Greece. This retrospective characterization of the book is justified. It is a novel that has perplexed readers, defeating attempts to smooth its ragged narrative edges into a comprehensible whole. It has, perhaps as a result, suffered two fates: the first is a lengthy chorus of academic criticisms that grapple with its contours and contexts; the second is a view that the book has become dated, a part of a '60s ethos that no longer holds true. While the latter statement is valid (though why this is the case bears investigation) and *Transnational Canadas* is participating in the perpetuation of the former, this chapter is most concerned with how this text treats questions of Canada, how it looks at borders, and how it transgresses them. Whereas texts concerned with mounting an international defence of Canada construct the nation in self-consciously problematic, yet still determined ways, Cohen's novel seems most interested in the defeat of categories, in the fractures within Canada (especially within Quebec and First Nations communities), in the explosion of myths, and in a defeated joy, or a joyous failure. Michael Ondaatje, in his 1970 book on Leonard Cohen, states that *Beautiful Losers* is a novel in which Cohen makes "heroes and saints out [of] the perverse," but adds that "these saints emerge by existing as fully as possible in the world around them, opening themselves to every sensual and mental energy."[1] The losers become saints in a nation composed, *pace* Lee, of "losers and quislings." All Canadians, one can extrapolate from this juxtaposition, might be wrapped up into this loss. There is a loss of the self, of confidence, of certainty in the novel, and it is through such loss that its characters become the perverse saints that Ondaatje describes. This idea of loss is important to thinking in turn about the centennial construction of the nation and the necessary critiques of it that were to follow. This chapter, then, also suggests the insight of the '60s and '70s nationalists, the self-awareness and self-critique that is implicit within work of the period. Their arguments for Canada and their awareness of the limitations of those arguments are necessary for those critiques that follow.

Beautiful Losers, by refusing to distill what its guru-character F.'s nationalism might mean, presents its readers with a complex vision of politics and representation on the cusp of a postmodern Canada. Cohen's novel is often celebrated as one that introduces a postmodern sensibility to Canadian writing, alongside texts by writers like Hubert Aquin, Robert Kroetsch, Ondaatje, and others. It is a sexually explicit, often disturbing and dark text that refuses to surrender its narrative, let alone its meaning, easily. Divided into three sections, it details the unnamed narrator's relationships with his friend-cum-lover-cum-mentor, F.; his wife, Edith; and Catherine Tekakwitha, a seventeenth-century Iroquois saint. The relationship between the narrator and F. recalls the failing buddy relationship between the characters Krantz and Breavman in Cohen's first novel, *The Favourite Game*, but is much more violent, homoerotic, and disturbing. The first section, written in the voice of the narrator, details these relationships after the deaths of F. and Edith (and the long-dead Catherine). The second part consists of a "long letter from F.," which supplements the first narrative, bidding the narrator to "go beyond" what his friend achieves.[2] The third and shortest part is said to be an epilogue, in which, critics have noted, F., the narrator, and possibly Catherine Tekakwitha's uncle seem to merge.[3] In this section, this composite character emerges from the countryside and moves into a Montreal that wants to both celebrate him as a champion of Quebecois separatism and convict him of child molestation. The text does not allow for an easy decision to be made either way, suggesting a confluence of these achievements—or crimes—as it concludes. Separatism comes to be equated with the rape of colonization, while the narrator's obsession with the history of the "mother church" in North America becomes part of a failing nostalgia for a past purity. This purity, in turn, is dismantled, repeatedly shown to be false; the text leaves the reader with a strong sense of irresolution on this score. Readers of the text have challenged the extent to which this irresolution and disruption might be seen as emancipatory, and this is a debate that continues as values and ideas of emancipation shift among its readers.

The emerging postmodernity that the novel captures in its collapsing structure suggests something about how liberatory politics shift in this period. In its depiction of F. and the narrator's participation in separatist politics, the text suggests the problems of nationalist politics, displaying both their unifying power and the inability of such narratives to hold true while the grand narratives of Western culture are failing. It is in such a context that the still-vital separatist movement of Quebec is seen as a relic of a former era, a notion that is not without political motives when voiced in English Canada. A number of textual details in *Beautiful Losers* indicate difficulties within Quebecois nationalism, and these, commingled with the text's disruption of subjectivity, contribute to the text's suggestions about possibilities for liberation. The novel is bleak, suggesting that the freedoms that F., Edith, and the narrator share are destructive— or at least come at a cost—but it also contests the sort of unified Canada in resistance to the United States that Atwood and Lee uphold despite their conscious reservations and lamentations. In doing so, *Beautiful Losers* leaves readers with an unresolved gesture towards a metaphysical bliss in which the text no longer believes, just as it celebrates a national revolution whose champion, F., disintegrates.

This chapter's secondary purpose is to examine how the reception of *Beautiful Losers* illustrates shifting possibilities for writing in Canada. Ondaatje notes the tempestuous initial reception of the text, stating that "the critics went at it with whips.... there was a howl of derisive triumph over the book" as Cohen, perceived as an egotist and eccentric, was declaimed for having written such a violent, dark, and perverse book.[4] This is a far cry from responses to the novel now, which range from allegations that the text is painfully dated to assertions that it plays a canonical role in defining Canadian literature. How to explain the difference between then and now? Dennis Lee, in his 1977 book *Savage Fields*, reduces *Beautiful Losers* to the "strife" between earth and the world, which stand in for a civilization versus nature dichotomy. Lee declares that his goal is to uncover "the prophetic pattern of Canadian history" through this reading of Cohen. Lee identifies prophecy first and foremost in F.'s teachings, which are, he states, designed "to produce ecstasy in the narrator." Lee is searching for a resolutionary reading, one in which he can perceive "the myth of Canadian history." This is a myth that, Lee contends, takes the shape of "a fall from grace, a period of exile, and a reascent to grace." Lee feels that this narrative is "literally true" in the case of Canada, but he suggests that Cohen is also affirming that "there is another perspective." Lee states that the third part of the book tries to "resolve the impasse" of the first two by merging its two main male characters, and, although he finds this section unconvincing, he concludes by affirming that "the illumination of the narrator is consummated at the end of the novel."[5] Lee's reading places the book in a spiritualistic or transcendental ethos, something from which literary criticism has since shied away. Instead, it seems that the novel concludes by opening up its meaning. It "rent[s]" out its final pages to "the Jesuits,"[6] undermining its closure, and proposes a collapse of subjectivities between F. and the narrator that challenges F.'s nationalist vision of Quebecois liberation and the narrator's lamentation of the failure of history to provide meaning.

A reading of these positions suggests an openness beyond history and beyond grounded narratives of belonging, and it may be this that concerns Lee. He maintains that "radical freedom means a plethora of alienated selves, free-floating I-systems, mocking a self which has been unselved of all but the will to create itself." To him, the way that *Beautiful Losers* portrays "the hunger, highs, and torment of this condition" of radical freedom is its achievement.[7] *Beautiful Losers* becomes, in effect, a morality tale, cautioning against the behaviour of its characters. Criticism has at times concurred with Lee, finding that the novel's portrayal of the central tensions of Canadian literature, or of the clash between the individual and the community, leads to "an alienation of the self, the soul, or the mind from the essential qualities of life."[8] This chapter of *Transnational Canadas* steps away from seeing the text as a morality tale; instead, the imposition of grounded selves through systems of limited belonging may in fact be what leads to an alienated self, one that is limited in terms of the lives it can perform. The will to create the self might, alternatively, lead to a sense of selfhood that is less restrained than Lee's vision of identity. Critics might be right in their arguments when they are arguing for Canada, and writing of the nationalist period does, indeed, seem at times to search for (re)integration of a divided selfhood. This search is surely a corollary of the spirit of the time, in which existentialism and psychoanalysis came together as dominant strains of intellectual discourse.[9] But it is this sort of (re)integration that is challenged in Cohen—and then in later writers—pushing towards a recognition of how Canadian writing might situate itself within an open, expansive global framework in investigating the politics of being and belonging. Cohen's text might be made to serve as a moral fable of sorts, but there are more readings of it available.

While Lee's reading, in its structured desire to achieve resolution, is problematic, his suggestion that *Beautiful Losers* "carries on an ontological debate with itself" is entirely apt.[10] By demonstrating an early postmodern sentiment, *Beautiful Losers* begins to articulate why a static notion of national belonging might be an inadequate stance for artistic modes of inquiry. The characters are caught within a world of expectations that they feel they cannot live up to in good conscience (F.'s role as a Member of Parliament being perhaps the most obvious example). But neither are they able to live their lives for long in their riotous abandon, given those expectations, as well as the physical toll of their contortions. They bear witness to the collapse of the ontological certainties of modernity and, while attempting to resuscitate or transform aspects thereof—the narrator attempts to continue with his pursuit of history all the while realizing its fleeting nature, just as F. pursues a troubling nationalist revolution—this collapse precipitates their own. The postmodern elements of the text participate in a dismantling of previous certainties, a dismantling that the characters have no conceivable way of integrating into their social milieu. They continue within it, but then fail; on the cusp of postmodernity, they become losers whose visions do not fit into the world. Cohen's novel thus offers an historical image that posits a political function to the postmodern, but this function is not realized. The lingering question is whether the characters are in the wrong (Lee's contention), or whether the world itself is.

The narrator troubles the grounds of history in the first section, which is entitled "The History of Them All." It is a history that, he says, he does "not want to write"; he is "a man who hates his memory and remembers everything."[11] The significance of this history is forever escaping him, as he searches to find meaning in the history of the A—— tribe, on which he is conducting research. At the same time, he contemplates the history of his relationship with F. and with his wife, Edith, who, we find out, is a member of this same Indigenous nation. While examining this group, whose "history is characterized by incessant defeat," the narrator ponders what "right" he has to pursue these narratives.[12] As an outsider to the group, he is in a dominant position given the colonial history in which his Anglo-Canadian forebears conquered both the French and the Indigenous peoples that predate them. Following Linda Hutcheon's lead, criticism has observed the structured hierarchization of the struggles in the novel, in which the A——s and other Indigenous peoples are oppressed by the French, who are in turn oppressed by the English, who are in turn oppressed by the off-screen Americans.[13] Hutcheon suggests that, in the novel, "Canadian history is patterned on the process of victimizer turned victim," as one oppressed group seeks to oppress another, with Indigenous people placed on the bottom rung of that ladder.[14] Each group is represented by one of the novel's main characters, Edith, F., and the narrator, and "this trio plays out the history and destiny of Canada, of her successive conquests (the deaths of the Indian, Edith, and the French, F.), and perhaps of her future fate (turning into an American movie)."[15] The narrator is in the position of the Anglo-Canadian, and he wishes to "rescue" the Iroquois Catherine "from the Jesuits," who are the early emissaries of the French.[16] But doing so places him in the difficult position of wishing to oppose the colonial past in which he is implicated. He struggles, recognizing his complicity, while admiring F., who is able to continue along his parallel path with ease, despite recognizing these same complicities. The narrator comes up with a long list of things that he wants to be able to do, which includes gaining acceptance by both "the Communist Party and the Mother Church," all the way through being "against the rich" and finding communion among "the Negroes," Jews, and Basques.[17] He finds himself unable, however, to ascribe to any of the doctrines that these groups offer. The politics of the past and the limited ways in which belonging is conceptualized in the present trouble the narrator, and he is caught, unable to participate in the world as his wife and his best friend / lover die. He is worried that he has "stumbled on the truth about Canada," and it is an ugly truth of arbitrary oppressions and deaths, leading to an inability to embrace a nationalist rhetoric. He speaks of running for Parliament, like F., and passing "off F.'s sayings as [his] own," but he seems not to believe these statements even as he utters them.[18] He witnesses political action and easy gestures of belonging, but is unable to participate because he lacks belief.

F., on the other hand, is untroubled by the past, and allows the domination of Indigenous peoples by the French to continue. He realizes that "of all the things which bind us to the past, the names of things are the most severe." He highlights how the "severe" process of naming fixes things in place, but he nevertheless participates in acts of naming and "colonizing."[19] His life is lived in contradiction to his teachings. F. successfully sets out to have sex with all the remaining women of the A——s, including Edith, thereby reenacting the history of sexual dominance by the French. This dominance parallels, in turn, Edith's childhood rape by French labourers, but F. pursues his conquests under the guise of sexual emancipation. F. is perhaps just more honest in his approach, however. The narrator's historical study of the A——s may also amount to little more than F.'s colonizing sexual endeavours, as both characters exploit the A——s to their own ends. But F. makes the contradictions apparent. His emancipatory politics are those of choosing sides, and he sides with Quebecois nationalism, becoming a member of the Canadian Parliament and siding with the cause of French liberation, even though he sees the limitations of both Canada and Quebec. He is content to embrace contingency. The narrator, in frustration, decries F.'s participation in this system in which neither can completely believe, telling F. that he is "a fake" and "a disgrace to Canada," and that his politics are "filthy."[20] The narrator is right, in that F.'s beliefs waver, but he is still able to choose some form of participation.

The choices that F. makes, given his recognition of their contingency, have been worrying to critics, but, more importantly, they also render national structures open. How can one choose, like the speaker of *Civil Elegies*, to turn back from the void in the world of *Beautiful Losers*? F. does it with self-conscious irony, exploiting the problems that his choices create. When F. and the narrator happen upon a separatist demonstration in Montreal, they go into the crowd and participate. F. embraces the crowd more readily than the narrator does. F. asserts that "it is a beautiful crowd" because the agitators "think they are Negroes" fighting for emancipation, and he is hailed by them as a hero of nationalism, as "a Patriot."[21] The narrator, however, sees the crowd's political actions as a displaced form of sex, and states that everyone there has "a hard-on, including the women."[22] He moves into the crowd and finds himself rubbing against a faceless and nameless woman, who reaches into his trousers and masturbates him nearly to the point of climax. He fails to come, however, just as does the promise of separatism. The parallel is not a chance one, and neither his erection nor the nationalist fervour can maintain itself. The nationalist rhetoric in which F. participates is conflicted: a young speaker in the crowd asserts that "History decreed that in the battle for a continent the Indian should lose to the Frenchman. In 1760 History decreed that the Frenchman should lose to the Englishman" and that, as a result, it is now time that "the English surrender this land…to the Frenchman."[23] The logic is imperfect at best: the conclusion of such a counter-history should be that the land be returned to the first-displaced people, the Iroquois and others whom the French defeated. But the sovereigntist narrative of liberation never arrives at this point. F.'s embrace of this separatist project illustrates a will to participate in power even though the rationale is flawed. He plans to blow himself up along with the statue of the Queen in Montreal's Victoria Square in order to attain separatism and martyrdom, an act that he calls "the happy exercise of the arbitrary."[24] He falls short of his stated goal, but nevertheless makes a physical sacrifice as he loses one of his thumbs. All the while, he maintains an awareness of the contingency of his revolutionary politics.

The teachings that F. offers to the narrator are arcane, even contradictory, perhaps as a result of this mixed recognition of the failure of grand narratives and his pragmatic approach. His teachings offer a hope for a future in which people will "connect nothing,"[25] in which narratives will be unhinged and rewritable, but his own life does not illustrate this directive. He asserts, against such an unhinged position, that "the world is made of races,"[26] for instance, and that this fact must be reckoned with. He is practical, cynically so, recognizing the problems of the world but still taking part. Frank Davey summarizes F.'s position as follows:

> *Beautiful Losers* can be read as a strong response to francophone Quebec nationalism of the 1960s.... F. is ... a political thinker who evolves from a narrowly nationalist and anticonscription position when he is elected to Parliament in the 1940s to a position that envisions a deterritorialization of both the body and politics—a position in which he can understand and sympathize with the sovereigntist rhetoric of the Parc Lafontaine speaker but can imagine a world without its boundaries or sovereignties.[27]

As such, F. counsels the narrator to "go beyond" his style in the posthumous letter that constitutes the second part of the book. He asserts that "God is alive" and that "magic is afoot," but then bids that the narrator should "interpret" and transcend him.[28] F. seems only partly to believe in his assertion that there is a secret code, God or magic, underlying the world; it is certainly a code to which he has had little access. He suggests these limitations in stating to the narrator, "I believed that I had conceived the vastest dream of my generation: I wanted to be a magician. That was my idea of glory. Here is a plea based on my whole experience: do not be a magician, be magic."[29] He allows that his participation in politics is imperfect, as he has proven unable to go beyond his understanding of the world. To replace the divine magic with the self, to become not transcendent, as F. tried, but, rather, to become transcendence itself is the dim possibility that F. holds out to the narrator. F. confesses that he "never saw the Québec Revolution clearly," and that, although he was aware of the problems of history and "tried to slip out of it," he "let History back because [he] was lonely."[30] His populist attachments drive him to a pragmatic position, one in which he falls back into an understanding of the past as a linear movement, just as he falls back into a limited mode of being, one that centres around national belonging. He sees the shortcomings of this position, but remains caught in it, bidding the narrator not to follow. He states that he wants the narrator to be free from "the useless history under which [he] suffer[s] in such confusion." F. suggests, finally, that those "who cannot dwell in the Clear Light ... must deal with symbols," the imperfection of language, and the limited modes of being into which they are interpolated.[31] He is among this crowd.

The sexual politics of the text, which have perhaps caused readers the most consternation, can be read through this lens, which involves looking for ways in which the liberating incoherence that the text calls for is pushed into more certain, but visibly failing narratives.[32] F. and the narrator's sexual congress is a point of anxiety, one that critics have found troubling, who argue that, ultimately, the characters' homoerotic encounters reinscribe heteronormativity, even while providing potential for the novel to open itself to alternative notions of gender. Critics assert that their sex is something readers need to deal with seriously. The novel may be, despite its expressions of queer desire and the ways in which it attempts to "disrupt complacent assumptions," "somewhat homophobic and certainly misogynist," as Terry Goldie suggests.[33] After they have sex, F. tries to assure the narrator that what they share "isn't homosexuality at all" because he is "not strictly male." While this statement gestures towards a disruption of gendered binaries, F. deflates the situation with the phony assertion that he "used to be a girl" prior to having "a Swedish operation."[34] The narrator, who grew up with F. in an orphanage, knows that F. is lying, and tells him so. Rather than dismantling sex/gender dualisms, F.'s flippant remark reinforces them, pushing the narrator to continue in his worries about being a "fairy" and of committing "queer horrible acts with F."[35]

F. asserts, as part of his liberatory project, that he wants to do away with "genital imperialism" by learning to recognize that "all parts of the body are erotogenic."[36] But this goal yields mixed results, and it contrasts with Edith's sudden inability to achieve orgasm through masturbation. She succeeds at length only with the help of F.'s manic Danish Vibrator, which takes on a life of its own, reaffirming "genital imperialism" as it feverishly gets her off. Edith, eventually, commits suicide beneath the elevator of her and the narrator's basement apartment. Her suicide is the result, it seems, of several factors: the history of colonization that she experiences, her use of holy water from the spring of Catherine Tekakwitha as a drug, and the clash between sexual emancipation and her husband's jealousy. We do not hear what her motives are, but are left to infer them from the facts of her life. The acts in which she participates lead the reader to suppose that her encounter with both violence and a terrifying freedom push her to suicide.

The novel ends with the narrative of the man who comes from the forest and into Montreal, to an amusement arcade on St. Lawrence Boulevard. There he is hailed as both "a Patriot" — as F., who has escaped from the asylum to which he is confined after his imprisonment — and as "a stinking cocksucker" — as the narrator, who has been living in F.'s former treehouse and molesting children.[37] The two can be confused or conflated because they both lack a thumb, the narrator having destroyed his when setting off a package of fireworks that F. arranged to have sent to him after his death. The timelines become incoherent, as critics have noted, the merging of identities deliberate. There is no reconciliation possible, but the suggestion remains that nationalism and perversion overlap. Although an alternative future is projected by F., one that might do away with conventional notions of history, the novel remains provisional, situated within a space that can witness alternatives but not live them. Linda Hutcheon argues that "the narrator has not learned from F.'s errors: he too seeks a system, an ordered vision,"[38] suggesting that the revolutionary promise of the novel goes unfulfilled. The grounded stories of nationalism, presented as cognitive maps of the '60s world, might not hold up under scrutiny. But new versions of the future are not available either, leaving F., the narrator, Catherine Tekakwitha, and Edith caught within cycles of history and hierarchies from which they cannot escape.

Notes to Chapter Four

1. Michael Ondaatje, *Leonard Cohen* (Toronto: McClelland and Stewart, 1970), 39, 54.
2. Leonard Cohen, *Beautiful Losers* (Toronto: McClelland and Stewart, 1966), 161, 169. Critics have often referred to the narrator of the book as "I," but this appellation seems awkward; this analysis sticks to a third-person elocution.
3. D.G. Jones first made the observation in *Butterfly on Rock* (Toronto: U of Toronto P, 1970), 80.
4. Ondaatje, *Leonard Cohen*, 45.
5. Dennis Lee, *Savage Fields: An Essay in Literature and Cosmology* (Toronto: Anansi, 1977), 63, 67, 74, 78, 91.
6. Cohen, *Beautiful Losers*, 259.
7. Lee, *Savage Fields*, 100.
8. F.M. Macri, "*Beautiful Losers* and the Canadian Experience," *Journal of Commonwealth Literature* 8.1 (1973): 90.
9. As signalled by the popularity of books like R.D. Laing's *The Divided Self* (New York: Pantheon, 1969).
10. Lee, *Savage Fields*, 76.
11. Cohen, *Beautiful Losers*, 61, 108.
12. Cohen, *Beautiful Losers*, 5, 3.
13. For example in Peter Wilkins, "'Nightmares of Identity': Nationalism and Loss in *Beautiful Losers*," *Intricate Preparations: Writing Leonard Cohen*, ed. Stephen Scobie (Toronto: ECW, 2000), 24–50, and David Leahy, "Re-Reading Linda Hutcheon on *Beautiful Losers, Prochain episode* and *Trou de mémoire*," *Studies in Canadian Literature* 18.2 (1993): 27–42.
14. Linda Hutcheon, "*Beautiful Losers*: All the Polarities," *Canadian Literature* 59 (1974): 45.

15 Linda Hutcheon, *Narcissistic Narrative: The Metafictional Paradox* (Waterloo: Wilfrid Laurier UP, 1980), 159.
16 Cohen, *Beautiful Losers*, 5.
17 Cohen, *Beautiful Losers*, 21–22.
18 Cohen, *Beautiful Losers*, 37.
19 Cohen, *Beautiful Losers*, 43.
20 Cohen, *Beautiful Losers*, 100, 142.
21 Cohen, *Beautiful Losers*, 125, 128. In stating it in this way, F. foreshadows Pierre Vallières' notorious 1968 book, *Nègres blancs de l'Amérique*, as Frank Davey observes in "*Beautiful Losers*: Leonard Cohen's Postcolonial Novel," *Intricate Preparations: Writing Leonard Cohen*, ed. Stephen Scobie (Toronto: ECW, 2000), 17.
22 Cohen, *Beautiful Losers*, 125.
23 Cohen, *Beautiful Losers*, 126.
24 Cohen, *Beautiful Losers*, 143.
25 Cohen, *Beautiful Losers*, 17.
26 Cohen, *Beautiful Losers*, 44.
27 Davey, "*Beautiful Losers*: Leonard Cohen's Postcolonial Novel," 20.
28 Cohen, *Beautiful Losers*, 161, 167, 169.
29 Cohen, *Beautiful Losers*, 175.
30 Cohen, *Beautiful Losers*, 173, 174. For an early reading of the treatment of history in the book, see Douglas Barbour, "Down with History: Some Notes towards an Understanding of *Beautiful Losers*," *Open Letter* 2.8 (1974): 48–60.
31 Cohen, *Beautiful Losers*, 200, 197.
32 See Patricia Morley, *The Immoral Moralists* (Toronto: Clarke, Irwin and Co., 1972) for a discussion of the book's function in the context of Canadian morality in the 1960s and '70s.
33 Terry Goldie, *Pink Snow: Homotextual Possibilities in Canadian Fiction* (Peterborough, ON: Broadview, 2003), 94–95. See also Andrew Lesk, "Leonard Cohen's Traffic in Alterity in *Beautiful Losers*," *Studies in Canadian Literature* 22.2 (1997): 56–65.
34 Cohen, *Beautiful Losers*, 18–19.
35 Cohen, *Beautiful Losers*, 31, 100, 50.
36 Cohen, *Beautiful Losers*, 34.
37 Cohen, *Beautiful Losers*, 256.
38 Hutcheon, "*Beautiful Losers*: All the Polarities," 49.

CONCLUSION TO PART ONE

In his 1965 conclusion to the *Literary History of Canada*, that seemingly inescapable document to which scholars of Canadian literature keep turning, Northrop Frye suggests that "the literature of protest" in Canada has become unhinged, detached from "any specifically Marxist or other political programmes." Such literature is, for Frye, an open-ended construct that can be formulated in a variety of ways, while remaining "a revolutionary garrison within a metropolitan society."[1] Linda Hutcheon, in *The Canadian Postmodern*, articulates a vision for Canadian postmodernism that is distinct from, for example, Jameson's, one that moves literatures of protest away from specific political programs similarly to Frye. For Hutcheon, Canadian postmodernism "render[s] the particular concrete" and "glor[ies] in a (defining) local ex-centricity."[2] She locates this practice particularly in novels that display a metafictive historiographic consciousness, such as Cohen's. In the period around the centennial, debates about protest are articulated through questions of the nation, as writing by Atwood, Lee, and Cohen shows, although these do not seem to have a necessary or even coherent political program. That said, this writing is articulated in continual reference to the nation. But the imagined national community becomes one of resistance to American neo-colonization, suggesting that oppositional logic maintains an important function at the same time as the signifier of "Canadian" lacks its own specific content. Atwood and Lee articulate the ambivalences with which Canada has both failed and succeeded as a nation, while Cohen's *Beautiful Losers*

67

pushes the argument towards a provocative incoherence. While Lee, following Grant, laments history, F. in *Beautiful Losers* looks towards a future in which history becomes malleable, transcendable. Although F. seeks an erasure of the past, his recognition that the national project remains always incomplete and provisional, limited by the competing claims of alternative nationalisms, is key. Atwood makes a strong claim for the nationalism that she supports, and creates a Canadian-centred narrative, in which this nation might be able to create a more positive version of belonging than that available elsewhere. And while nationalism as a defence against international imperialism holds sway, she balances her narrative with a descent into nature that demonstrates the logical impossibility of the national construct in which *Surfacing*'s narrator grounds herself. While Canada is buttressed in the constructions of the '60s and '70s discussed in Part One, its construction also bears the seeds of an inchoate nature. As literary studies began dismantling notions of privilege alongside the culture wars, and as intellectual discourse became more attuned to notions of difference, the limitations of Canadian nationalism became increasingly evident through literary works. In choosing to be a magician, F. can only beguile the masses into following him. When those masses learn his contradictions, the nuances, struggles, and problematics become more and more apparent.

Notes to Conclusion to Part One

1 Northrop Frye, Conclusion to *Literary History of Canada: Canadian Literature in English*, ed. Carl F. Klinck (Toronto: U of Toronto P, 1965), 833–34.
2 Linda Hutcheon, *The Canadian Postmodern* (Toronto: Oxford UP, 1988), 19.

PART TWO

INDIGENEITY AND THE RISE OF CANADIAN MULTICULTURALISM

INTRODUCTION TO PART TWO

One last citation from Northrop Frye, to provide continuity with Part One:

> The writers of the last decade, at least, have begun to write in a world which is post-Canadian, as it is post-American, post-British, and post everything except the world itself. There are no provinces in the empire of aeroplane and television, and no physical separation from the centres of culture, such as they are.[1]

That Canada can be read, as Frye suggests, as existing in a decentred world suggests possible ways of reading Canadian texts that clash with national programs—depending on how the nation is conceived. In Part One, *Transnational Canadas* was concerned with how Canadian texts have debated the national as a means of resisting transnational capitalism, especially as embodied by the United States. Such resistance involved constructing an alternative centre of power in Canada with which to identify. Such centres of power are shifting more and more in the Frygian "empire of aeroplane and television."

At the end of Part One, Leonard Cohen's *Beautiful Losers* disrupted what the nation might mean during a moment of heightened nationalism. Following Cohen, postmodern writers of English fiction in Canada have examined how Canadian literature might be constructed in an open manner around social alternatives—similar to Hutcheon's notion of revelling in the ex-centric. This practice might allow, in the words of Robert Kroetsch, "*this place*, with all its implications, [to become] available to us for literary purposes."² Kroetsch's writing here pursues the social construction of space—the ways in which writing and discourse create a sense of space and place—as a means of moving towards self-definition, focusing on regional writing. He attempts, among many things, to see space not as negatively burdened by the past, unlike in the history that Dennis Lee laments (although new questions are raised in this process). Wolfgang Klooß suggests that such a localizing approach has allowed "the formerly ex-centric a central position and a decisive voice in Canadian literature" in writers such as Rudy Wiebe, Margaret Laurence, and others, a list that we might expand radically.³

Part Two is interested in examining what Klooß calls the ex-centric (picking up on the work of Hutcheon) and how this social category has responded to the nation. If Atwood, Lee, and Cohen present a nuanced and troubled look at writing in Canada, then the authors in Part Two further trouble such perspectives as they present a decentring and disruptive vision of the WASP mentality that they see as dominating Canada. The writings upon which Part Two focuses—all first published in the 1980s—take place in a milieu in which discourses of equity and identity politics are vibrant and passionate, and it looks for ways in which belonging might be reconceived. Part Two takes writing in Canada well into a postmodern ethos and beyond, into a space that is insistently aware of the extent to which transnational and transborder debates are key to an understanding of the self. These discussions are equally ontological and political, examining a world of exclusions and inclusions, as will also emerge in Part Three.

This examination is located in the territory of what has been identified as multicultural writing. This is a difficult label, one that might problematically circumscribe texts within the terrain established by the Canadian government in its Multiculturalism Act and related policies. That said, the label is useful here for several reasons. Liberal philosopher Charles Taylor associates multiculturalism with the concept of recognition, which he sees as a prime demand coming from "minority or 'subaltern' groups, in some forms of feminism and in what is today called the politics of 'multiculturalism.'"⁴ Taylor's equation of the subaltern and the multicultural should render readers wary of the politics of domination involved in questions of voice and coming to speak. The Canadian Multiculturalism Act and its policies broaden the definition of what it means to be Canadian in order to include people who do not come from a Euro-Western background (or even a Western European one), and legislates tolerance of cultural difference. As such, it attempts to perform the distinction that Will Kymlicka proposes for dealing with the "polyethnic" diversity that is encountered in the age of globalization, "manag[ing]" rather than "resolv[ing]" the "politics of difference."[5] For Kymlicka, this process is consistent with the notions of freedom and social justice attached to liberalism, but it might not be completely innocent, either. The Multiculturalism Act has been critiqued in numerous ways, for instance for defining Canada as a pluralistic society, all the while actively subordinating "other" cultures to the twin linguistic—and by extension cultural— hegemonies of English and French (as defined through the Official Languages Act), and for essentializing people's cultures of origins as coming from "outside" Canada. Adam Paul Weisman summarizes the situation when he asserts that "the Canadian understanding of multiculturalism is that an individual's ethnic identity is inherent, group-oriented, grounded in a geographical territory, linguistic, and—most important— unrecombinant," unlike theories of the American melting pot.[6] Donna Bennett further alleges that "by institutionalizing multiculturalism, Canada has encouraged identity through alterity. In doing so, it has effectively institutionalized marginality."[7] Further critics, from Himani Bannerji to Smaro Kamboureli to Eva Mackey, have examined multiculturalism's function in the management of Canadian diversity, identifying policy shortcomings and the consequences of how the Act has been put to use.

The picture is complex. In essence, Canadian multiculturalism has expanded the nation, decentred it, and made diversity a category around which the nation can be organized. Difference need no longer be a disruptor of the national project—quite the reverse, in fact: the celebration of difference has become a part of Canadian nationalism. The Multiculturalism Act seeks to recognize the multiplicity of experiences lived by residents of Canada, all the while seeking to bring these experiences in under the label of "Canadian," even if they disagree with that term. This process is one that writers variously challenge and adopt in their rewritings of how Canada might be understood. Texts that give voice to previously subaltern subjects, whose voices have been unable to be heard by the dominant—or by members of other communities, either—are inserted into national narratives through the act of publication. And those texts that are read widely have been those that the reading public is most able to recognize. This has been an immensely important process.

At the same time, there is an anxious push to exoticize and market difference in this process, alongside the desire to avoid such exoticization. By articulating different bodies that seek recognition, writers assert their place within Canada and are frequently approved of for seeking inclusion (reform) rather than radical disruption (revolution). This movement may be desirable; at the same time, this gesture of inclusion has appeared at times to reify existing power structures by implicitly validating the power of the bodies that recognize difference as such. A bid for social inclusion can be a troubling thing if it leaves the core values of the nation intact. This book's use of the term "multicultural literature" should evoke this problematic. At its best, what *Transnational Canadas* calls multicultural literature in Canada demonstrates that belonging is always already transnational, suggesting that the structures of Canada are impermanent, open, and modifiable. Borders shift, and that is a good thing. Part Two is interested in the dialectic between bids for inclusion that reinforce the norm and those that manage to successfully contest it.

This part, therefore, is concerned with how narratives of Canada have been challenged and/or dismantled through narratives that focus upon the limitations of the nation, especially in terms of questions of ethnicity and race. It is interested in how postcolonial and Indigenous interventions into poststructural and Marxist discourse push criticism to account adequately for difference, and it highlights how, in Canada, these discussions have aligned themselves with debates around multiculturalism, as either a state apparatus or a set of lived (and literary) experiences. A great deal of the literature discussed in Canada has come to be writing that deals with racialization and ethnicity, with a tense dyad in play between exoticizing difference and challenging the construction of the nation. For now, Part Two is concerned with the latter half of the dyad. However, the neo-liberal realignment of Canada also results in a marketing strategy for the country as the site of multicultural difference. In this climate, as Part Three discusses in more depth, difference is something that is attractive for its market value, and the cultural marketplace, as a result, is interested in commodified and exoticized visions of diversity. The national position of seeing Canada as a potentially anti-colonial space in resistance to American imperialism is uprooted at some of the sites of Canadian literature that will be highlighted in that final part to this book, which focuses upon such commodification and exoticization—and resistance to these processes. This is a position that is arrived at through both that uncomfortable national celebration and the ways in which questions of ethnicity and race have worked and reworked the nation.

Part Two is concerned, then, with ways in which racially marked writing posits a challenge to Canadian narratives—and to how one conceptualizes the nation. A discussion of postcolonial studies, a field whose workers have seemed to be transforming themselves into specialists in diaspora or globalization—although the postcolonial is by now an entrenched mode in literary studies—is key to arriving at a broader conceptualization of both the national and the transnational, as is a focus on debates in Indigenous studies, which influence questions of the nation in a global framework and trouble notions of multiculturalism. Theorists of transnational economics and cultures have repeatedly argued that the contemporary moment can no longer be seen as one of decolonization or postcolonialism, but rather as one of brutal recolonization or neo-imperialism, from Baghdad and Abu Ghraib to Israel–Palestine to Tibet to Afghanistan and beyond. Postcolonialism has even been read by Michael Hardt and Antonio Negri—who will be discussed in much more depth in Part Three—as mirroring the methods of a contemporary imperialism that colonizes the globe in the name of an economics that celebrates difference while consolidating capitalist power.[8]

Theorists of the postcolony have questioned whether Canada should be seen as a postcolonial country in light of analyses of the ways in which imperialism is today alive and thriving.[9] This question is a vexed one in Canada, given its history as a settler-invader nation-state and the continuing struggles of Indigenous peoples to have their rights recognized (and the United Nations' damning reports of Canada's treatment of Indigenous people, as well as the Harper government's decision to vote against the UN's declaration on the rights of Indigenous peoples). This part begins, as a result, with a discussion of transnational issues in postcolonial studies. This discussion is followed by readings of multicultural and Indigenous literary productions in Canada. These work with Len Findlay's exhortation to "always indigenize," which is, as he puts it, "a strategically indeterminate provocation to thought and action on the grounds that there is no *hors-Indigène*, no geopolitical or psychic setting, no real or imagined *terra nullius* free from the satisfactions and unsettledments of Indigenous (pre)occupation."[10] Findlay's exhortation is an ethical call to action that *Transnational Canadas* strives to incorporate. Postcolonial and Indigenous thought, as it has emerged in theoretical discussions, responds to Western thought, although it need not rely upon Western dictates for its roots or validation. Postcolonialism has sought to incorporate and interrogate useful aspects of Marxism and poststructuralism, putting them to new political ends. The repeated Western denial of indigeneity, however, makes the call to indigenize a challenging one; this call is increasingly taken up by critics whose perspectives remain important here as this part moves through postcolonial arguments and into Indigenous thought.

Chapter Five opens this discussion by considering some of the legacies of postcolonial studies. In this chapter, Gayatri Spivak's ongoing interaction with the strong Marxist traditions of the Third World and poststructural questions are the focus, especially as they are discussed in her *Critique of Postcolonial Reason* and her ongoing grappling with questions of subalternity. Spivak's methods derive from a long-term engagement with Derrida, but her work profoundly disrupts many of Derrida's foci in its insistent recognition of women and the global South.

This chapter is followed by an investigation of the oft-cited and much-taught *Obasan* by Joy Kogawa, a text that has been repeatedly discussed in analyses of multicultural writing. This text, as much as it contests racism, has also been used to reinforce and validate Canadian notions of multiculturalism and the nation-state. These discourses are placed in the conversation in order to suggest some of the reasons why this text has proven as lasting and important as it has. Chapter Six goes on to look at criticism that has seen the text, in Roy Miki's terms, as either resolutionary or revolutionary. The social valence of this text is both challenging and sometimes problematic, but it is, certainly, a Canadian text that exemplifies many of the tensions of state multiculturalism.

If *Obasan* manages to challenge the state and push towards its reconfiguration, this is not always a straightforward or even apparent process in multicultural writing. Chapter Seven examines Michael Ondaatje's bestselling novel *In the Skin of a Lion*, a book that has often been discussed in terms of its revolutionary politics. These politics are seen as working towards a recognition of both workers and non-Anglophone Canadians. The terms in which the text has been discussed are, frankly, somewhat confusing; the text is read here as one whose politics largely evaporate under close scrutiny. As much as the text focuses upon communities engaged in acts of dissent, the content of those politics seems to be lacking. Celebrations of this text as one that seeks to rewrite narratives of Canada are therefore of interest. What content does the multicultural nation-state maintain? Does such a literary text challenge that content in a globalizing era? How so? *In the Skin of a Lion* poses several problems for any uncritical acceptance of state-sponsored notions of difference. They need close scrutiny, both in this text and more generally.

The discussions of Kogawa's and Ondaatje's interventions enable the following one, in which Indigenous knowledges in contemporary North America are considered through an examination of Jeannette Armstrong's novel *Slash*. Chapter Eight considers Indigenous challenges to how the transnational might be viewed within the colonial nation-state, and allows for an articulation of the relationship between Frank Davey's *Post-National Arguments* and *Transnational Canadas*. Questions of representation and value here become questions about sovereignty and political representation. The discussion of *Slash* is approached through a reading of the contrasts between Muskogee-Creek scholar Craig Womack's *Red on Red: Native American Literary Separatism* and Kahnawake Mohawk scholar Taiaiake Alfred's *Peace, Power, Righteousness: An Indigenous Manifesto*. These texts are read against one another in order to think through the complexity of Indigenous national resistance. Attempting to follow Linda Tuhiwai Smith's call to avoid conducting research "through imperial eyes,"[11] this chapter reads these texts and *Slash* as books profoundly concerned with (de)colonization but also with more than just the white settler-invader populations, and looking towards questions of community revitalization and growth.

Notes to Introduction to Part Two

1 Northrop Frye, Conclusion to *Literary History of Canada: Canadian Literature in English*, ed. Carl F. Klinck (Toronto: U of Toronto P, 1965), 848.
2 Robert Kroetsch, "On Being an Alberta Writer," *Open Letter* 5.4 (1983): 76.
3 Wolfgang Klooß, "From Colonial Madness to Postcolonial Ex-Centricity: A Story about Stories of Identity Construction in Canadian Historiographic (Meta-) Fiction," *Historiographic Metafiction in Modern American and Canadian Literature*, ed. Bernd Engler and Kurt Müller (Paderborn, Germany: Ferdinand Schöningh, 1994), 58.
4 Charles Taylor, *Multiculturalism and "The Politics of Recognition"* (Princeton: Princeton UP, 1992), 25.
5 Will Kymlicka, *Multicultural Citizenship: A Liberal Theory of Minority Rights* (Oxford: Clarendon, 1995), 193.

6   Adam Paul Weisman, "Reading Multiculturalism in the United States and Canada: The Anthological vs. the Cognitive," *University of Toronto Quarterly* 69.3 (2000): 708.
7   Donna Bennett, "English Canada's Postcolonial Complexities," *Essays on Canadian Writing* 51–52 (1993–1994): 194.
8   Michael Hardt and Antonio Negri, *Empire* (Cambridge: Harvard UP, 2000), 137–39.
9   On the question of Canada's postcolonial status, see Laura Moss, ed., *Is Canada Postcolonial? Unsettling Canadian Literature* (Waterloo: Wilfrid Laurier UP, 2003).
10 Len Findlay, "Always Indigenize! The Radical Humanities in the Postcolonial Canadian University," *Ariel: A Review of International English Literature* 31.1–2 (2000): 309.
11 Linda Tuhiwai Smith, *Decolonizing Methodologies: Research and Indigenous Peoples* (London: Zed, 1999), 56.

CHAPTER FIVE

Critique of Spivakian Reason and Canadian Postcolonialisms

This chapter works with the thinking of Gayatri Chakravorty Spivak, who has been one of the most vocal postcolonial cultural critics. Her discussion of representation and the subaltern is brought here to Canadian literature's discussions of multiculturalism and cultural difference because her struggles are indicative of some of the convulsions through which Canadian literature has gone. She has maintained a long and complex relationship with Marxist and poststructural theorists, continually seeking to bring non-Western contexts and women into these arguments. The focus here, her 1999 book *A Critique of Postcolonial Reason*, rewrites Spivak's earlier famous essay "Can the Subaltern Speak?" — a rewriting that illustrates her continual grappling with similar political and literary themes. Importantly, her answers to some of her own questions about contemporary Third World women shift in her revision. The original essay has been hailed as among the "ur-texts of postcolonialism," one that contributed to understanding deconstruction in the context of anti-imperial resistance movements.[1] It is in this spirit that Spivak has worked through Derrida, Jameson, and others, noting the limits of these thinkers by stating, for example, that Derrida "cannot know the connection between industrial capitalism, colonialism, so-called postindustrial capitalism, neocolonialism, electronified capitalism, and the current financialization of the globe, with the attendant phenomena of migrancy and ecological disaster," given his situation.[2] Derrida remains for Spivak a somewhat myopic if amiable Westerner who, while useful in his thinking, remains outside the fields of postcolonial and transnational studies. One of her tasks is thus to read through Marxism, deconstruction, and poststructuralism, looking for spaces in which the subaltern woman—the woman subjected in the Third World to the intersecting oppressions of patriarchy, racism, and capitalism—might begin to represent herself, rather than being represented by a Western, male voice, however benevolent.

While positioning herself as being on the political left, and often as a Marxist, Spivak reads Marx not only as enabling a reading of the interconnection between capitalism and imperialism, but also simultaneously contributing to the difficulties of representation. Marx signals an interest in the rise of transnational capitalism, and, although non-European perspectives remain largely occluded in his writing, he provides the means of beginning to articulate the oppressions of capitalism when it is transposed across territories. In *The Communist Manifesto*, Marx and Engels argue that "the need of a constantly expanding market for its products chases the bourgeoisie over the whole surface of the globe" and that "the bourgeoisie has through its exploitation of the world market given a cosmopolitan character to production and consumption in every country."[3] These statements identify the capitalist tendency towards imperialism that is analyzed in Marx's writing, although he was unable to deliver upon the initially planned fifth and sixth volumes of *Capital*, which were to have focused upon international trade and the world market, respectively.[4] Nevertheless, Marx's analysis of transnational capitalism can be traced in the extant volumes of *Capital*, especially the chapter "Foreign Trade" in volume three. Here Marx discusses how "the expansion of foreign trade" is "the specific product of the capitalist mode of production," given the necessity for capitalism to create ever-expanding markets in order to foster growth.[5] Imperialism is an integral component of capitalism in Marx's reading. This combined imperialist and capitalist process is analyzed in the chapter "The Modern Theory of Colonization" in the initial volume of *Capital*, where Marx discusses the manner in which the creation of the worker is a necessary component of imperialism. The creation of the worker is necessary to imperialism given the worker's supposedly non-subordinated status prior to colonization, which is founded in his ownership of the means of small-scale production (Marx's worker is, of course, male). Subordination to a foreign power comes through the adoption of the capitalist model. This dependence upon the capitalist organization of labour, Marx notes, "must be created through artificial means" in the colonies, and it is one of the oppressive effects of imperialism there.[6]

Spivak notes difficulties with Marx's representations of the world outside the West, of the colonies that capitalism creates. She highlights, in particular, problems in Marx's sketch of what he terms the "Asiatic Mode of Production" in his *Contribution to the Critique of Political Economy*. Spivak critiques Marx's *Contribution* and other writing for reducing the Asiatic and the Western to two opposed masses in which the latter is privileged. Marx is worth citing here at some length from his *Surveys in Exile*; for him, the Indian village is

> the solid foundation of Oriental despotism.... England, it is true, in causing a social revolution in Hindustan was actuated by only the vilest interests, and was stupid in her manner of enforcing them. But that is not the question. The question is, can mankind fulfill its destiny without a fundamental revolution in the social state of Asia? If not, whatever may have been the crimes of England she was the unconscious tool of history in bringing about that revolution.[7]

This passage has been discussed repeatedly.[8] Marx advocates colonization in the name of progressing towards a communist future, given that communism is, in his theory, the result of the capitalist system's internal contradictions. Such an ideology becomes, in Spivak's reading, a reiteration of her idea that imperialism argues for the necessity of "white men saving brown women from brown men" through the process of colonization.[9] This act of "saving" is used, she argues, to legitimize colonization as a benevolent act, and it ties into the issue of representation.

This concomitant issue surfaces in another of Marx's phrases that has been a focus for postcolonial critics, his classic formulation in *The Eighteenth Brumaire of Louis Napoleon* that "they cannot represent themselves; they must be represented."[10] This line is situated towards the end of a lengthy text dealing with Louis Napoleon and French politics since the 1789 revolution. The line itself deals with what Marx terms the "small-holding peasants," a group that is difficult to assess because of its disparity. The problem is with how they will be represented politically, and for

Marx this is of course an issue of class. As far as he can tell, this group forms a class insofar as they share a common method of production, one that divides them from the other classes as subordinates engaging in production for their own sustenance. But, at the same time, because they have "no national linkage and no political organization, they do not form a class." As a result, Marx reasons, they are "incapable of asserting their class interests in their own name."[11] They therefore require political representation from another body, since they cannot be represented by themselves in any coherent form. Representation is needed, in Marx's reading, when a group does not become uniform enough to articulate its class concerns. Attempts to represent itself would dissolve into solipsism. The answer, for Marx, is to provide political representation that speaks to what *should* be the relevant class interest.

This concern connects to authors coming to speak from minoritized positions. Who could fairly speak on behalf of an ethnic, cultural, gendered, or classed group was among the most important literary debates of the 1980s and '90s in Canada, culminating in the widespread furor around the Writing Thru Race conference in 1994 in Vancouver, which excluded white participants in order to create a space for racialized writers.[12] The problem of representation extends, as it does for Spivak, beyond Marx's concern for class and into broader questions. Representation is, in its several forms (political, linguistic, metaphorical), indeed one of the central issues addressed in "Can the Subaltern Speak?" In the essay, Spivak focuses on "how the third world subject is represented within Western discourse," via Gilles Deleuze and Michel Foucault,[13] prior to moving to a discussion of attempts by Indian women to articulate themselves despite their subaltern status. Spivak reads these articulations through the 1926 suicide by hanging of Bhuvaneswari Bhaduri, which she sees as a rewriting of the sati-suicide, that is, as a rethinking of the Hindu practice of widow-burning through self-immolation.[14] Spivak reads the practice of widow-burning as one that belongs to the largely privileged classes, and summarizes the history of its being outlawed by the English. Local reasons for resistance to the British legislation were invalidated in this history by reading sati from a Western perspective as a simple case of patriarchal subordination. Spivak wishes to create a more nuanced picture and to note the layers of colonial significance that are added to sati through the British ban. In her later rewriting of the essay, she notes that "it is the place of the free will or agency of the sexed subject as female that is successfully effaced" by situating sati as a cultural debate between the British—the imperialist white men—and the Hindu men—the brown men from whom the white men are saving the brown women.[15] The position of the women is overwritten, erased.

If the continuation of sati resists the imposition of Western values, the English attempt to outlaw it speaks of the universalization of their beliefs under imperialism. Bhuvaneswari Bhaduri's suicide is read as an attempt to articulate resistance on several levels. Spivak asks whether "the ideology of *sati*, coming from the history of the periphery" can "be sublated into any model of interventionist practice" or, in other words, whether the transformation of sati into suicide functions as a means of articulating resistance to oppression in the context of both imperialism and patriarchy.[16] Spivak traces after-effects of the suicide, noting that the woman's nieces thought of the suicide as "a case of illicit love," despite Bhuvaneswari Bhaduri's attempts to demonstrate otherwise.[17] Spivak concludes, as a result of the failure of her own family to acknowledge her resistance, that "the subaltern as female cannot be heard or read" and, consequently, that "the subaltern cannot speak."[18] In the context of imperialism, women's dissenting attempts to speak themselves, even through death, are bound to fail, as women do not have the agency to be heard. As a disparate group without a unified self-conceptualization or stated class interest, they cannot represent themselves.

The details to Spivak's argument are more instructive than a glancing look at her classic essay would be today.[19] Her argument is useful because for her it does not necessarily follow that these women *must* be represented, in line with Marx. If the subaltern woman cannot speak or be heard, stepping in and representing her concerns is a fraught project. While the subaltern cannot represent herself, engaging in representing her must be thought through beyond Marx's formulation—as must any eventual coming-to-speak of the subaltern herself. For Gyan Prakash, Spivak's conclusion that the subaltern woman cannot speak demonstrates in turn "the limits of historical knowledge," and results in a resistance to "a paternalist 'recovery' of the subaltern's voice and frustrates our repetition of the imperialist attempt to speak for the colonized subaltern woman."[20] The question of representation is not straightforward. It does not simply follow that one should engage in representation on behalf of dominated women. The question of representation becomes one whose answer varies based upon the locatedness of the speaking subject, its proximity to the voices for which it might be speaking. Imperialism may represent the speech of the subaltern in order to effect its own agenda, while the subaltern herself may recognize the futility of speech or of being heard and attempt to transgress beyond subordination. The different locations of subjectivity are important and have been central in Spivak's ongoing struggles with the issue of subaltern speech.

This dialogue on the subaltern woman, after some twenty years' discussion on Spivak's part, is ongoing. While her first writing of the essay states that the subaltern woman cannot speak, her revisions of the piece have led her to the position in her *Critique* that "it was an inadvisable remark."[21] Looking back, she states that in the early essay, she "was so unnerved" by the "failure of communication" between Bhuvaneswari Bhaduri and her nieces that she determined that the subaltern could not speak, working from her case study to a generalization that women, defined as subordinated and without agency in a subaltern context, are unable to be heard and are thus unable to speak. The process of revising this position into its newer form in the chapter titled "History" in the *Critique* is a long one. When Donna Landry and Gerald MacLean were assembling *The Spivak Reader*, she refused their request to publish the original essay, instead agreeing to an interview on the subject. In the interview, the editors note that her decision came from the fact that the revision that was soon to appear in the *Critique* "made the original version obsolete."[22] At nearly the same time as the reader appeared, Spivak published an essay in which she derided "Can the Subaltern Speak?" as "a turgid piece," and she continues the story of the suicide into the present in light of the fact that the woman's "eldest sister's eldest daughter's eldest daughter's eldest daughter" had become an executive member of "a US-based transnational" corporation—and has thereby, Spivak argues, become complicit in the imperialism against which she positioned the original suicide. This revelation leads Spivak to suggest that she "hanged herself in vain."[23] While Spivak expresses some doubt about her original despair over the subaltern woman, she continues to question the ability of others to hear subaltern speech. In the interview with the editors of the reader, Spivak asserts that the original essay is "too complicated," given that her answer to her question was often misrecognized as a more literal statement about speech. Instead, Spivak suggests that she means that "even when the subaltern makes an effort to the death to speak, she is not able to be heard."[24] It is this failure of the cycle of communication that prompted the initial expression of despair.

Spivak has displaced the question of communication in subsequent thinking by reconsidering the concept of subalternity. The difficulty, Spivak notes, is that "subaltern insurgency... *is* an effort to involve oneself in representation, *not* according to the lines laid down by the official institutional structure of representation."[25] But this involvement in representation is difficult, given how the subaltern has been thought. Spivak returns in her *Critique* to Antonio Gramsci's conceptualization of the subaltern in his *Prison Notebooks*, in which Gramsci defines the group as those who are systematically excluded from the exercise of power by the hegemony: "the subaltern classes," Gramsci states, "are not unified and cannot unite until they are able to become a 'State': their history, therefore, is intertwined with that of civil society, and thereby with the history of States and groups of States."[26] The subaltern is thus similar to Marx's small-holding peasants.

Spivak builds upon both Gramsci and the elaborations of the Subaltern Studies Group, and especially upon the definition of subalternity forwarded by Ranajit Guha, who defines the Indian subaltern as s/he who is excluded from any position of dominance, as determined by the elites who control the means of representation: for Guha, "subordination cannot be understood except as one of the constitutive terms in a binary relationship of which the other is dominance."[27] This opposition creates a suppressed group whose identity consists in "*the demographic difference between the total Indian population and all those whom we [describe] as the 'elite.'*"[28] This group, shifting according to its differences from the elite, has been, Guha argues, overlooked by historians, or else read as a part of resistance movements connected to the elites. The utility of Guha's definition for Spivak is that it is one "that can only be an identity-in-differential."[29] For Spivak, the practice of the subaltern studies group "is closer to deconstruction" than anything else, affording her an opening into the subject.[30] That is, the subaltern is a subject whose identity cannot be conceptualized as static, as s/he is subject to the mobile workings of elite power. We get a concept of identity that is determined by a process of *différance*: the subaltern is determined through difference and deferral, as s/he remains in flux. Spivak's position in the *Critique* that "knowledge of the other subject is theoretically impossible" is amplified, as this other is one who can be known only in reference to the elite that excludes her/him.[31] By definition, in this sense, the subaltern cannot speak in that s/he cannot be heard, as Spivak suggests. Radically tied to a context of domination, attempts to speak on the part of the subaltern result either in not being heard or in transcending the position of subalternity.

This second proposition is increasingly important in Spivak's engagement with the question of subaltern speech: being heard, she argues, lends a modicum of agency that is by definition impossible for the subaltern and is therefore connected to movement into the elite or the dominant. Spivak makes the point in her conclusion to the rewritten version of "Can the Subaltern Speak?" that

> when a line of communication is established between a member of subaltern groups and the circuits of citizenship and institutionality, the subaltern has been inserted into the long road to hegemony. Unless we want to be romantic purists or primitivists about "preserving subalternity"—a contradiction in terms—this is absolutely to be desired.[32]

As soon as the subaltern is heard, s/he moves into a position of alignment with the dominant in a quest for adequate (self-)representation. At this point of recognition, the difference of the subaltern can be spoken and thought within the parameters of the dominant. Prior to this recognition, the concept of one subaltern group or another remains impossible within the dominant. The consequence in Spivak's rewriting is that the women whom she discusses can no longer be seen as "purely" subaltern. In a somewhat wrought phrase, she states that "for the (gender-unspecified) 'true' subaltern group, whose identity is in its difference, there is no unrepresentable subaltern subject that can know and speak itself."[33] As long as these identities remain deferred, the subaltern cannot know her- or himself as s/he is not self-defining, not having the agency of speech. Once s/he can know and speak her- or himself, on the other hand, s/he ceases to be the "true" subaltern. The women whom Spivak discusses, then, can no longer be seen as subaltern, as the modicum of repressed speech that they do achieve leads to the beginnings of representation.

Spivak's rewriting, then, manoeuvres around the question of whether the subaltern can speak. The implication of Spivak's thought is that the process of incorporation removes subaltern groups from their identity-in-differential and leads them into representation, with the concretization of identity positions that accompanies the shift into articulable language. The difficulty for some of retaining resistant and unfixed identities remains. As a deconstructive theorist, Spivak recognizes the certain necessary openness of identity, but the road to the hegemonic onto which she places her subaltern suggests a valorization of a position that requires different sorts of struggles. These struggles are uneven; coming to speak still relies on the hearer, and the power of the hearer continues to affect how the marginalized are heard. A great deal of power differential remains between the fixing power of the dominant and the marginalized former subaltern on the road to hegemony. Coming to speak demonstrates a modicum of power, as one participates in the hegemonic in some way. Spivak emphasizes that this position needs to be understood as a good thing when the alternative is to remain unheard.

The global complexities of representing a subordinated group—be it subaltern or marginalized—further highlights issues of value, both literary and economic. One of the central issues that emerged through identity politics was a reconsideration of the construction of canonicity (emblematized by the debates between Robert Lecker and Frank Davey in Canada).[34] What constitutes literary value has been paramount in these discussions, especially as Eurocentric models of writing have been challenged. Self-representations by previously marginalized groups have been valorized as a shift from being represented by the dominant. This process is caught up within the movements of the dominant, as groups coming to self-representation move onto Spivak's "long road to hegemony." Spivak elaborates on the connected notion of value in her "Scattered Speculations on the Question of Value," in which she reads the idea of literary value in the context of Marx's discussion of the production of surplus value. Spivak examines how "the issue of value surfaces in literary criticism with reference to canon-formation." Representation becomes a function of value in the capitalist context, mediating the transformation of value into money, which is in turn transformed into capital.[35] That is, value is something that requires representation. In the context of capitalism, representation is money; in literary studies, that representation is canonicity—a text's *currency*—but the underlying values need interrogation.[36] These transformations from value to capital constitute a series of displacements, which Spivak reads in the context of "universal equivalents" like money, such as the concept of "'universal humanity'—both psychological and social—as the touchstone of value in literature and society."[37] The growing value of minority or multicultural literatures, in this context, derives from their ability to produce surplus value, both in the basic sense of producing revenue for publishers and in the context of creating cultural worth. The potential for complicity

87

or alliance between literary production and capitalism is a tension that will remain; it is necessary in this context to avoid romanticizing authorship, and it is productive to see equity-seeking texts as co-existing with commercially minded literary products in a marketplace governed by economics. How texts may or may not challenge how representation functions in Canada is the more immediate focus for now, however, as Part Two is interested in how texts have served as a broadening force whose represented subjects join the trek towards the hegemony. These have functioned as a challenging and disruptive force that alters how meaning is made in Canada.

This concern with representation and value helped many writers to emerge from non-Western perspectives, challenging ways in which diverse populations have been represented in mainstream texts. Many writers in Canada have seen their work as a part of coming to speak for themselves or for their communities, and this participation in what Spivak sees as the path to hegemony has indeed often been valorized. Such work has challenged national visions of Canada but also exists in a difficult relationship to these, especially considering the ways in which minority writing has worked with, alongside, and against Canada's state visions of multiculturalism. Multiculturalism is, as Eva Mackey sees it, a tool for management, and "recognizing difference" has been, she suggests, "integrally linked to state management of difference" in Canada.[38] Multicultural texts, in this context, can also participate in the hegemonic processes of social management even as they contest how Canada has been constituted. It is within this nexus of problems that this part of *Transnational Canadas* is situated, examining how subaltern or suppressed voices in Canada have come to speech, along the way altering how Canada has constituted itself. At times these voices participate in state processes and, at other times, they reject them entirely. The problematics of speech are not simply those of ensuring that all voices are represented within the polis. Instead, coming to speech is a fraught process, and it has become necessary to look beyond mere ideas of inclusion in understanding difference in our globalizing world.

Notes to Chapter Five

1 Neil Larsen, "Marxism, Postcolonialism, and *The Eighteenth Brumaire*," *Marxism, Modernity and Postcolonial Studies*, ed. C. Bartolovich and N. Lazarus (Cambridge: Cambridge UP, 2002), 204, 214.
2 Gayatri Chakravorty Spivak, "Ghostwriting," *Diacritics* 25.2 (1995), 68.

3 Karl Marx and Friedrich Engels, *The Communist Manifesto* (London: Penguin, 1967), 83.
4 This plan was laid out in a letter to Engels written April 2, 1858 (*Selected Correspondence, 1846–1895: Karl Marx and Friedrich Engels*, trans. D. Torr (New York: International, 1942), 104). Although Marx died in 1883, Engels assembled volumes two and three of *Capital* posthumously; the rest remained unwritten, although the plan appears to have changed over time.
5 Karl Marx, *Capital*, vol. 3, trans. D. Fernbach (London: Penguin, 1981), 344.
6 Karl Marx, *Capital*, vol. 1, trans. B. Fowkes (London: Penguin, 1976), 937.
7 Karl Marx, *Surveys from Exile*, ed. D. Fernbach (London: Pelican, 1973), 306–307.
8 In *Orientalism*, Edward Said argues that Marx never wavered in his belief that "even in destroying Asia, Britain was making possible there a real social revolution," and that, for Marx, "as human material the Orient is less important than as an element in a Romantic redemptive project. Marx's economic analyses are perfectly fitted thus to a standard Orientalist undertaking, even though Marx's humanity, his sympathy for the misery of the people, are clearly engaged" (New York: Vintage, 1978), 153–54. Aijaz Ahmad argues for a more nuanced take on both Marx's India and orientalism, arguing against seeing the passage as paradigmatic in *In Theory* (London: Verso, 1992), 222–23, while Pranav Jani tracks how Marx's "conceptual shifts" led him away from such Eurocentrism in "Karl Marx, Eurocentrism, and the 1857 Revolt in British India," *Marxism, Modernity and Postcolonial Studies*, ed. C. Bartolovich and N. Lazarus (Cambridge: Cambridge UP, 2002), 83.
9 Gayatri Chakravorty Spivak, "Can the Subaltern Speak?" *Marxism and the Interpretation of Culture*, ed. C. Nelson and L. Grossberg (Urbana: U of Illinois P, 1988), 296.
10 Karl Marx, "The Eighteenth Brumaire of Louis Napoleon," *Later Political Writings*, ed. and trans. T. Carver (Cambridge: Cambridge UP, 1996), 117.
11 Marx, "The Eighteenth Brumaire," 117.
12 On the question of appropriation and Writing Thru Race from the perspective of the conference participants, see especially Roy Miki, "Sliding the Scale of Ellision: 'Race' Constructs / Cultural Practice," *Broken Entries: Race, Subjectivity, Writing* (Toronto: Mercury, 1998), 125–59; and Dionne Brand, "Whose Gaze, and Who Speaks for Whom" and "Notes for Writing Thru Race," *Bread Out of Stone: Recollections on Sex, Recognitions, Race, Dreaming and Politics* (Toronto: Vintage, 1994), 113–31, 187–92. Stephen Henighan reports dissenting views in "'Appropriation of Voice': An Open Letter," and "The Terrible Truth About 'Appropriation of Voice,'" *When Words Deny the World: The Reshaping of Canadian Writing* (Erin, ON: Porcupine's Quill, 2002), 59–61, 63–69. Brand's and Miki's targets are Neil Bissoondath and Robert Fulford, inter alia, the former as an apologist for those who would speak for the marginalized, and the latter as the embodiment of Canada's white establishment.
13 Spivak, "Can the Subaltern Speak?" 271.
14 For an extended discussion of sati, in part motivated by Spivak's writing, see Lata Mani, *Contentious Traditions: The Debate on Sati in Colonial India* (Berkeley: U of California P, 1998).
15 Spivak, *A Critique of Postcolonial Reason* (Cambridge, MA: Harvard UP, 1999), 235.
16 Spivak, "Can the Subaltern Speak?" 307.
17 Spivak, "Can the Subaltern Speak?" 308.
18 Spivak, "Can the Subaltern Speak?" 308.

19 Doing so also prevents some of the pitfalls of the easier criticisms made of her statement—a statement that has been, surely, one of the most debated in postcolonial studies. Spivak has been accused of silencing the subaltern on numerous occasions, but also lauded on many others. One useful starting point for such reading is Sandhya Shetty and Elizabeth Jane Bellamy, "Postcolonialism's Archive Fever," *Diacritics* 30.1 (2000): 25–48.
20 Gyan Prakash, "Postcolonial Criticism and Indian Historiography," *Dangerous Liaisons: Gender, Nation, and Postcolonial Perspectives*, ed. A. McClintock et al. (Minneapolis: Minnesota UP, 1997), 494–95.
21 Spivak, *Critique of Postcolonial Reason*, 308.
22 Gayatri Chakravorty Spivak, "Subaltern Talk: Interview with the Editors," *The Spivak Reader*, ed. D. Landry and G. MacLean (New York: Routledge, 1996), 289.
23 Gayatri Chakravorty Spivak, "Diasporas Old and New: Women in the Transnational World," *Textual Practice* 10.2 (1996): 262–63.
24 Spivak, "Subaltern Talk," 288, 292.
25 Spivak, "Subaltern Talk," 306.
26 Antonio Gramsci, *Selections from the Prison Notebooks*, ed. and trans. Q. Hoare and G. Smith (London: Lawrence and Wishart, 1971), 52.
27 Ranajit Guha, Preface to *Selected Subaltern Studies*, ed. R. Guha and G. Spivak (New York: Oxford UP, 1988), 35.
28 Ranajit Guha, "On Some Aspects of the Historiography of Colonial India," *Selected Subaltern Studies*, ed. R. Guha and G. Spivak (New York: Oxford UP, 1988), 44.
29 Spivak, *Critique of Postcolonial Reason*, 271.
30 Gayatri Chakravorty Spivak, "Subaltern Studies: Deconstructing Historiography," *Selected Subaltern Studies*, ed. R. Guha and G. Spivak (New York: Oxford UP, 1988), 4.
31 Spivak, *Critique of Postcolonial Reason*, 283.
33 Spivak, *Critique of Postcolonial Reason*, 310.
33 Spivak, *Critique of Postcolonial Reason*, 272.
34 See Robert Lecker's article "The Canonization of Canadian Literature: An Inquiry into Value," *Critical Inquiry* 16.3 (1990): 656–71. Robert Lecker, defending his article, argues "Canadian literature today reflects a displaced form of nationalism that is conveyed through a mimetic literature that comprises what we commonly refer to as the Canadian canon" in his "Response to Frank Davey," *Critical Inquiry* 16.3 (1990): 682. Davey argues that Lecker provides too "unitary conceptualizations" of the Canadian canon in "Canadian Canons," *Critical Inquiry* 16.3 (1990): 672, and provides an indirect refutation of Lecker in his book *Post-National Arguments* (Toronto: U of Toronto P, 1993), among other writings, by arguing that Canadian literature is becoming postnational. Lecker's book *Making It Real: The Canonization of English-Canadian Literature* includes the initial essay and expands the argument (Toronto: Anansi, 1995).
35 Gayatri Chakravorty Spivak, "Scattered Speculations on the Question of Value," *In Other Worlds: Essays in Cultural Politics* (New York: Routledge, 1988), 154, 158.
36 This model of value varies from Pierre Bourdieu's also useful model of capital, in which economic capital is merely one form of capital, while cultural capital might be said to describe the value that attaches to canonicity.
37 Spivak, "Scattered Speculations on the Question of Value," 164.
38 Eva Mackey, *The House of Difference: Cultural Politics and National Identity in Canada* (Toronto: U of Toronto P, 2002), 62.

CHAPTER SIX

Multiculturalism and Reconciliation in Joy Kogawa's *Obasan*

It is in the spirit of interrogating the politics of inclusion that this chapter turns to Joy Kogawa's *Obasan*. *Obasan* is a novel that appears to have had a measurable impact upon culture in Canada beyond its textual confines—something that is rather rare. Joy Kogawa has not only created the text—and a children's version of the novel, as well as a sequel, first titled *Itsuka* and recently edited and republished as *Emily Kato*—but she has also been active in the Japanese redress movement. This is a movement that has, with substantial success, sought both acknowledgment of and compensation for the fact that Canadian citizens of Japanese descent were imprisoned, displaced, and in some cases deported during and after the Second World War by the Canadian government. When Brian Mulroney's Progressive Conservative government announced its settlement with the Japanese Canadian redress movement on September 22, 1988—some two months after the Crown's assenting to the Multiculturalism Act—*Obasan* was cited in the House of Commons as evidence for the errors of previous governments. Kogawa's childhood home in Vancouver has also been a recent focus of conservation efforts, as the house was threatened by demolition. Conservationists have successfully argued that the house needs to be preserved as a part of maintaining awareness of Canada's history of racism and intolerance. *Obasan* has also played an important role in establishing Asian Canadian writing. First published in 1981, it can be seen as a forerunner to the successes of Japanese Canadian writers such as Roy Kiyooka (who was already working by then but was less well received), Roy Miki, Hiromi Goto, and a much wider array of Asian Canadian writing. It is a book that renders visible and recognizable a segment of Canadians who were marginalized. As a result, it plays an important role in expanding what sorts of writing might be read, valorized, and canonized. In *Itsuka*, the character Emily Kato states that the community of Japanese Canadians is "being eaten up...because others define us."[1] *Obasan* and Kogawa's work is part of contesting just such a process of being defined from the outside.

The uses to which this text has been put suggest some of its politics of recognition. *Obasan* is built around a series of silences, about people wanting to forget the histories of violence and racism that they have faced in order to live in Canadian society. Their attempts at integration fail, however, because racism in Canada, in both its subtle and explicit forms, leads to white Canadians' failure to recognize the novel's narrator, Naomi Nakane, and her family members as Canadian. This failure comes about despite Naomi's aunt Emily's vigorous assertions of Canadian belonging. Much of the family seeks inclusion through an erasure of their origins and pasts (in varying ways), but the novel concludes that a recognition of the past is needed in order to dismantle structures of racism in the present and achieve inclusion. It is not enough to change oneself in the hopes of inclusion. Instead, it is necessary that Canadian society be forced to recognize its racism and to change its attitudes. The novel follows Naomi and her family from her childhood in Vancouver through their internment in the small town of Slocan, in the British Columbia interior, and then near Granton, Alberta, where Naomi's aunt and uncle live in their old age, with Naomi living nearby. The novel traces Naomi's coming to understand her family history and the pain that has been concealed from her. Naomi wishes to forget the past and move on, but she is forced by her aunt Emily, again and again, to recognize the legacies of Canadian racism and to talk about them; Emily argues that it is impossible to move on without doing so. At the novel's conclusion, when Naomi realizes that her mother was wounded, disfigured, and eventually killed by the American bombing of Nagasaki in 1945, she acknowledges that reconciliation with the past is necessary and proposes a new way of being in the world, one that seeks to incorporate these histories.

Critics have often situated the novel in relation to the rise of a multicultural Canadian mindset. Guy Beauregard suggests that, in reading *Obasan*, "we" confront "profound ethical questions about how we read, discuss, and teach racialized texts in contemporary literary studies."[2] Thinking about who is encompassed by this "we" is an important dimension to thinking through how such ethical questions might be addressed. *Obasan* was repeatedly discussed in the terms Homi Bhabha offered in *The Location of Culture* (when Bhabha was *de rigueur*) as a book that posits a hyphenated or hybrid form of Canadian being that embraces difference and pushes the nation to broaden how it recognizes its citizens. Roy Miki observes that *Obasan* demonstrates the manner in which "a one-dimensional oppositional positioning is hardly an adequate basis for new cultural forms which can represent localized subjectivities," in part by displaying the efficacy of more multidimensional modes.[3] *Obasan* works towards a position in which opposition, marginality, and the norm all become implicated in one another in its discussion of the incoherence of Canadian practices of labelling and prejudice. However, the productive multidimensionality that Miki identifies is less likely today to be reduced to a simplistic hybridity. The theorizations of hybridity that were prevalent in literary studies until a few years ago resembled the celebratory phase of poststructuralism that was criticized for its lack of a definitive politics (the lack that Derrida counters through his encounter with Marx). Border crossing and blending is not necessarily a radical act, although it can be. Careful analysis is needed to wade through the layers of meaning and cultural politics that have accumulated around *Obasan*.

As this book has already suggested, the politics of state multiculturalism can be troubling, and *Transnational Canadas* is concerned with interactions between these official discourses and cultural works. If one supports the Canadian nation and the powers that it affords its citizens, then one might, indeed, approve of the ways in which multiculturalism expands the scope of what it means to be Canadian. However, none of these things can just be assumed: the existence and practice of the Canadian nation, who is and is not a citizen (and how so), what it means to be Canadian, and who gets to define the term. The multicultural model is often criticized for the ways in which it encodes diverse subjects within monolithic labels, imposing a theoretical unity on ethno-cultural groups that it proceeds to consolidate through nation-building projects. This labelling process imposes its own exclusions: being Japanese Canadian is associated, as Naomi notes, with a traditionalism grounded in that subject's putative place of origin. So do other, similarly hyphenated labels. These processes, in turn, reinforce the normativity of unmarked, white Canadians. Roy Miki voices part of his suspicion of multiculturalism as follows: in its "inscription of the terms 'race' and 'racial' as essentialized signs in a national social text, people of colour, or 'non-white,' are produced as ethnic and racial identities that differ from the constitutional base."[4] The limited possibilities of such origins fail to account for many subjects who cross the sorts of hyphenated boundaries discussed in postcolonial theories. Given the diversity of people living in Canada, benevolent discourses of multiculturalism, observing the other within a normative enclave, at times multiply hyphenated labels in order to preserve the white origin of the nation. This may not be what was intended by the writers of the Multiculturalism Act or its related policies, and it isn't exactly what people are clamouring for either. These labels ultimately signal their own descriptive failure, pointing to limits in projects of producing identities in discourses of multiculturalism.

It is therefore productive to focus on questions of both multiculturalism and state discourse in *Obasan*. This problematic is embodied by Naomi's aunt Emily. Emily is a vibrant character who works untiringly for political change, seeking redress for Japanese Canadians, but she is mocked for her efforts. Naomi disparages Emily's insistence upon the need for speech and the recognition of history, stating that she wants "to get away from aunt Emily and her heap of words."[5] She states, with a flippant tone, her opinion that Emily is "crusading" towards "the goal" of integration in Canada by having the Nisei—second-generation Japanese Canadians—"prove themselves Canadian."[6] This rendition of Emily's activism is, however, accurate, as Emily worries about how Japanese Canadians "will ever get a chance to prove" themselves to Canada, implicitly accepting the challenge from the white hegemony.[7] Naomi situates her silent noncompliance with white norms as a counterpoint to Emily's seemingly assimilationist stance. At other points, however, Naomi recognizes that Emily is a good person, a "General Practitioner of Just Causes," "one of the world's white blood cells."[8] Emily is someone who attends to "women's rights [and] poverty" in addition to the oppression faced by Japanese Canadians.[9] The reader is given a limited and—especially early on—mostly negative view of her, one in which she appears to be unbalanced, "shouting 'Democracy' to keep the enemy at bay."[10] Naomi tells Emily's story through her own imaginative rendition, picturing her in Toronto "trying to find the right mix that strikes home" with white Canada in order to gain acceptance.[11]

Emily has not fared well in critical discussions, which sometimes take on Naomi's slightly exasperated tone towards her. Emily's acts, mediated by the narrator, are appraised by critics who read in her, for instance, a "determination to be Canadian, not Japanese."[12] Such appraisals, while largely accurate, also create barriers to understanding her role in helping Naomi towards her reconciliation with the past, and they tidy the text up more than is possible. Emily plays a more important role than simply that of foil to Naomi. Her role can and should be problematized rather than dismissed, as Smaro Kamboureli suggests in a sustained consideration. She states that it is not

> easy to understand how a woman as politically astute and passionate as Emily, who is capable of recognizing that "[i]n one breath we are damned for being 'inassimilable' and the next there's fear that we'll assimilate," can regard "Canadian" as the quintessential liberal national identity. Emily dedicates her life to restoring dignity to her community, but she draws her energy and political will from her unproblematized notion of Canada as a democracy. Because Emily never conceded that racialization is embedded in the foundation of the Canadian state, she unwittingly reproduces the liberal ideology that justifies racism within a democratic framework.[13]

For Kamboureli, Emily's awareness and dissidence are undermined by a reliance upon the signifier of Canada, which Emily assumes to be stable. Moreover, this position makes her complicit with state multiculturalism as a method of managing and regulating difference, as Eva Mackey sees it. Yet some critics have been more approving. Matthew Beedham, for example, suggests that "rather than turning white or disappearing, Emily speaks out loudly to ensure her visibility," thus becoming "the foundation of the community's resistance."[14] Kamboureli grants that "*Obasan* attempts to deconstruct [Emily's] liberal ideology in subtle but still powerful ways,"[15] quoting Emily's remark that "none of [them]...escaped naming" as other by white Canada as they "were defined and identified by the way [they] were seen."[16] Emily's dissidence, if relying on an "unproblematized notion of Canada as a democracy," is also, at times, aware of its problematics and takes on a broader role in the narrative. Ideologies of liberal humanism pervade Emily's resistant stance, but these are not necessarily static. They become, instead, productive over the course of the novel, pushing Naomi into a recognition of the past and helping her personally, just as Emily works to help the community as a whole. By the end of *Itsuka*, moreover, her liberal notions of tolerance and difference assist the Japanese Canadian community in achieving redress, as her complaints are framed in ways that are recognizable by the Canadian government as demands for accommodation.

It is therefore useful to see the productive ambivalences of Emily's position. Her blind faith in democracy seems naïve, but her allegiance to Canada is not as monolithic as it appears. One can note, for example, that Emily's allegiance shifts with her use of the terms "us" and "them." She positions herself at different times both inside and outside Canada, sometimes siding with Japanese or Japanese Canadian perspectives and often with dominant or white Canadian ones.[17] Emily suggests a need to redefine what being Canadian means when she overlaps with these multiple communities, which are thought of separately because of the artificial restrictions of the nation-state. She suggests the inadequacy of nationalist ideologies that would render Canada homogeneous in contrast to, for example, the United States, as I argued above that Margaret Atwood and Dennis Lee self-consciously attempt to do. Emily's politics are compromised by her reliance upon the nation as the ultimate ground for working through the complexities of being of Japanese descent in Canada, as the continual racism she faces denies her the belonging she desires. However, her renegotiations of the terms of marginalization have the potential to perform anti-racist work, as the public uses of *Obasan* suggest. Emily's identification with Canada is both emotional and strategic, an identification rather than a rigid identity. Emily is able to identify "the exact moment," we are told, at which she "first felt the stirrings of identification with" Canada, and wavers in her diary between feelings of belonging and betrayal.[18] She celebrates the fact that she lives "in a democracy and not an officially racist regime," but later changes to a position of disbelief, asking whether one can "wonder that there is deep bitterness among the Nisei who believed in democracy."[19] Emily becomes disillusioned with Canada and tries to recuperate time and space by seeking a redress that would allow her to recover her faith in the nation. She insists upon her citizenship, and, while she can be criticized for using the terms of nationalism, her position can never be static because she is attempting to renegotiate that very positioning.

This analysis may have to work against how *Obasan* has been read by critics who treat Emily as ineffectual. Miki suggests that *Obasan*, as it is read in much criticism, rejects "the political (as embodied by Aunt Emily) in favour of a 'universal nature' as the totalizing source of meaning."[20] As a result, he argues, *Obasan* is read in terms that are "resolutionary" rather than "revolutionary," a reading that proposes an ending in which tranquility and universality are achieved. Miki is suspicious of such a reading, even though the book's Christian elements point towards a universalism upon which the narrator does not substantially comment. Such universalizing readings are, as Arun Mukherjee has argued, consistent with benevolent Western reading practices that value difference only insofar as it can be assimilated to mainstream knowledges.[21] Such universalizing strategies are also of a piece with a Canadian vision of multiculturalism that appreciates difference primarily for how it informs the dominant. It seems that such resolutionary readings have often been desired by the text's critics. Beauregard suggests that

> the shape of Kogawa criticism needs to be understood as a symptom of the cultural politics of contemporary Canadian studies, in which literary critics attempt to discuss a "racist past" in a "multicultural present" ... attempting to manage the implications of a particular moment in Canadian history *by remembering it in a particular way*.[22]

Criticism has often seen the ending of *Obasan*, in which Naomi returns to the open prairies that she visits with her uncle at the beginning of the book, as a moment of transcendence. Beauregard argues that this reading is the result of a desire to situate racism as something of the past and to celebrate the diversity of the present. This ending becomes a moment in which Emily's speech-making and the alternative of oppressed silence come together in a synthesis in which Naomi can mourn the past and move into the future.[23] Beauregard suggests that this reading is a palliative for critics' own guilt. Criticism here participates in the managerial function of multiculturalism through the selective recognition and recounting of difference.

This implicit, if unintended, critical complacency can be contested. Such a totalizing ending for *Obasan* is undermined in its final pages. After

Naomi returns to the prairie, remembering the past, the text adds a three-page excerpt from a document that reminds readers of the ongoing consequences of Japanese Canadian internment. The document is a statement from "the Co-operative Committee on Japanese Canadians," and it asks the government to address the displacement of Japanese Canadians in the post-war period.[24] It is signed by three men bearing Anglo-Saxon names, leading Miki to note that, at the very end of the text, "Japanese Canadians are still *spoken for*."[25] They have not transcended their subaltern status, as they cannot represent themselves. Kamboureli suggests that this document is a reminder that "we should...read against [Naomi's] intention" of imposing resolution and recall that "a progressivist view of history reproduces the transcendental truths that posit homogeneity as normative."[26] If readers succumb to a reading in which the racist problems of the past are "solved" by Naomi's own arrival at reconciliation, the result is a fall into a linear past of ruptures and resolutions, one that posits a synthetic conclusion as the outcome of the dialectic between opposing forces. The final interruption of the text, the inserted document, forecloses such a movement towards closure and reasserts a dynamic of unresolved dialogue about the experience of marginalization. If Emily does not succeed as a result of her reliance upon a racist nation-state, she has at least provided the groundswell of words necessary to stage a dialogue between her and Naomi that renders their marginalization mobile, capable of being changed. Emily's insistence upon speech, her desire for history, and her attempts to renegotiate centres and margins illustrate a resistance to pre-emptive closure that is reinforced at the text's disjunctive ending.[27]

Evaluating Naomi's resolution to the problem, given her privileged status as the text's narrator, goes a long way towards determining what to make of Emily's attempts at national recuperation. Naomi begins the novel staunchly opposed to Emily's insistence upon narrating the past. She seeks silence in response. The novel prevaricates between two statements in the brief, italicized section that comes before the paginated narrative begins: "there is a silence that cannot speak" and "there is a silence that will not speak," we are told. This prevarication between ability and will suggests an undecidability between a subaltern inability to speak and an unwillingness to participate. This uncertainty is embodied by Naomi, who is separate from her community in Alberta for reasons that go beyond the fact of her racialized body: she feels that her silence is misunderstood by those around her as intransigence, when it might be more rightly described as shy politeness (one that is not shared by her white Albertan neighbours). As the novel continues, Naomi recounts childhood experiences of sexual abuse, of becoming distanced from her brother, Stephen, and her father, and of the long process of "political expediency, race riots, the yellow peril" that has influenced the course of her life.[28] The Japanese Canadian internment emerges as the primary disjunctive force in the lives of the Japanese Canadians in the novel, Naomi included. As it is retold, Naomi reaffirms her resolve to stay silent, stating that she can best live by letting the past rest—something that she is not, ultimately, able to do. She maintains early on, nevertheless, that the community's "memories were drowned in a whirlpool of protective silence" and that "what is past recall is past pain."[29] She segregates the past from the present, seeing it as a rupture across which no communication can ensue.

After her uncle's death, however, Naomi learns more of the family history from which she has been protected and from which she has chosen to exile herself. She comes to desire reconciliation with that past. She recognizes that she and her Obasan are "trapped...by [their] memories of the dead," still wondering, in Naomi's case, why her mother never returned from Japan after the war.[30] These unanswered questions spur her to seek answers in the past. She goes through Emily's documents on the internment, heeding Emily's insistence that "the past is the future," that "you are your history," and that "if you cut any of it off you're an amputee."[31] Initially, these files—especially Emily's diary—confirm Emily's naïve belief in Canadian democracy, but they eventually unravel the perversity of state-endorsed racism. Emily demonstrates that Japanese Canadians have been "defined and identified by the way [they] were seen"—that is, as being of the "Japanese race."[32] Naomi wishes "to break loose of the heavy identity, the evidence of rejection" that the past foists upon her, but her ignorance of that past at the book's opening hardly prevents her from being rejected in the present.[33] As she opens up to the past, she states that she does, indeed, "need to be educated," even though she does not understand "what good" Emily's words might do.[34] However, when Naomi learns through these documents of her mother's maiming in the American bombing of Nagasaki in 1945, she comes to desire speech, opting for a recognition of the past and its brutal consequences. She states that she and her mother "were lost together in [their] silences" and that their "wordlessness was [their] mutual destruction."[35] In her desire to understand the past, Naomi comes to seek a politics of recognition that parallels Emily's. She rejects Emily's activism insofar as it rails against the present—she prefers to be content in the present, understanding the past and moving beyond it in the final scene—but she accepts the ethos of understanding upon which Emily builds her foundations.

Naomi's acceptance of Emily's insistence upon history suggests a parallel acceptance of Emily's desire for inclusion within the Canadian body politic. This parallel emerges in what begins as an apostrophe by Naomi to the land:

> Oh, Canada, whether it is admitted or not, we come from you we come from you.... We come from our untold tales that wait for their telling. We come from Canada, this land that is like every land.... Obasan, however, does not come from this clamorous climate. She does not dance to the multi-cultural piper's tune or respond to the racist's slur. She remains in a silent territory, defined by her serving hands.[36]

By cutting herself off from Obasan, from the older and more "traditional" generation, Naomi aligns herself with Canada and pushes for an integration through storytelling. As a result, *Obasan* can be seen as a text that in turn pushes for recognition within the constructs of Canadian literature, at the same time as it broadens the scope of the term "Canadian" itself. This broadening is not something that should be negated. The text has shown a capacity for performing anti-racist work and has been effectively used in teaching tolerance and advocating inclusion. These are productive developments, and the Japanese Canadian redress movement can also be seen as a unique and welcome reconciliation, one in which Kogawa's text has participated. Critical hesitation, however, begins when querying what sort of inclusion is entailed in this process. Emily, in her collection of papers, erases difference as a means of opposing exclusion, as she crosses out instances in which Japanese Canadians are referred to as being "of the Japanese race," replacing this phrase with "Canadian citizen."[37] Emily's position approaches an assimilationist one. She cuts herself off from a community with which she shares many affinities, that of people living in Canada with Japanese ancestry but without formal citizenship. Her reliance upon citizenship as the final category of inclusion does not solve all problems. Rather, it continues to exclude many. Emily seems at times to wish to be integrated in white Canada's norms, as does Naomi's brother,

Stephen, who leaves home in order to become a concert pianist, disdaining things that are "too Japanese."[38] And yet, it is Naomi's markedly Japanese vision of herself that is the more troubled one. It is seen as self-silencing, a process that is connected to her failure to reconcile with the past. Stephen disidentifies with his heritage in order to succeed in the white world, but Naomi is unable to do so. She both silences the past and avoids substantial engagements in the present. The novel's reconciliation with the past suggests a movement towards integration founded upon an inclusion that borders on an erasure like Emily's. In the end, *Obasan*'s vision of acceptance and inclusion expands the definition of Canada only slightly, leaving the nation substantially unchallenged and its white norms (those from whom Emily seeks recognition) largely unchanged.

Assimilation, though, tends to pose serious difficulties for racialized characters. Naomi remarks that "Emily toiled to tell the lives of the Nisei in Canada in her effort to make familiar, to make knowable, the treacherous yellow peril that lived in the minds of the racially prejudiced.... But the heart was not there."[39] Emily's efforts fail because they go unheard. And while Stephen is successful in his career as a pianist and musician, we are not made aware of the struggles that he faces. However, in a parallel instance, in Tomson Highway's *Kiss of the Fur Queen*, when Cree protagonist Jeremiah Okimasis works to become a concert pianist, his assimilationist denial of Indigenous selfhood leads him down a self-destructive path that immobilizes him in the world of "whiteman music."[40] What little reconciliation is available comes to him through his brother, the dancer Gabriel, whose parallel path of self-destruction leads to his death from AIDS. There is comparatively little discussion in *Obasan* of the side-effects of assimilation. But the text makes it apparent that white people in Canada are not willing or able to include people of Japanese ancestry in their conception of the norm. What appears to cause self-destruction — or at least Emily's self-abnegation, her long-suffering activism — is exclusion from the option of national inclusion. But no matter how assimilated *Obasan*'s characters become, the politics of recognition fails since it involves acts of recognition on all sides, and white people in the text do not enact the ideals of the state's then-nascent multicultural project.

By the time Naomi has progressed into full participation in redress activism in *Itsuka*, we see an acceptance of assimilation to mainstream norms as an apparent expression of neo-liberalism. Naomi states with rapture, while in Hawaii, that it is a pure pleasure to be "able to eat Japanese food and speak English" at the same time, a statement that evokes one of the tropes of multiculturalism as consisting of the commodified diets of minoritized cultures within an Anglo-white norm.[41] Although Naomi should not be read too easily across the two volumes, the relationship between ethnicity and citizenship in Kogawa's work is uncertain. Naomi moves into an acceptance of the redress movement that champions Canada as the vessel that might contain the diverse peoples who have come to or were born in it. As we will see in the next chapter's discussion of Michael Ondaatje's *In the Skin of a Lion*, the politics of ethnicity and multiculturalism do not always cohere, and a more critical focus on the concept of the nation and the problematics of national belonging will be necessary for understanding Canada from a literary perspective in a transnational world.

Notes to Chapter Six

1. Joy Kogawa, *Itsuka*, rev. ed. (Toronto: Penguin, 1993), 239.
2. Guy Beauregard, "After *Obasan*: Kogawa Criticism and Its Futures," *Studies in Canadian Literature* 26.2 (2001): 6.
3. Roy Miki, *Broken Entries: Race, Subjectivity, Writing* (Toronto: Mercury, 1998), 107.
4. Miki, *Broken Entries*, 149.
5. Joy Kogawa, *Obasan* (Toronto: Penguin, 1981), 201.
6. Kogawa, *Obasan*, 32–33.
7. Kogawa, *Obasan*, 110.
8. Kogawa, *Obasan*, 33, 35. This last is a loaded term that certainly relates to discourses of racialization, pitting Emily in opposition to the "yellow peril" that she and her family are made to represent to white Canadians.
9. Kogawa, *Obasan*, 33.
10. Kogawa, *Obasan*, 46.
11. Kogawa, *Obasan*, 43.
12. Arnold Davidson, *Writing Against the Silence: Joy Kogawa's* Obasan (Toronto: ECW P, 1993), 29.
13. Smaro Kamboureli, *Scandalous Bodies: Diasporic Literature in English Canada* (Don Mills, ON: Oxford UP, 2000), 188.
14. Matthew Beedham, "*Obasan* and Hybridity: Necessary Cultural Strategies," *The Immigrant Experience in North American Literature: Carving Out a Niche*, ed. K. Payant and T. Rose (Westport, CT: Greenwood, 1999), 142.
15. Kamboureli, *Scandalous Bodies*, 190.
16. Kogawa, *Obasan*, 118.
17. See Kogawa, *Obasan*, 36, 38, 44, 61, 112.
18. Kogawa, *Obasan*, 42.
19. Kogawa, *Obasan*, 87, 93.
20. Miki, *Broken Entries*, 141.

21 Arun Mukherjee, "The Vocabulary of the 'Universal': The Cultural Imperialism of the Universalist Criteria of Western Literary Criticism," *Oppositional Aesthetics: Readings from a Hyphenated Space* (Toronto: TSAR, 1994), 17–29.
22 Beauregard, "After *Obasan*," 14.
23 See for example Marilyn Rose, "Politics into Art: Kogawa's *Obasan* and the Rhetoric of Fiction," *Mosaic* 21 (1998): 220; Davidson, *Writing Against the Silence*, 74–75.
24 Kogawa, *Obasan*, 272–74.
25 Miki, *Broken Entries*, 117.
26 Kamboureli, *Scandalous Bodies*, 220.
27 That said, it may not be possible to read the ending of *Itsuka* in the same way. There, another document ends the text, this time the Government of Canada's statement of redress to Japanese Canadians, an insert that announces precisely the sort of closure that the document in *Obasan* undermines.
28 Kogawa, *Obasan*, 17.
29 Kogawa, *Obasan*, 22, 48.
30 Kogawa, *Obasan*, 26.
31 Kogawa, *Obasan*, 45, 54.
32 Kogawa, *Obasan*, 126.
33 Kogawa, *Obasan*, 201.
34 Kogawa, *Obasan*, 207, 208.
35 Kogawa, *Obasan*, 267.
36 Kogawa, *Obasan*, 247–48.
37 Kogawa, *Obasan*, 34.
38 Kogawa, *Obasan*, 238.
39 Kogawa, *Obasan*, 43.
40 Tomson Highway, *Kiss of the Fur Queen* (Toronto: Doubleday, 1998), 256. A further parallel to the impact of white music is found in Dionne Brand's *What We Long For*.
41 Kogawa, *Itsuka*, 86.

CHAPTER SEVEN

Multicultural Postmodernities in Michael Ondaatje's *In the Skin of a Lion*

Michael Ondaatje's novel *In the Skin of a Lion* (1987) offers a reading of Toronto, and by extension Canada, as a racialized space that excludes many of its citizens and denizens from official history. It uncovers alternative histories as a means of demonstrating the fundamental emptiness of national myths, and turns instead to focus upon specific localities as the sites of meaning-making. *In the Skin of a Lion* does so by recording the histories of the workers who build the city, but the text's politics are famously unstable. In the context of the late 1980s that Eva Mackey evokes in the following statement, the novel can be seen (and has been seen by some) as a cynical gesture to include surface-level discussions of politics and ethnicity that have very little substance. "By the late 1980s," Mackey states, "global capitalism enters the picture as a justification for multicultural policy.... Canada's 'multicultural heritage' is now a resource. The cultural politics of pluralism, it is argued, make good business sense."[1] The cultural politics of pluralism certainly have made for good business here: *In the Skin of a Lion*, celebrated for its postmodern pastiche style of recording the narratives of Canadian immigrants, was the first winner of CBC's Canada Reads competition in 2002, a win that increased the novel's sales by eighty thousand within the following twelve-month span.[2] The novel includes images of resistance to power and of attempts to subvert structures of domination, and shows how, at both a physical and an imaginative level, marginalized actors within urban spaces and rural Canada inhabit and construct spaces beyond the dictates of those who are officially in control. At the same time, the alternative modes that are offered in the text have been questioned. It seems that the politics of difference ends up requiring that ethnically marked bodies give up their marks of difference in order to be integrated into Canada, a troubling position that abuts some of the difficulties in *Obasan* (and a demand that is impossible for *racialized* bodies). It also requires, it seems, an acceptance of capitalist narratives of history in order to secure the participation of the marginalized, a stance that negates the novel's suggestions of alternatives to the dominant.

This chapter reads this novel within the continuum of the 1980s and '90s multicultural critique of the 1960s and '70s period of national consolidation. It is interested in how the text thematizes political organization, but the chapter veers somewhat from criticism that takes issue with the text's surface-level politics. A critical tradition contends that the text's explicit politics are empty, and while it may be true that the text uses participation in political projects in a way that has been characterized as making "'use' of the unempowered to create bourgeois art,"[3] this chapter is interested in the text's less overt concepts of politics, especially how notions of history in the text relate to those concepts. The novel records an attempt, mostly by the character Patrick Lewis, to recover the untold histories of workers and the oppressed. This is a theme to which Ondaatje has returned often, as he does in the recent novel *Divisadero*, in which the character Claire notes of a book of interviews of her mother and others that the marginalized seem to possess "a sense that history was around them, not within them."[4] *In the Skin of a Lion* seeks to restore a sense of history to the workers who built Toronto, arguing for their inclusion within the city by virtue of their labour. The stories of characters like Nicholas Temelcoff, immigrants to the country, are retold to readers in order to insert them into history. Therein, it seems, *In the Skin of a Lion* finds its political purpose, its postmodern methods of producing an ex-centric historiographic metafiction. This historical recovery, the book implies, is one that will right historical wrongs, or perform an act of Foucauldian counter-memory.[5] The novel pursues the lives of immigrants to Toronto, both internationally and from within Canada, revisiting the history of the construction of two of Toronto's landmarks, the Bloor Street Viaduct and the R.C. Harris Filtration Plant. It records the lives of workers and immigrant families, focusing on their political gatherings and anti-institutional organizing. It thereby appears to thematize overt politics at the same time as the less visible cultural politics of class and ethnicity. It does so, however, without naming anyone's political affiliations, and ends with Patrick Lewis's ambivalent, abortive attempt to blow up the filtration plant and his subsequent travel with his stepdaughter, Hana, to find his former and future lover Clara.

Critics have seen this text as one that prevaricates. Such appraisals are dominant. The text does play an important role in performing what Winfried Siemerling has termed "writing the other."[6] However, the text's explicit politics are rendered problematic by how it performs this writing. Julia Beddoes proposes that the novel's "postmodern aesthetic practices neutralize — or even oppose — its tentative thematizing of a radical class politics."[7] Criticism has proposed that although readers may wish to see the book's thematization of historical redress as a political act in itself, the novel should not, Beddoes goes on to argue, "make us believe that because a work raises questions about its narrator and official history it is necessarily an instrument for social change."[8] Christian Bök goes further in his appraisal of the text, arguing that it "in fact present[s] revolutionary ideology as itself potentially oppressive, an ideology of which the protagonists must always beware in order to sustain their individual humanity," echoing other arguments about the novel's tendency to favour the individual over the collective.[9] The novel's erstwhile and seeming interest in labour; union organizing, as embodied by the character Cato's work in the logging camps of northern Ontario; and anarchism or socialism, embodied by Alice Gull, Cato's former partner and Hana's mother, is undercut by the novel's focus upon history, upon individualism, upon aesthetics. Its show of politics, which is alluring, is challenged by analysis that shows how unstable these politics are. Its challenge to what it terms "official history" makes it an inviting text, but an analysis that stops there, without examining what alternatives to the official history are being offered, is incomplete.

Although its apparent politicization of history has rendered *In the Skin of a Lion* a deeply teachable and likely canonical text, problems remain.

Robert Stacey suggests that the overt politics upon which critics have focused are simply not there, and proposes a displacement from the urban to the pastoral as a means of getting past criticisms of the text that lament the lack of substance to the text's promise of leftist organizing.[10] It is useful to step past the overt politics in order to think about the politics of history here. This is a text that, Jody Mason finds, lacks adequate differentiation between immigrant populations. What she calls its "nomadic metaphysics" record the historical movements of peoples across space and the self, but that process proposes an equivalence between characters that undercuts the model of "cosmopolitan citizenship" that the novel holds up.[11] This model of equivalence seems to be one that is based within neo-liberal notions of the state and history. Readers need to contend with the sort of history given and the sort of options granted to immigrant and other oppressed groups for action. *In the Skin of a Lion* is a novel that allows only narrow forms of belonging as the means to rectify exclusion. In this it is comparable to the way in which *Obasan*'s Aunt Emily is unable to imagine any justice shy of that achieved through equal participation in the Canadian state (even though this participation can exist only with the assent of the white Canada against which she rails; such participation through assent by one group for another is always already asymmetrical, undercutting her goal).

In Ondaatje's novel, equivalence is offered through participation in capitalist models of organizing history and knowledge. That is, full participation in politics, in society, and in history comes through becoming a property owner. The history of the workers is not simply recovered: it is recovered in ways that evidence the structuring of history as a history of the progress of the workers into the society of owners. A passage that focuses on Nicholas Temelcoff highlights this process. Temelcoff is the daredevil worker who, early in the novel, works on the Bloor Street Viaduct, taking the dangerous jobs shunned by others, and rescues a nun who falls from the bridge, who emerges later in the novel as Alice Gull. At this later point, we learn that Temelcoff has become "a citizen here, in the present, successful with his own bakery."[12] Patrick, who has returned to Toronto after a prison sentence for setting fire to a resort in the Muskokas, presents Temelcoff with a photograph from his earlier life working on the viaduct. The photo becomes a crystallizing moment. Looking at it, the narrator suggests that Temelcoff thinks that this is what history means. He came to this country like a torch on fire and he swallowed air as he walked forward and gave out light. Energy poured through him. That was all he had time for in those years. Language, customs, family, salaries. Patrick's gift, that arrow into the past, shows him the wealth in himself, how he has been sewn into history. Now he will begin to tell stories.[13]

What does it mean to be "sewn into history"? On the surface, it means to be granted participation or entry, and the artifact of the photo validates Temelcoff's presence. But how this entry takes place is noteworthy. At the same time as he enters history through the documentary record, Temelcoff also gains access to storytelling through his participation in the logics of capital — that is, thorough ownership. We are reminded immediately before this section that his ownership of the bakery is what has rendered him a citizen, and this passage uses the metaphor of wealth in order to describe Temelcoff's inner workings.

Although this is a small portion of the narrative, the novel proceeds in a similar manner, arguing that ending oppression and gaining a voice comes through successful participation in a fundamentally unchanged system that retains the potential to oppress. The practices of class — as well as of multiculturalism — within this framework have the potential to be exclusionary. Not all of the workers, surely, will go on to become successful entrepreneurs. And this reading of Temelcoff's participation in capitalist forms of exclusion parallel other critics' takes on questions of race in the novel. The novel is seen as blurring identity formations, opening spaces for immigrants in the Canada of the novel, and upsetting racial assumptions by seeing the city as being forever under construction. But the novel also uses the imagery of colour in specific ways in order to remain fixed, argues Jodi Lundgren, "within a racialized logic that ties liberation to the shedding of coloured skin and/or the attaining of whiteness."[14] That is, the novel's recasting of history becomes, upon further analysis, not a radical act of creating social change, but an act of creating enfranchisement for the oppressed through successful participation in social patterns of oppression. When Caravaggio paints himself blue to match the ceiling of the Kingston Penitentiary in order to facilitate his escape back to the Toronto in which he and Patrick will attempt to demolish the filtration plant, he demonstrates how colour allows borders to be refashioned. The border between Caravaggio and the background disappears, just as, incrementally, the border between immigrant newcomers and English-speaking Canadians disappears as the former shed their accents by imitating stage actors. In this disappearance, however, Caravaggio also suggests an unruly excess to the logic of participation in the nation, as his disappearance allows his escape from prison and, possibly, from the historical process in which others become enmeshed. Participation is the desired goal for Temelcoff and many immigrants, however, and while those who are excluded from participation are explicitly thematized in their rebellions against power, the achievement of similarity, of passing, seems to be enough.

Spivak's arguments are pertinent here. She argues in her *Critique of Postcolonial Reason* that women can enter into the historical record only when they participate in the mode of production narrative that underlies history itself. History, in her sense, is in fact the history of economics, of production. If one does not produce, one disappears. Similarly, neo-liberal understandings of the end of history were predicated on economic models, on the idea that history as such is the history of class antagonisms, the transcending of which enables the end of the dialectic. If history, the idea of history in the West, is in fact the history of economics, then it is important to ask precisely how radical or progressive it is to restore the historical record. The act of writing or rewriting history, in this sense, may amount to little more than an act of reinscription that forecloses the transformation of either history or social structures that rely on narratives of production, oppression, and exclusion. This is the point at which it is difficult to share the rancour of critics who take issue with *In the Skin of a Lion* for failing to be as political as they wish it to be. What kind of politics does the novel enable? If it carried out its promise of political action, it might offer only a politics of reinscription. At its most radical moments, we are told that it is necessary to "name the enemy" and to "destroy his power."[15] But what happens after that point—what the political model for the novel's radical characters might be—is never discussed and is, indeed, not the point. What we might get if that were the point would be a fuller vision of historical participation as a part of joining Spivak's road to hegemony, a point that is distinctly unromantic. It is necessary, as a result, to ask about the valence of historical representation within Canada, particularly as the novel's initial impression of participating in revolutionary politics clashes with its model of history.

Notes to Chapter Seven

1. Eva Mackey, *The House of Difference: Cultural Politics and National Identity in Canada* (Toronto: U of Toronto P, 2002), 68.
2. Laura Moss, "Canada Reads," *Canadian Literature* 182 (2004): 6.
3. Frank Davey, *Post-national Arguments: The Politics of the Anglophone-Canadian Novel since 1967* (Toronto: U of Toronto P, 1993), 146.
4. Michael Ondaatje, *Divisadero* (Toronto: McClelland and Stewart, 2007), 10–11.
5. On acts of counter-memory in the novel, see Meredith Criglington, "The City as a Site of Counter-Memory in Anne Michaels's *Fugitive Pieces* and Michael Ondaatje's *In the Skin of a Lion*," *Essays on Canadian Writing* 81 (2004): 129–53.
6. Winfried Siemerling, "Oral History and Writing of the Other in Ondaatje's *In the Skin of a Lion*," *CLCWeb: Comparative Literature and Culture* 6.3 (2004). http://clcwebjournal.lib.purdue.edu/clcweb04-3/siemerling.html.
7. Julia Beddoes, "Which Side Is It On? Form, Class, and Politics in *In the Skin of a Lion*," *Essays on Canadian Writing* 53 (1994): 206.
8. Beddoes, "Which Side Is It On?" 206.
9. Christian Bök, "The Secular Opiate: Marxism as an Ersatz Religion in Three Canadian Texts," *Canadian Literature* 147 (1995): 13.
10. Robert Stacey, "A Political Aesthetic: Michael Ondaatje's *In the Skin of a Lion* as 'Covert Pastoral,'" *Contemporary Literature* 49.3 (2008): 439–69.
11. Jody Mason, "'The Animal Out of the Desert': The Nomadic Metaphysics of Michael Ondaatje's *In the Skin of a Lion*," *Studies in Canadian Literature* 31.2 (2006): 66–67.
12. Michael Ondaatje, *In the Skin of a Lion* (Toronto: Vintage, 1987), 149.
13. Ondaatje, *In the Skin of a Lion*, 149.
14. Jodi Lundgren, "'Colour Disrobed Itself from the Body': The Racialized Aesthetics of Liberation in Michael Ondaatje's *In the Skin of a Lion*," *Canadian Literature* 190 (2006): 17. See also Glen Lowry's "The Representation of 'Race' in Ondaatje's *In the Skin of a Lion*," *CLCWeb: Comparative Literature and Culture* 6.3 (2004). http://clcwebjournal.lib.purdue.edu/clcweb04-3/lowry04.html.
15. Ondaatje, *In the Skin of a Lion*, 124.

CHAPTER EIGHT

Dismissing Canada in Jeannette Armstrong's *Slash*

Because of the struggles that critics have with *In the Skin of a Lion*, it is useful to examine writing that, while written in the context of Canadian cultural diversity and its attendant debates, does not seek approval from the nation (as *Obasan* does in this book's reading, and as Ondaatje's novel seems to do, albeit less explicitly). If multiculturalism posits only a partial challenge to the structures of Canada, it is productive to see how writing that does not easily fit into that category deploys issues of difference. In some cases, racialized writing that cannot easily be called multicultural provides more substantial challenges. Many Indigenous writers, such as Jeannette Armstrong, provide strong examples. Armstrong's novel *Slash* provides a damning critique of the colonial governments of North America—and does so without needing to focus solely on that colonial relationship either, moving into an indigenized terrain that relates to Canada, but that does not rely upon it. *Slash* strives, rather, to dismiss it.

Slash is concerned, as is much (though by no means all) Native writing, with sovereignty and nationhood. In the face of having been represented by colonizing voices that had an interest in "preserving" or "saving"

Native cultures for their own consumption, Indigenous critics have been engaged in processes of self-representation, searching for forms of autonomy through the writing process as part of struggles for self-determination. These struggles abut Spivak's concerns about entering the hegemonic, but Indigenous texts such as *Slash* challenge the configuration of the dominant, rather than simply reifying it. The differences are important. Wresting control of what Chantal Mouffe and Ernesto Laclau term "the means of representation" is an extension of wresting control over geographic space, and the contemporary imperialist project is connected to both processes. Grappling with Western incursions into representational practices has been one important approach to reclaiming Indigenous perspectives in scholarship. The representations of nationhood and sovereignty in *Slash* and other writing thus connect to the deployment of these same concepts in Indigenous scholarship. This chapter examines two recent texts that explore Indigenous concepts of autonomy before it reads *Slash* in order to illustrate Indigenous struggles over questions of self-determination, and considers how these texts relate to aspects of transnational theory in Part Three. The focus is on Craig Womack's *Red on Red: Native American Literary Separatism* and Taiaiake Alfred's *Peace, Power, Righteousness: An Indigenous Manifesto*. These texts make for a strong contrast because, while they were both published in 1999, they come to different conclusions about how to approach concepts of Indigenous autonomy and resistance. The tribal groundings of both critics — Womack is Muskogee Creek and Cherokee (from contemporary Oklahoma), while Alfred is Kanien'kehaka or Mohawk — are important in terms of the ways in which they discuss pan-Native consciousness and nationalism.[1] Alfred seeks a form of autonomy that is based in nationhood but not sovereignty, while Womack is interested in a form of national sovereignty that sees Western models of the nation as inapplicable to his Creek nation. Their struggles are also connected to the colonial states within which their nations are situated, Canada and the United States, respectively. The differences between these perspectives highlight questions of representation, literary value, and the ways in which resistance can be formulated. These perspectives say a great deal about how the politics of transnationalism might be thought today, given the inter-, multi-, and transnational alliances into which Indigenous nations have been thrust by colonialism — and which in many cases predate European contact.[2] Alfred and Womack offer parallel models for anti-imperial resistance grounded in geographical locatedness, demonstrating a recurrent if at times difficult position from which to begin theorizing.

Their perspectives—and others offered by Indigenous critics—are useful for thinking about transnational capitalism and for questioning the role of the nation within the contemporary world. Many of the critics whom *Transnational Canadas* has so far dealt with dismiss the nation, particularly Derrida and Spivak. For them, nationalism is based upon the construction of absolute differences. Benedict Anderson's *Imagined Communities* has been taken as a paradigmatic text for ways in which nations have been conceptualized: as communally derived fictions that take on the authority of rigid codes, those based upon, among other things, racial segregation. This generalization is commonplace enough that transnational theorists Michael Hardt and Antonio Negri—who will be dealt with in depth in the next chapter—see the foundation of any nation as being based upon "the construction of absolute racial difference" from any other.[3] At the same time, many critics engaging in transnational fields of inquiry see the nation as the only means, as Frank Davey has argued in a Canadian context, of "defending...against multinational capitalism."[4] This chapter is concerned with Frank Davey's reading of *Slash* in his book *Post-national Arguments* on this score. The long history of various nationalisms is relevant here, especially of ones that rely on the Western conceptualization of the nation historicized by Eric Hobsbawn. In much anti-colonial thinking, this nation is a vexed inheritance. In successful liberation movements, it has been often deployed by those who come into power in order to exclude others. These exclusions led Franz Fanon, in his advocacy for anti-imperial nationalism, to argue that any anti-imperial nationalist consciousness requires "rapid transformation into a consciousness of social and political needs" at the moment at which freedom from colonization is achieved.[5] That is, anti-imperial nationalism requires rethinking after liberation in order to avoid reproducing the oppressions of the colonial system. This argument has mixed applicability for Canada, in part because Canadian nationalism has not been constructed upon racial exclusions in the late twentieth century. Rather, at an official level, Canada has been deliberately constructed over the past quarter century as a nation that is founded upon racial and ethnic diversity. And the concomitant multicultural nationalism does not seem to have been an effective means of defending Canada against capitalism. Instead, multicultural nationalism has enabled Canada to position itself at the forefront of cosmopolitan globalism. Canada is now a global brand whose distinguishing feature is its diversity, its supposed liberal tolerance of difference. Canadian nationalism has shown itself to be of a piece with neo-liberalism. This strategy is one that profits from images of diversity, rendering multicultural literary products susceptible to appropriation by a nation that promotes itself through those visions of inclusion. This marketing is alarming in a country that is still colonial from an Indigenous perspective. Liberation has not been achieved for the land's first inhabitants. From an Indigenous perspective, the cosmopolitan nation, with its roots in Western thought, can only be problematic at best — as it has been, also, to many of the theorists of transnationalism. But the Indigenous challenge to Western nationalism is different, as it looks at alternative modes of thinking the nation or the community.

What Alfred and Womack offer are conceptualizations of non-Western nationalism. In some ways, their approaches parallel aspects of anti-nationalist Western analyses of politics in the context of global capitalism. In Womack's *Red on Red*, Native nationalism is a means of creating a Native-based scholarship about indigeneity. This is a book that has had a large impact on Native scholarship and has aligned Womack with Indigenous scholars, such as Daniel Heath Justice and Jace Weaver, who argue for a nationalist model. Protesting the appropriation of Native voices by white academics, Womack creates a practice in which criticism is based in knowledge of the specific tribal contexts out of which works emanate. At *Red on Red*'s foundation lies "the conviction that Native literature, and the criticism that surrounds it, needs to see more attention devoted to tribally specific concerns."[6] Womack develops this agenda through readings of texts in the Creek tradition, from the oral tradition to Joy Harjo and beyond, creating not only a sense of national continuity, but also one of change and movement into the future, one in which queer Indigenous voices, for example, challenge the supposedly static identities of Native people. Womack builds on Indigenous nationalists such as Howard Adams, who suggests that "red nationalism is essential to Indian/Métis liberation" and states that "native separatism" is necessary "for a temporary transitional period" as Indigenous peoples rebuild. Adams notes that Indigenous efforts must "not imitate those of mainstream bourgeois society," and he aligns Indigenous liberation struggles with the left.[7] To advocate Indigenous nationalism is part of an ongoing tradition, and Womack's contribution is to examine this tradition from a literary perspective that provides a less-fixed concept of the nation than earlier ones.

Central to Womack's discussion is an idea of nationalism that is different from dominant Euro-Western modes. For Womack, this nationalism is tied to sovereignty: "Native literature, and Native literary criticism, written by Native authors, is part of sovereignty," he argues, maintaining that "sovereignty is inherent as an intellectual idea in Native cultures, a political practice, and a theme of oral traditions; and the concept, as well as the practice, predates European contact."[8] To Womack,

> sovereignty... is an ongoing, dynamic process, rather than a fixed creed, and evolves according to the needs of the nation. This "unfixing" of the idea of nationhood is needed to avoid some of the problems that Edward Said and other postcolonial writers discuss regarding the problem of the emergent nation simply becoming a "colored" version of the old oppression.[9]

Nationalism, via the concept of sovereignty, is unmoored from racialized ("colored") bases and made to respond to specific and changing tribal situations. Sovereignty, Womack states, "might be used as a model for building nations in a way that revises, modifies, or rejects, rather than accepts as a model, the European and American model."[10] The goal is to create an Indigenous nationalism that is responsive, not relying on a too-easy insider–outsider split based upon genealogies and bloodlines (as have been often required by colonial administrations). His concept of nationalism is, Womack argues, more culturally engaged, based upon community participation and social practice. Critic Michelle Henry suggests that Womack's "fluidity of culture and identity" is precisely what enables him to develop a concept of national authenticity. Defining belonging through cultural practice rather than genetics extends an idea of authenticity that is in turn built around a fundamentally "inauthentic" self—but only if one reads through the colonizer's codes.[11] Examining the Muskogee Creek concept of authenticity enables Womack to create an authentic national subject precisely through inauthenticity: Womack's reworked concepts of belonging foreground an unfixed sense of nationhood at the base of a broad quest for Indigenous sovereignty.

Womack's position contrasts with that advocated by Taiaiake Alfred in *Peace, Power, Righteousness*. There Alfred argues that it is sovereignty that is an inappropriate concept in Indigenous struggles, stating that the concept "must be eradicated from politics in Native communities."[12] The contrast between Womack and Alfred is striking, but the goals are similar: both are theorizing means of achieving decolonization and resisting imperialism. For Alfred, Indigenous "respect for individual autonomy" means that Native governance systems must reject sovereignty, which is, for him, "the idea that there can be a permanent transference of power or authority from the individual to an abstraction of the collective called 'government.'"[13] He sees sovereignty as "an exclusionary concept rooted in an adversarial and coercive Western notion of power."[14] In its place, Alfred advocates a more contingent form of leadership, one in which mobile interests "pool their self-power in the interest of collective good."[15] A traditional Indigenous model of governance would consist, for Alfred, in vesting leadership in suitable persons only for so long as their actions reflect the consensus of the community. Power would derive from a broad mandate, but remain provisional. Alfred suggests that the goal is to recover

> a set of values that challenge the destructive and homogenizing force of Western liberalism and free-market capitalism; that honour the autonomy of individual conscience, non-coercive authority, and the deep interconnection between human beings and the other elements of creation.[16]

Alfred unthinks the colonial models of governance that have been thrust upon Indigenous people, and gestures towards a non-coercive or unfixed consensual nationhood that recognizes the interconnections between colonization and the contemporary disparities of capitalism. He acknowledges the role of economics in the genocide of Indigenous people while conceptualizing ways of rebuilding fragmented communities.[17]

Alfred's discussion of sovereignty reflects the concerns of his manifesto. His goal is "resistance to foreign notions of power and control," and he conceptualizes an equitable Indigenous polity that is based on "a self-conscious traditionalism" towards this end.[18] To Alfred, this is a way to think past models of exclusive power-wielding and towards a consensual and less centred form of community. A "'Native American' political tradition," for him, would consist of "commitment to a profoundly respectful way of governing, based on a worldview that balances respect for autonomy with recognition of a universal interdependency."[19] While Alfred is not always clear about how to achieve this model, and he has been criticized for not providing examples of how such a vision would operate in a world of overwhelming overlaps with colonial populations,[20] his attempt to conceptualize governance rooted in national identifications that forgo the notion of sovereignty is useful. Alfred seeks an unfixed political body capable of self-representation on behalf of the consensual group that supports it. This concept, drawn from Alfred's sense of traditionalism, revises Western notions of the nation. It parallels, also, some aspects of Western examinations of nationalism in the context of globalization.

The contrasts between Womack and Alfred are indicative of a struggle to think Indigenous autonomy in a geography that purports to be postcolonial or progressively multicultural despite its occupation of Indigenous lands. Womack and Alfred create gendered discourses of national belonging in a context in which many writers are concerned with dismantling male-centred forms of resistance or decolonization, seeing such gendering as an aspect of imperialism itself. Bonita Lawrence argues that "it is crucially important...to understand the central role that the subordination of Native women has played in the colonization process...as a *collective* sovereignty issue," and records Canada's history of disenfranchising Indigenous people by imposing a patrilineal system of inheritance.[21] Alfred's and Womack's masculinist responses to colonization risk complicity with colonial processes. It is in this vein that Lee Maracle remarks that "the denial of Native womanhood is the reduction of the whole people to a sub-human level."[22] Womack's and Alfred's voices contest aspects of the colonial inheritance in their challenge to nationhood and sovereignty; these challenges need to extend through to analyses of gender (a direction in which Womack moves) in order to thoroughly rethink the colonial relationship.

These discussions are reflected in Western thinking about nationalism and sovereignty. The difficulty with the nation and the nation-state as a Western structure of sovereign control has been taken up in provocative ways by Giorgio Agamben, whose analysis of modern Western society is based on the readings of biopolitics of Michel Foucault. Agamben picks up Foucault's analysis of the ways in which the disciplinary societies of modernity extend their control to the very processes of the body and suggests that modernity begins at the point at which the "simple living body become[s] what is at stake in a society's political strategies." This body, or "bare life," as Agamben calls it, is ruled by the structures of sovereignty, and "the inclusion of bare life in the political realm constitutes the original—if concealed—nucleus of sovereign power."[23] Sovereignty is founded upon the state of exception, the suspension of rules for the sovereign, who, by virtue of being granted the power to make the rules, simultaneously suspends them, because changing the rules is against the rules for everybody else. This state of exceptionality becomes more and more common in Agamben's analysis of life in the West, so much so that the exception eventually becomes the rule. A state of permanent exception, in which biopolitical forces rule over the bodies of others, is exemplified for Agamben in the concentration camps of Nazi Germany. Such an analysis has appealed to analysts of globalization interested in the ongoing states of exception surrounding the United States' so-called war on terror. Sovereign power creates fundamental contradictions where the rules exist but, because they can be changed by the sovereign—who does not exist purely inside or outside of this state of affairs—the exception can become normalized. The extension of sovereign power over bare life, into the realm of biopolitics, gives the state of exceptionality the potential for increasing its coercion and broadening its territory, such that bodies themselves can be ruled, as they are in the concentration camps, in a permanent state of exception.

This argument leads Michael Hardt and Antonio Negri to their rejection of nationalism as a structure of the sovereign exception in their two-part exploration of contemporary imperialism and globalization, *Empire* and *Multitude*. Their exploration views global capitalism as an Empire that is consolidating a new form of sovereignty beyond the older boundaries of the nation-state. Michael Hardt, in interview with Thomas Dumm, states that while he is skeptical about Agamben's placement of the concentration camp at the apogee of modern sovereignty, he and Negri agree with him in taking a position "against sovereignty in all its forms," including "imperial sovereignty" and the nation-state.[24] Reliance upon the Western sovereign nation, for them, fails to recognize how contemporary capitalism operates. Hardt and Negri equate the reinforcement of the nation as a means of collective empowerment with anti-colonial nationalisms: they state in *Empire* that "the nation is progressive strictly as a fortified line of defense against more powerful external forces."[25] For them, the possibility of radical change lies in the possibilities of a postnational multitude, and they insist

> on asserting that the construction of Empire is a step forward in order to do away with any nostalgia for the power structures that preceded it and refuse

any political strategy that involves returning to the old arrangement, such as trying to resurrect the nation-state to protect against global capital.[26]

Hardt and Negri maintain that political agency must ultimately reside in efforts at "autonomously constructing a counter-Empire" through the maturation of the multitude.[27] The nation-state becomes, in *Multitude*, an aspect of Empire itself, since, Hardt and Negri maintain, "today imperial administration is conducted largely by the structures and personnel of the dominant nation-states."[28] Statist nationalism makes little sense in this context, as the dominant nation-states that rely on such sentimental attachments are themselves tools of the developing Empire. Stronger nation-states lead, in this line of analysis, to a strengthened Empire. Dominant nation-states use their strength in order to extend the global domination of their forces. The grounds for struggle, Hardt and Negri argue, should cross geographies, taking on nomadic formations based upon alliances that privilege forms of democracy that reject the nation.

Canada, in this context, is a part of Empire, and multicultural reorganizations of the nation, while playing a crucial role in intervening in state racisms, have also been subsumed into the transnational brand that Canada has become. This is a country that continues to oppress Native communities while claiming its diversity as its strength. Womack's and Alfred's concepts, rather than adopting a deterritorialized position (such as that of Hardt and Negri), advocate a rooting of political struggles within specific contexts that challenge Western sovereign nationalisms. This rooting enables thinking about broader connections such as pan-Native struggles. A reconfigured nationalism becomes a political strategy. Such projects challenge the constructs of Canada, since Canada has proven very able to incorporate writing from people who have immigrated to Canada or descended from immigrants. Indigenous writing poses a different problem. The less racially exclusive models of Indigenous belonging that Womack discusses suggest the potential for belonging to work through the problems of the nation, but this model might not, in the end, vary a great deal from Canadian models of citizenship. Rejecting sovereignty's structures, however, offers something different — a challenge to notions of belonging that needs further consideration.

It is productive to turn to *Slash* with this in mind. Western notions of sovereignty become ridiculous in an Indigenous context, as they do in Thomas King's oft-anthologized story "Borders." In this story, a young

Blackfoot boy and his mother attempt to drive from Standoff, Alberta, to Salt Lake City, Utah, in order to visit Laetitia, the boy's sister. On arriving at the U.S. border, the mother refuses to give her nationality as anything other than Blackfoot, leading the border guards to deny them entry. They then turn back and face the same exclusion at the Canadian border. They end up circling for several days before being let pass when the media descend. The story demonstrates the artificiality of the forty-ninth parallel border and shows the impositions of colonial sovereignties upon people who previously spanned both sides of the border. It also shows how Indigenous people are compelled to reconcile themselves to national labels that do not fit with their lives, or else to disappear—to head back home and stay out of the way, as the narrator and his mother are pushed to do. Their bodies are ruled biopolitically, located on marginal land in their reserve. This reserve system is a state of exception to the juridical norms of citizenship that one might be extreme and inaccurate, but far from original, to compare to the concentration camps of Agamben's analysis.[29] *Slash* delves into these rifts, working away at the impossible and false binary of assimilation or disappearance that is foisted upon Indigenous people. It recognizes that "there [is] really no border that [is] recognized by Indians," and moves to discuss the legacy of Indigenous activism across North American since the 1960s.[30] It pushes for a "third choice" for Indigenous people in Canada,[31] one that is rooted in what are deemed traditional values and that transcends colonial impositions. In so doing, it queries the issue of integration into Canada, contesting indigenist bids for inclusion in federal policy and settling upon a sense of being that is founded upon site-specific concepts of belonging.

It is instructive to read this text in order to further suggest skepticism for what has become of the project of multiculturalism. This has become a project that, from a First Nations perspective, might be used to reinforce the colonial history of Canada. It does so by celebrating Canada's diversity in such a way that it justifies the state: Canada's advertisement of multicultural tolerance reinforces the idea that Canada is a welcoming country to all, a celebration that downplays the history of colonization. The legacy of *Obasan* and the discourses of tolerant Canadian nationalism, while combating elements of Canada's everyday racism, have led to viewing texts marked by their ethno-cultural difference as pieces of a national mosaic that attest to how good the country is—or might be in the future. A text like *Slash*, written for and distributed to a very different audience than *Obasan* or *In the Skin of a Lion*, upsets that notion of reconciliation with the past. While multicultural fictions have reconfigured the appearance of Canada by seeking to broaden it, they may implicitly accept the nation-state as a predetermined fact, thereby reifying it. *Slash*, by navigating its protagonist Tommy Kelasket, also known as Slash, away from Canadian national structures, creates a more nuanced vision of the state's relationship to cultural diversity. It challenges Diefenbaker- and Trudeau-era notions of belonging, beginning with legislation to allow Indigenous people in Canada to vote so that they "would be equal,"[32] through to the 1969 White Paper, which advocated Indigenous assimilation, and beyond. It contends that rights-based equality is a misnomer when it comes to Indigenous peoples.

Slash is a complicated text despite its seeming simplicity. Its plot tracks Tommy Kelasket as he meanders through the activism of Indigenous people across Canada and the United States since the 1960s. The book is a virtual catalogue of events and uprisings, from the beginnings of the American Indian Movement to the occupation of Alcatraz to the strife at Wounded Knee and the Pine Ridge Reservation. Slash attends the Trail of Broken Treaties caravan and witnesses confrontations with the Bureau of Indian Affairs, culminating in the occupation of their offices in Washington, D.C. He participates in a parallel caravan from Vancouver to Ottawa, as well as a brief occupation of the offices of the Department of Indian Affairs. At the same time, the text incorporates numerous dialogues between Indigenous activists, elders, and others, all of which, collectively, describe the struggles within and across Indigenous communities. George Ryga, in his foreword, summarizes the book as "a story of colonialism in Canada and the rest of the continent," a story that reflects both the personal and communal levels at which colonialism has had its effects.[33] The book tracks Slash's growth into adulthood, as well as the growth of the modern-day resistance movement. The eventual position that Slash assumes in his community is one of traditionalism, but the book is far from one-sided, and offers a great deal of open-ended dialogue.

The criticism of the text is indicative of the interpretive anxieties that discourses of difference have created in critics. The text's open-endedness is difficult for some, but, for the most part, the anxious critical responses to *Slash* have been written by white readers who struggle with their personal difficulties in teaching or reading it. It is a book that makes these readers uncomfortable. Helen Hoy argues that the novel "insists upon its own cultural tradition and resists quite dramatically the imposition of extraneous literary and critical criteria" — like those of white academic methodologies — finding that it is "not readily assimilable into a western literary tradition." It is a book that resists all forms of assimilation, and falls into an uncomfortably interstitial space for many. Hoy concludes that she both "can't teach it" and "can't not teach it."[34] White readers routinely evidence what Manina Jones has aptly termed "critical embarrassment" in reading the novel.[35] It is written against imperialism and confronts white critics' and teachers' benevolently multicultural impulses in attempting to include it in their work. It implicitly accuses them of participating, actively or passively, in the grossest forms of racism. Margery Fee notes in her reading of *Slash* that "Canadians have consolidated their identity through means of a symbolic transaction with the constructed figure of the Imaginary Indian," and observes that it is worth "pondering the extent to which any account of [Indigenous] novels published in a journal called *Canadian Literature*" — which publishes her article — "is in itself an act of colonization."[36] That is, even in discussing the book, Fee is participating in the reinscription of Indigenous peoples within the Canadian nation-state. It is at the same time an ethical imperative, as Hoy notes, that Armstrong's critique be recognized.

Slash has been hard to work with because it accuses the educational system in which critics participate of oppression. Starting with residential schools, *Slash* is clear in its assertion that "schools are meant to teach the young of the middle class the best way to survive their society and maintain its system. They are not meant to instruct those who do not have the values of that society."[37] The formal model of education on display in the book is of this sort. It challenges the traditionalism of the elders in Slash's community, pushing him towards assimilation in white culture. Critics are left trying to find an adequate means of reading the text. It does not fit with the postcolonial approaches prevalent in literary studies of the 1990s, Armstrong notes in an interview.[38] This is a point that Thomas King has made for all Indigenous literatures: for King, the term "postcolonial" — a term that is implicit in the arguments that Canada makes for itself through its deployments of multiculturalism — is inappropriate for discussing Native literature. It is a term that, King argues, reduces all Native literatures to ones that deal with the colonial encounter and that assumes a temporal progress beyond colonialism. While "post-colonial might be an excellent term to use to describe Canadian literature," King maintains, "it will not do to describe Native literature."[39] Julia Emberley proposes, in her reading of *Slash*, a distinction between postcolonial and "decolonial" critical practice as a result, but it is clear that any celebratory use of terms like "hybridity" to conceptualize anti-colonial approaches is out of synch with Indigenous epistemologies.[40] This debate is itself central to the novel as it queries the grounds for political action for Indigenous peoples. It finds these grounds in ways that clash with the project of multiculturalism, as well as with much of the theory that has fallen under the label of postcolonial.

This critical struggle appears at its most interesting in Frank Davey's *Post-national Arguments*. While Davey is one of Canada's most astute and knowledgeable critics, editors, and writers, his proposal for reading *Slash* has been seen as problematic. Davey asserts that his study addresses assumptions that his focal texts "take for granted and which become identifiable as political in the context of different assumptions brought to the text by the reader."[41] He is interested in the implicit constructions of the Canadian nation in texts written since 1967, finding that these reduce the Canadian polity to an atomized individualism that rests upon specific places and identities. His study sets out to contest such an atomization, relying upon the statement, quoted in shorter form earlier, that "participating in the arguments of a nation that is being continuously discursively produced and re-produced from political contestation" is "the only means" that Canadians "have of defending themselves against multinational capitalism."[42] Davey reiterates the common national/global dichotomy, one that *Transnational Canadas* disagrees with at the same time as it shares his sympathies. Contemporary Canadian literature written in English evidences a thread of texts that argue, explicitly or not, that the contemporary world does, indeed, shift away from the politics of nationalism, but these also find other ways of challenging global capital. Davey suggests that his study announces "the arrival of a post-national state—a state invisible to its own citizens, indistinguishable from its fellows, maintained by invisible political forces, and significant mainly through its position within the grid of world-class postcard cities."[43] It seems, however, that the Canadian nation-state has always been contested—even while it was being constructed—and that despite centennial and other celebrations, it has always remained problematic. The turn to the global simply leads to new twists.

The state, of course, is invisible to only some citizens. It is very present in the Indigenous communities with which *Slash* is concerned. Davey's reading is important to consider in this context. To Davey, *Slash* is "paradoxically both more comprehensively 'Canadian' and more 'North American' in the signs it deploys than almost all post-centennial Canadian novels."[44] He argues that the book relies upon an "oppositional politics" that forces it to render both of those positions more solid than they might otherwise be. It is oppositional in that it resists "Western conventions for framing the aborigine" and, as a result, takes "Canada and North American as single fields of action" for resistance. For Davey, the characters of the novel "construct Canada as a homogeneous field for political action, and North America as everywhere 'Indian territory'" as a result of the "underlying historically constituted commonality" between Indigenous people—that is, the history of colonization.[45] This position is apt insofar as the novel identifies its oppressors as the colonizers, those who, in the words of Slash's father, are "sneaking in from somewhere and pushing [their] way in."[46] Davey's homogenizing read of *Slash*'s reification of Canada is, however, contestable. Some critics have read the novel differently, noting how it maintains its cultural specificity in its Okanagan setting, one from which Tommy Kelasket departs and to which he eventually returns.[47] Manina Jones, arguing against the national reification that Davey suggests characterizes the novel, argues that the novel is self-conscious in working across terrains: she states that it "deliberately registers a pointed contradiction, a kind of foundational wound, within its own narrative utterance: speaking with a 'Native' voice is both a powerful motor of political agency...and problematic cultural grounding," given the specificities of Indigenous cultures.[48] Its construct of Native identity can be seen, instead, as a provisional one that is the result of colonization and is active in questioning itself.

The provisionality of pan-Native consciousness is apparent in the text. The elder Pra-cwa recognizes the frailty of Indigenous solidarity when he notes that the Okanagan people have become divided as a result of colonization. He states that the "people are two now," split between traditionalists and assimilationists.[49] This is the primary divide in the community, one that the text seeks to heal. Slash is himself divided between these positions, between his childhood friend Jimmy's goal of becoming more white—a goal that the text makes clear is founded in self-hatred—and the more traditional ways of Slash's family. These strike him in the early stages of the novel as being too far removed from the contemporary context. The traditional ways of living, white people and assimilationists keep on insisting, are vanishing. Jimmy asserts that the people "can't ever go backward," a direction that he associates with "following tradition."[50] Jimmy, predictably, struggles and is not accepted by whites. And these divides multiply when looking across different groups. Slash notes that Indigenous people everywhere are impoverished and oppressed, but he is careful to note differences between individual reserves in Canada and reservations in the United States. Each community is distinct. Armstrong notes in an interview that "there is no such thing as an Indian person."[51]

De-solidifying the text's pan-Indianism might help, in turn, to witness its contesting of Canada. Davey argues that "without the Canadian federation assumed by *Slash* the various political goals of its Indians would have no meaning; there would be no common ground for negotiation, no reliable framework to guarantee an agreement."[52] The characters of the book reify the Canadian state and in so doing, he suggests, validate it. While Davey's observation is astute in noting that contesting some*thing* assumes that that thing exists *a priori*, and that this is a troublesome concession from an Indigenous perspective, the novel expresses considerable ambivalence on this point. One of the final movements of the novel consists of a sustained discussion of whether Indigenous people should participate in the patriation of Canada's constitution in 1982. The people are far from unanimous in opting for inclusion in the discussions, and Slash challenges the idea that Indigenous people should be included in the constitution. Doing so would entail an acknowledgement that Canada has a right to exist. His partner, Maeg, is succinct in her alternative analysis, one that seeks inclusion. She is skeptical about the notion of human rights under the constitution, noting that "equal rights is no rights." This is what Indigenous people will have forced upon them, she argues, if they do not secure specific rights through the constitutional process. She argues that "Canada is here to stay" and that Indigenous people need to "join Canada in a way that is not too harsh."[53] Slash disagrees and joins the caravan of protestors going to Ottawa. He concludes that it is necessary to reject the constitution, stating that the people "would finally have to take a real stand to resist this [constitution] or [their] children would have nothing. Nothing but equality in a slave market to the corporations."[54] His rejection of the state and the peoples' ambivalence are found throughout the novel, especially over land claims debates. The people argue about whether to refuse to settle small land claims because achieving settlement would implicitly validate Canada. When some of the bands agree to negotiate with the B.C. government, the people's energy is dissipated. The government requires that all demonstrations cease until the claims are settled before they agree to proceed. The text is deeply ambivalent about acting within the political spheres of the settler-invader culture.

The text is, furthermore, very careful in its deployment of language related to these issues. Armstrong states that using English is, for her, "a continuous battle against... rigidity," against the limited forms of expression that the language allows.[55] The terms that Womack and Alfred discuss, "sovereignty" and "nationhood," are used sparingly as a result. The concept of the nation is first mentioned by a speaker at the Washington, D.C., occupation of the Bureau of Indian Affairs. This speaker states that their "leaders are no different" than other visiting dignitaries to the Capitol, because "they are the spokesmen of [their] Nations."[56] This phrasing suggests a strategic use of the term in order to gain recognition. On the following page, Native reservations are, similarly, referred to as "Sovereign Nations."[57] The term reappears only at the very end of the text and, again, it is spoken in relation to the colonizing government. Slash suggests that Indigenous people are constituted by "different nations... not just one large conglomerate group called Indians, the way government would prefer it."[58] Using the term to insist upon the peoples' legitimacy in the oppressors' language is a strategic action, and it appears three more times thereafter, each time in reference to the Canadian government or the United Nations.[59] The term "sovereignty" is deployed similarly, entering the text during a band meeting near Slash's home. Another unnamed speaker discusses the people's sovereignty, which, he emphasizes, has not been signed away in the treaties. Theirs is a set of rights that, he states, the people "want to keep."[60] If the text is sparing in its use of nationhood, this single mention of sovereignty as a noun situates it as a concept that preceded colonization, as it is connected to the peoples' ancestral rights. Sovereignty is paralleled, moreover, by the text's repudiation of the "system of dependency" that colonialism has taught Slash's people, a system that makes it necessary for them to become "self-sufficient" once again.[61] Slash illustrates such progress from dependency to self-sufficiency in his final return home, a return in which he learns to articulate his resistance through acts of living and in bringing up his son, Marlon, after Maeg is killed in a car accident.

If *Slash* were a text that reified the state, then it would need to include a more approbatory endorsement of political process. This reading has been focusing on Davey's reading here partly in order to suggest how *Slash* differs from mass-market Canadian novels marked by cultural difference. While novels like Kogawa's and Ontaatje's are able to suggest that Canada is a nation-state imbued with a history of racism, they are often limited by a critique that suggests Canada might be made better by recognizing its flaws and admitting broader segments of society into its inclusive whole. This has been a radical political position, but just as 1960s nationalism became mainstream, such discourses of multiculturalism have become widely recognized; Ashok Mathur has recently argued that

> the critical and political components of literary production [by writers of colour were] evacuated...in favour of "marketable" books. Mainstream Canadian literature so completely absorbed writers of colour through the maw of capital that we became indistinguishable from the corpus of Canadian literature.[62]

Slash suggests, against such an appropriation, that Canada is a nation-state that has a questionable right to exist at all, and that it has even less right to include Indigenous discourses in its self-conceptualization. Multiculturalism and indigeneity are not, of course, one and the same. It is therefore not surprising that Canadian critics have had a response of embarrassment in discussing *Slash* and texts like it. *Slash* is ultimately *not* a Canadian novel (although it will continue to be discussed under the rubric of CanLit), and critics' discussions of it as such risk reducing its challenges. Rather, it renders the question itself ridiculous. Instead of working within the terms that are allowed for Indigenous people by the state, the book sees what its activist character Mardi terms "a third choice": "you see they only give us two choices," she tells Slash. "Assimilate or get lost. A lot of us are lost. We need to make a third choice."[63] This statement has been recognized as the book's central and didactic thesis: finding another way through an Indigenous-centred worldview is the key, one that is not only rooted in the past and the land, but that is adaptable to the present-day lives of the Okanagan people. As such, *Slash* seeks, in the words of Margery Fee, to "expose the fake ideas and debunk the 'choices' that white acculturation has forced on Native peoples in Canada."[64]

It is a novel that does not accept Canada at face value, that writes scripts that exceed its logic, and that roots itself in a worldview that is not easily assimilable to the norms of the colonial state.

The response of embarrassment is therefore part of the novel's purpose. Armstrong has said that the novel was designed as a fictionalized means of encoding the recent history of Indigenous protest movements for a high school audience.[65] It has an explicit "moral emphasis," as Davey notes,[66] one that rewrites the possibilities available to the Okanagan people. While it concludes with Tommy Kelasket at home and recently widowed with his young son, rejecting activism and living his politics through inhabiting the land, it also synthesizes gender relations. It has a doubly instructional purpose: of reconciling Slash to an Indigenous third way beyond assimilation or extinction, and of reconciling his earlier masculinity to a feminine aspect. The solutions that the novel proposes are simple, but their simplicity demonstrates the brutality of colonization and the need to develop decolonizing approaches. Slash asserts that it is important simply to "tell people that it's okay to be an Indian," a disarmingly simple strategy. This strategy is needed because the root of their problems is not merely a "lack of money or opportunity," as Jimmy suggests early in the novel. Rather, people "feel inferior and shitty just for being Indian."[67] That fact needs to be countered with a path through the binary splits offered by colonization. Undoing Western scripts of gendering play a role in this healing process, and Slash distances himself from his earlier exploitation of "chicks" to a deep appreciation of women, who work "harder than anybody realize[s]" to effect political change.[68] He strives to work beyond gender roles and finds solace in his partner, Maeg. Armstrong is explicit in this anti-sexist project, evincing impatience with "the male ego" in an interview, and writes the character Slash so that he can change his gendered roles.[69] As much as Armstrong writes the novel in order to deny the dichotomous choices on offer from white society, she is also working to disrupt the gender systems that she sees in Okanagan and Indigenous societies. But these are systems that derive, the novel suggests, from colonization.

Slash finds peace in recognizing that he is "part of all the rest of the people," but "the people" is a term that the novel uses quite specifically.[70] It refers to an awakening pan-Native sense of self, but Slash's recovery from violence and substance abuse also occurs through a rooting in his own community, one in which he discovers that he is "necessary" as a "keeper of the ways."[71] The ultimate political act, he discovers, is existence: "respecting people and being a good teacher just by your actions is enough," he is told while in Oregon. The conclusion, Slash states, is "to find out what things were left of the old ways... and make it usable in [their] modern Indian lives."[72] These ways are specific to the lands and to the plants and animals that exist there. The novel's pan-Native consciousness is set alongside Slash's Okanagan roots, and it refuses to see these two positions as being opposed.

Slash is, therefore, a text that pushes readers to recognize the limitations of how the label of Canadian might be applied to writing that takes place in Canada. Instead of wishing for a more inclusive form of belonging within the colonial nation-state or a Western notion of sovereignty, *Slash* pushes for forms of belonging that are rooted in ancestral communities while still being responsive to the present, while contesting the gendered norms of white Canada. *Slash* seeks a locus for coming to speech that cannot be assimilated to however welcoming a notion of colonial belonging. *Slash* challenges the notion of Canada, upsetting those who would normally view the Okanagan as a white space (one that is designated as a space of agriculture, recreation, and holidaying, rather than colonization). If it is possible to relinquish ingrained notions that Canada is necessarily a good place to be—something that is radically contestable from an Indigenous point of view—then it might be possible to recognize the anti-colonial critiques of *Slash*, as the text itself invites and asks of its readers.

Notes to Chapter Eight

1. It should be noted that in this chapter in particular, *Transnational Canadas* pays little heed to the Canada–U.S. border, which is, as Thomas King notes in *The Truth about Stories: A Native Narrative*, "a figment of someone else's imagination," one that "doesn't mean much to the majority of Native people in either country" (Toronto: Anansi, 2003), 102.
2. In Alfred's case, his nation at Kahnawake has been involved in the Rotinohshonni Confederacy of Six Nations since long before colonization. Womack traces how the Creeks have constituted themselves through their confederation as a nation that includes diverse ethnic groups both prior to and since contact.
3. Michael Hardt and Antonio Negri, *Empire* (Cambridge: Harvard UP, 2000), 103.
4. Frank Davey, *Post-national Arguments* (Toronto: U of Toronto P, 1993), 24.
5. Franz Fanon, *The Wretched of the Earth*, trans. C. Farrington (New York: Grove, 1963), 204.

6 Craig Womack, *Red on Red: Native American Literary Separatism* (Minneapolis: U of Minnesota P, 1999), 1.
7 Howard Adams, *Prison of Grass: Canada from a Native Point of View*, rev. ed. (Saskatoon: Fifth House, 1989), 168–69.
8 Womack, *Red on Red*, 14, 51.
9 Womack, *Red on Red*, 59.
10 Womack, *Red on Red*, 60.
11 Michelle Henry, "Canonizing Craig Womack: Finding Native Literature's Place in Indian Country," *American Indian Quarterly* 28.1–2 (2004): 33.
12 Taiaiake Alfred, *Peace, Power, Righteousness: An Indigenous Manifesto* (Don Mills, ON: Oxford UP, 1999), xiv.
13 Alfred, *Peace, Power, Righteousness*, 25.
14 Alfred, *Peace, Power, Righteousness*, 59.
15 Alfred, *Peace, Power, Righteousness*, 25.
16 Alfred, *Peace, Power, Righteousness*, 60.
17 A third perspective is offered by Robert Warrior, who suggests that Indigenous struggle "is a struggle for sovereignty, and if sovereignty is anything, it is a way of life," thereby redefining the concept in *Tribal Secrets: Recovering American Indian Intellectual Traditions* (Minneapolis: U of Minnesota P, 1995), 123. The concept of "intellectual sovereignty" is key in Warrior's formulations.
18 Alfred, *Peace, Power, Righteousness*, xiv, xviii.
19 Alfred, *Peace, Power, Righteousness*, xvi.
20 For example by Kristina Fagan in "Tewatatha:wi: Aboriginal Nationalism in Taiaiake Alfred's *Peace, Power, Righteousness: An Indigenous Manifesto*," *American Indian Quarterly* 28.1–2 (2004): 25.
21 Bonita Lawrence, *"Real" Indians and Others: Mixed-Blooded Urban Native Peoples and Indigenous Nationhood* (Vancouver: UBC P, 2004), 46.
22 Lee Maracle, *I Am Woman: A Native Perspective on Sociology and Feminism* (Vancouver: Press Gang, 1996), 17.
23 Giorgio Agamben, *Homo Sacer: Sovereign Power and Bare Life*, trans. D. Heller-Roazen (Stanford: Stanford UP, 1998), 3, 6.
24 Michael Hardt and Thomas Dumm, "Sovereignty, Multitudes, Absolute Democracy: A Discussion between Michael Hardt and Thomas L. Dumm about Nardt and Negri's *Empire*," *Empire's New Clothes: Reading Hardt and Negri*, ed. P. Passavant and J. Dean (New York: Routledge, 2004), 166.
25 Hardt and Negri, *Empire*, 106.
26 Hardt and Negri, *Empire*, 43.
27 Hardt and Negri, *Empire*, xv.
28 Michael Hardt and Antonio Negri, *Multitude: War and Democracy in the Age of Empire* (New York: Penguin, 2004), 60.
29 Carlos Embry, in fact, devoted a book to such a theme back in 1956: *America's Concentration Camps: The Facts about Our Indian Reservations Today* (New York: David McKay, 1956).
30 Jeannette Armstrong, *Slash* (Penticton, BC: Theytus, 1985), 92.
31 Armstrong, *Slash*, 70.
32 Armstrong, *Slash*, 18.
33 George Ryga, Foreword to *Slash* by Jeannette Armstrong (Penticton, BC: Theytus, 1985), 9.

34 Barbara Hodne and Helen Hoy, "Reading from the Inside Out: Jeanette Armstrong's *Slash*," *World Literature Written in English* 32.1 (1992): 68, 82.
35 Manina Jones, "Slash Marks the Spot: 'Critical Embarrassment' and Activist Aesthetics in Jeannette Armstrong's *Slash*," *West Coast Line* 33.3 (2000): 48. The reception of the novel, Jones argues, "has to a substantial degree been an account of the difficulties academic readers have in addressing the novel at all" (49). Essays such as Matthew Green's "A Hard Day's Knight: A Discursive Analysis of Jeannette Armstrong's *Slash*" thus routinely begin with apologias like his disclaimer that he is "a White, heterosexual male" in *The Canadian Journal of Native Studies* 19.1 (1999): 52.
36 Margery Fee, "Upsetting Fake Ideas: Jeannette Armstrong's 'Slash' and Beatrice Culleton's 'April Raintree,'" *Canadian Literature* 124–125 (1990): 178, 177.
37 Armstrong, *Slash*, 212.
38 Katja Sarkowsky also notes this point in "A Decolonial (Rite of) Passage: Decolonization, Migration and Gender Construction in Jeannette Armstrong's *Slash*," *Zeitschrift für Anglistik und Amerikanistik* 49.3 (2001): 233. Armstrong's questioning of postcolonialism takes place in Hartwig Isernhagen, *Momaday, Vizenor, Armstrong: Conversations on American Indian Writing* (Norman: U of Oklahoma P, 1999), 178.
39 Thomas King, "Godzilla vs. Postcolonial," *Unhomely States: Theorizing English-Canadian Postcolonialism*, ed. Cynthia Sugars (Peterborough, ON: Broadview, 2004), 185.
40 Julia Emberley, *Thresholds of Difference: Feminist Critique, Native Women's Writings, Postcolonial Theory* (Toronto: U of Toronto P, 1993), 4.
41 Davey, *Post-national Arguments*, 3.
42 Davey, *Post-national Arguments*, 24.
43 Davey, *Post-national Arguments*, 266.
44 Davey, *Post-national Arguments*, 56.
45 Davey, *Post-national Arguments*, 56, 58, 61.
46 Armstrong, *Slash*, 23.
47 See Gabriele Helms, *Challenging Canada: Dialogism and Narrative Techniques in Canadian Novels* (Montreal and Kingston: McGill-Queen's UP, 2003), 100; and Noel Elizabeth Currie, "Jeannette Armstrong and the Colonial Legacy," *Canadian Literature* 124–125 (1990), 140.
48 Jones, "Slash Marks the Spot," 58.
49 Armstrong, *Slash*, 42.
50 Armstrong, *Slash*, 84.
51 Janice Williamson, "Jeannette Armstrong: 'what I intended was to connect...and it's happened,'" *Tessera* 12 (1992): 116.
52 Davey, *Post-national Arguments*, 63.
53 Armstrong, *Slash*, 243.
54 Armstrong, *Slash*, 248.
55 Jeannette Armstrong, "Land Speaking," *Speaking for the Generations: Native Writers on Writing*, ed. Simon Ortiz (Tucson: U of Arizona P, 1998), 194.
56 Armstrong, *Slash*, 101.
57 Armstrong, *Slash*, 102.
58 Armstrong, *Slash*, 235.
59 Armstrong, *Slash*, 239, 241, 243.

60 Armstrong, *Slash*, 135.
61 Armstrong, *Slash*, 218.
62 Ashok Mathur, "Abstract," TransCanada One: Literature, Institutions, Citizenship Conference website, 2005, http://www.transcanadas.ca/transcanada1/mathur.shtml. The ideas from this presentation entered, in slightly different form, into his essay "Transubracination: How Writers of Colour Became CanLit," *Trans.Can.Lit: Resituating the Study of Canadian Literature*, ed. Smaro Kamboureli and Roy Miki (Waterloo: Wilfrid Laurier UP, 2007), 141–51.
63 Armstrong, *Slash*, 70.
64 Fee, "Upsetting Fake Ideas," 168.
65 Williamson, "Jeannette Armstrong: 'what I intended was to connect,'" 122 ff.
66 Davey, *Post-national Arguments*, 57.
67 Armstrong, *Slash*, 147, 149.
68 Armstrong, *Slash*, 153.
69 Williamson, "Jeannette Armstrong: 'what I intended was to connect,'" 119. Armstrong's choice to write about a male protagonist has led to a fair amount of critical ink, as Julia Emberley notes in *Thresholds of Difference*, 147–49.
70 Armstrong, *Slash*, 203.
71 Armstrong, *Slash*, 203, 205.
72 Armstrong, *Slash*, 210.

CONCLUSION TO PART TWO

The readings of the three focal texts in Part Two should not be seen as signalling a rejection of multicultural writing. The questioning of the political uses to which such writings are put leads to an interrogation of why certain texts are read—and continue to be read—and whose purposes those readings serve. As is the case with *Obasan*, a book can serve specific political uses within a community, while still creating a role for itself within the dominant narratives of the nation. As much as books like *Obasan* and *In the Skin of a Lion* pose challenges to the official narratives of the nation in which they situate themselves, the risk remains that readings of these books will reinforce the terrain of the dominant rather than reformulate it. Such is this section's sense of the politics of class in Ondaatje's novel, as well as that novel's perspective on ethnicity and racialization. However, seeking inclusion is also a progressive political action (in a liberal, humanist vein), and was all the more so when those novels were written. It seems preferable, however, to challenge the politics of power upon which notions of belonging are founded. *Slash*, in its attempt to carve an alternative epistemological ground upon which to rethink notions of power and the legacy of colonialism, works at creating a greater ambivalence in critics. This ambivalence indicates the useful difficulty of assimilating the text to dominant Canadian notions of selfhood.

Each of these texts exists in a distinct milieu, and this section's comparisons might not always be fair. Beyond the obvious risk of homogenizing them vis-à-vis white Canada as representing otherness, each maintains its own relationship to its readership and the market. These relate to their social function: *Obasan* is reprinted as an inexpensive Penguin paperback and reaches a wide-ranging audience, from high school students to the broader reading public. *In the Skin of a Lion* circulates as a paperback from Vintage and is situated as a part of the literary establishment. *Slash*, in turn, is published by Theytus, an independent and Indigenous-run house connected to the En'owkin writers' centre with which Armstrong is associated, and as a result frames a more specific audience, one that is more intimately concerned with Indigenous issues. The first two texts play a more active role within the realm of Bakhtinian "official discourse" about the nation, while *Slash* exists in a more ambivalent position. Working to reformulate or challenge Canada is a complex process in *Obasan* and *In the Skin of a Lion*, as each adopts an insider-and-outsider perspective. *Slash*, on the other hand, thinks of itself as being primarily outside Canada. All tactics are important and should be read for their merits.

PART THREE

CANADA IN THE WORLD

INTRODUCTION TO PART THREE

Part Three turns to texts that place Canada in dialogue with today's global order. Here the concept of hegemony that Spivak discusses will need further consideration, as will the broader problematic of the transnational. In a sense, this book has already arrived here. The pan-Native, yet still very specific positions offered by Womack and Alfred provide models for thinking about alliances across national boundaries, as does Armstrong's discussion of Slash's perambulatory participation in activist movements. Understanding how alliances are being thought in the context of globalization derives from such located knowledges. The politics of transnational alliance hinge upon the potential for being open to multiple strategies. And the politics of writing in the globalizing world are mixed, frequently subsumed to the dictates of neo-liberalism but also offering competing visions. The writing upon which this book has been focusing should give readers a way of thinking about the possibilities and risks faced by writers in this context. Part Three focuses first upon the development of an articulated field of transnational theory. *Transnational Canadas* has established some of the intersections between Marxism, poststructuralism, postcolonialism, and Indigenous thinking towards this end. Part Three proceeds from there to interrogate recent writing in Canada that examines the world through a transnational or globalizing lens. Some writing in Canada is attesting to a vision of the nation as progressive and cosmopolitan despite the ongoing legacies of colonialism. Other writing, however, works to shift notions of subjectivity and belonging, challenging such a vision. Tracking the rise of a transnational mindset involves a parallel process of tracing how subjects think themselves and their belonging—and work to challenge these notions. This tracing is the challenge of this final part. As Chapter Nine discusses, theorizations of the global present difficulties by variously misrepresenting totality or by reasserting notions of universality. Therefore, the later chapters in Part Three trace discourses of globalization in three texts in order to put such totalizing concepts into question. There is a shuttling between positions, an engagement with questions of scale and re-scaling, and a continued concern with disrupting structures of domination in these chapters. Part Three will suggest that the debates about the Giller Prize and Vincent Lam's recent book, *Bloodletting and Miraculous Cures*, signal a cosmopolitan multiculturalism that functions well as a marketing tool for Canada. The challenges posed by Roy Miki in *Surrender* and Dionne Brand in *What We All Long For* prove to be more engaged in issues of transnational politics as they relate to questions of subjectivity. The terrain is mixed as writers grapple with their responses to global capitalism, voicing concern alongside necessary moments of hope. Understanding where their hope lies is crucial to assessing how literatures of this country have shifted notions of the political from the national to the transnational, altering notions of subjectivity as they do so.

Part Three begins with a discussion of recent transnational studies. Many theorists working from leftist positions are examining how the increasing economic disparities of the world can be solved by transforming or dismantling capitalism, and these discussions are useful for situating discussion of the issues underlying writing in Canada. The most controversial theorists of these issues to date have been Michael Hardt and Antonio Negri, whose book *Empire* has been both discussed as a new *Communist Manifesto* for the twenty-first century and harshly critiqued from many quarters. Their sequel, *Multitude*, deals with some of these criticisms while pushing their formulations further.[1] Chapter Nine uses Hardt and Negri's work as a focal point, but also discusses the range of transnational studies, looking for openings to work with Canadian literature. Transnational or global studies remain diverse, uneven, and contradictory, but if there is a common thread to be traced through them, it is that global capitalism creates political and cultural problems that require innovative approaches. These approaches come on a scale that is both local and global, all the while challenging the divide between the two. The role of literature within global politics, economics, and culture is complex. The socio-political answers that are being proposed are united, if at all, by their recognition of the need for a diversity of answers. Such a nuanced take will force this book to move beyond the totalizing efforts of much global discourse to date, Hardt and Negri's in particular, in order to assess literature in this context.

Part Three moves from this balancing of theories of transnationalism to literary works written since 2000. That this book skips over literary works written in the 1990s might be seen as unusual, as many excellent books were written and discussed during the decade. Many people will consider it to have been a good decade for Canadian letters. *Transnational Canadas* discusses works from the period in passing, though none have ended up being focal texts in this book. This was a decade that saw a consolidation of the Canadian publishing industry as an international force and the successful marketing of CanLit globally. However, a book like *In the Skin of a Lion* was very much a portent for much of the work that was widely received during the '90s, and, rather than producing a strict literary history, this present analysis is more invested in the specific texts that are read here. Part Three moves, then, to considering the politics of the Giller Prize and Vincent Lam's 2005 book *Bloodletting and Miraculous Cures* in Chapter Ten. The popularity of this book of stories—especially its winning of the 2006 Scotiabank Giller Prize—suggests something of the ubiquity of its sentiments, which have been read as a complex, troubling instance of a mainstreamed multiculturalism. The argument traces ways in which discourses of difference come, in that book, to confirm the society in which it is situated and to which it is marketed.

Getting into the vexed politics of *Bloodletting and Miraculous Cures* leads to an inquiry for more thorough responses to contemporary capitalism's drive to the commodification of difference. Part Three moves from Lam's text to Roy Miki's 2001 book of poetry, *Surrender*, in Chapter Eleven. This book provides the chapter with a way of looking at mobile responses towards global capitalism through the lens of subjectivity. Miki's book is focused upon how subjectivity functions under globalization. The reading of his volume follows the ways in which a poststructural, destabilized subject—one who disavows fixed forms of identity to the point of negating the first-person singular "I"—might foster anti-oppressive spaces. At the same time, this book highlights the difficulties of such an open-ended approach. This chapter is careful to read Miki's discourse on subjectivity in a way that accounts for the controlling structures of Empire.

Dionne Brand's *What We All Long For* then intervenes as a final look at the possibility for a resistant politics to articulate itself through concepts of subjectivity that take readers beyond identity politics. Taking an approach more founded in realism than Miki's *Surrender*—a difference partly brought in by its genre—*What We All Long For* follows the lives of a number of characters whose families immigrate to Toronto. Their struggles to liberate themselves within a racist society illustrate the perils of decentred forms of subjectivity under contemporary, imperial forms of capitalism, but also point towards spaces in which the self can push towards an open-ended future, the sort of openness to the other that we saw Derrida advocating in his reading of Marx. Not all of Brand's characters succeed in freeing themselves. For some, an open—or "drifting"—approach leads to painful encounters with the disciplinary structures of the state. For others, however, the chaos of the city and the world provides them with spaces in which to begin constructing another world, one that is built collectively and from below, across borders and between communities.

Part Three brings together three different voices responding to a similar set of conditions. All point towards the importance of considering global perspectives and routes of migration in considering what it might mean to write in contemporary Canada. This part is guided by the problematics of this book so far: while the world may be one of Empire today, it is not enough to seek simply a multitude in opposition to it, as Hardt and Negri seek to do. Instead, Part Three pursues a coalitional politics. But it remains especially cognizant of the critiques offered by Spivak and others, which suggest that one cannot make any easy generalizations about the oppressed in the contemporary world of war and imperialism.

Notes to Introduction to Part Three

1 See especially Slavoj Žižek, "Have Michael Hardt and Antonio Negri Rewritten the Communist Manifesto for the Twenty-First Century?" *Rethinking Marxism* 13.3–4 (2001): 190–98. Timothy Brennan and Atilio Boron continue to be Hardt and Negri's harshest critics.

CHAPTER NINE

Transnational Multitudes

Michael Hardt and Antonio Negri's two-part contribution to debates of globality has attracted critics because of the writers' sheer optimism and incorporation of a vast array of the knowledges produced about globalization. At a time when many theorists of the left sounded increasingly glum about global capitalism and the ongoing state of war, Hardt and Negri injected vigour into debates by claiming that the world is improving and that a future of what they term "radical democracy" is around the corner, coming to us through the global movements that many critics were decrying. This argument, stated by two well-situated theorists on either side of the Atlantic, has prompted debate and given critics a substantial amount of material with which to engage.

The initial arguments of *Empire* and *Multitude* are straightforward. Hardt and Negri build on their earlier co-authored *Labor of Dionysus* to provide an interdisciplinary focus upon contemporary tropes of hegemony and resistance. They read the political and cultural problems that they see in the globalizing world while formulating ways of escaping from the disparities of corporate globalization. Modelling their thinking on Marx, they portray globalization as a new form of domination, just as Marx read industrial capitalism. For Hardt and Negri, the new form of domination is conceptualized under the term "Empire." Their Empire is not tied to any nation-state, and it is best thought not with reference to national frameworks, given what they see as the growing obsolescence of the state. Empire consists of the mobile, decentred, and deterritorialized forms of dominance projected by a new form of global sovereignty. Its political bodies have not yet been formalized, although bodies like the United Nations, the World Bank, and the International Monetary Fund are incipient forms thereof. Empire absorbs national projects into the capitalist whole. For Hardt and Negri, Empire "establishes no territorial center of power and does not rely on fixed boundaries or barriers. It is a *decentered* and *deterritorializing* apparatus of rule that progressively incorporates the entire global realm within its open, expanding frontiers."[1] While American power remains hegemonic, for them the nation-state serves the broader functions of Empire, as capitalism within the state model is transposed onto a transnational stage. As a result, Hardt and Negri state that "the United States does not, and indeed no nation-state can today, form the centre of an imperialist project."[2] Empire is, rather, a broader series of conditions that determines the political and economic situations of an ever-larger portion of the globe.

The task facing the left, Hardt and Negri claim, is to dismantle sovereignty itself as a structure of implicit injustices and hierarchies, and to realize a form of politics founded upon a mobility similar to that of Empire. They see the future of political movements arising through Empire itself because they see in its contradictions the beginnings of its inevitable demise and the arrival of "a democracy of the multitude."[3] This sense of inevitability, almost messianic, leads Timothy Brennan to suggest that Hardt and Negri develop "a revealingly theological tone" in this aspect of their discussion.[4] For Hardt and Negri, however, the multitude is what is created when Empire dismantles the barriers between the mass of disenfranchised labourers, citizens, and refugees. This multitude is "an alternative" to imperial rule: it is "the set of all the exploited and the subjugated, a multitude that is directly opposed to Empire," who no longer have any mediation between them as a result of Empire's systematic, yet still incomplete, removal of borders.[5] This multitude is "the living alternative that grows within Empire."[6] These sorts of movements are thought of as rhizomatic, in the sense that Deleuze and Guattari discuss, that is, as connecting "any point to any other point... not necessarily linked to traits of the same nature."[7] The multitude that Hardt and Negri theorize exemplifies Deleuze and Guattari's nomadic, poststructural thinking, challenging leftist models based upon notions of class solidarity and unity, claiming primacy for movements that maintain only loose connections and that shift continuously.

This conceptualization of resistance is open to critique from many quarters. While many critics have recognized the usefulness of the critique or voiced a general agreement, many have criticized the books. Critics have focused on the (in)accuracies of many of Hardt and Negri's diagnoses, disproving their theses through analyses of material conditions that contradict, for instance, the claim that the nation is a receding form.[8] Other criticisms have supported mass movements and workers' struggles as the primary grounds for anti-capitalist resistance, while Hardt and Negri argue that the contemporary world privileges immaterial forms of labour and that, as a result, resistance should be founded on more mobile grounds. Hardt and Negri are, additionally, caught within broader debates about the valence of the term "globalization." Timothy Brennan notes that Hardt and Negri are unwavering in what he calls their "devotion to New Times credos," and this belief in the radical difference of the present from the past has been debated repeatedly in discourses of globalization.[9] Whether the global order presents us with a genuinely "new" form of capitalism in its neo-liberal, post-Fordist forms or if the shifts are gradual progressions has determined many analysts' reception of discourses of the global—and of Hardt and Negri. The "term *globalization*," Masao Miyoshi notes, "is nearly as abused as *postcoloniality*."[10] Its breadth effaces differences between regional economies, giving the impression that there is a level playing field in contemporary capitalism, and creates an image of a present that is different from the past. All of these are debatable (and debated) points. There have been and continue to be perceived differences between the past and the present, however: Eric Hobsbawn, for example, separates the present from the past on the basis of its "ultra-rapid, fundamental and unprecedented socio-economic transformations."[11] Hardt and Negri, similarly, rely upon such a narrative.

There are several consequences to how Hardt and Negri approach their arguments. For them, feminist, anti-racist, and queer liberation struggles, among other social movements, form an important component of the struggles of the multitude.[12] Fredric Jameson has wondered whether these social movements are "consequences and aftereffects of late capitalism," rather than genuinely revolutionary changes.[13] To Hardt and

Negri, this question may be moot, as they see all change as coming from within Empire. The broader question is one of organization or political strategy. Hardt and Negri eschew the socialist emphasis upon strategy in favour of more contingent tactics. Whereas socialist politics have emphasized the class struggle, the politics of the multitude valorize struggles at all levels. There can be no overall politics in this framework, but that lack becomes itself a politics, one that is de-hierarchized and open-ended. This lack of strategy is something that critics of the book have found frustrating, but it allows Hardt and Negri to avoid being overly programmatic, thereby allowing them the breadth of argument that they attempt.

Hardt and Negri do, however, offer a contingent list of demands at the end of *Empire*, which becomes the broader political project in *Multitude*. *Empire* concludes by invoking a future multitude and democracy to come and provides three demands: "global citizenship," "a social wage and a guaranteed income for all," and "the right to reappropriation" of information.[14] These goals are articulated alongside a discussion of the potential of the multitude, whose maturity they await. In the sequel, the politics of this body are articulated in more depth. There, the "project of the multitude" becomes one of employing new "weapons" for undermining global capitalism and creating a form of democracy founded upon a distinction between constituent and constituted power.[15] The task is to use "weapons that are not merely destructive but are themselves forms of constituent power," weapons that are capable of "creating the social relations and institutions of a new society."[16] They seek forms of power that are mobile, existing at the level of articulated potential, rather than being constituted into crystallized forms of sovereign power. The open-endedness of such constituent power begins in their theory of participatory democracy. The tools or "weapons" that they invoke are of interest. *Transnational Canadas* has seen cultural production and literature as tools that might be capable of constructing new social relations despite their absorption within capital and the machinery of the nation-state. Cultural acts such as writing retain the potential to create social movement, growth, or recognition across differences. These sorts of changes vary over time, as has been argued of the '60s and '70s national vision and the movement of discourses of difference into the national body through the rhetorics of multiculturalism and cultural difference. This perspective on the efficacy of culture is, of course, a long-advocated one, notably by

Shelley in his famous declaration that poets are the "unacknowledged legislators of the world." The power of cultural interpretation is important to Hardt and Negri's formulations of Empire and the multitude, and the authors also leave room for literary acts to create change.

Their version of global resistance and counter-Empire becomes complicated, however, in its distinction between constituent and constituted power. The distinction is somewhat elusive. They usually distinguish between the already-solidified power of nation-states and other institutions, and power that remains merely potential, within the broad circulation of human power. This second, constituent power retains the ability to constitute the multitude and is privileged because it remains unfixed. Its potential is always greater than that of any constituted power. It is, as Negri suggests in *Insurgencies*, "the source of production of constitutional norms" and "the power to establish a new juridical arrangement."[17] It is the power to take action and to create a new state of affairs. Hardt and Negri suggest that "the power to act is constituted by labor, intelligence, passion, and affect in one common place" and that those abstract concepts, acting in common, are what "configure a *constituent power*."[18] This constituent power contrasts with the already-constituted power of sovereign state systems, with their structures and exclusions. "Keeping the formative capacity of constituent power itself in motion," Negri writes, is key to formulating a new constitutional model, since "sovereignty presents itself as a fixing of constituent power, and therefore as its termination, as the exhaustion of the freedom that constituent power carries."[19] Within Empire, the constituent power lying within human potential dictates an eschewal of tactics. As long as power remains always potentially greater than that which is realized, any tactics remain provisional. Moreover, given Empire's deterritorializing nature, strategy becomes virtualized, able to respond to an expanding whole. This point leads Hardt and Negri to aver that "the virtual center of Empire can be attacked from any point."[20]

The idea of constituent power, while productive, falls short for those who wonder, as Slavoj Žižek does, what "the 'multitude in power' [would] look like."[21] His point is pertinent. Neil Smith suggests that Hardt and Negri fail to note that the Deleuzian idea of deterritorialization upon which they rely is always countered by acts of reterritorialization, that "reterritorialization counters deterritorialization at every turn,"[22] a point to which this section will return in its discussion of Roy Miki's and

Dionne Brand's work. That is, the deterritorialized Empire that Hardt and Negri conceive is not simply open-ended; it is also engaged in an active process of constructing new borders. One site for contesting Empire might not, as a result, have an equal valence as any other. Empire has a specific, as-yet-unmapped geography, like the postmodern world that Jameson suggests should be countered through processes of cognitive mapping. In power, Žižek suggests, the multitude's lack of tactics might be untenable; in resistance, it might be unproductive. Although this is, indeed, one of Hardt and Negri's concerns, they defer to the hopeful spirit of contestation that animates their work. Malcolm Bull suggests that, in *Empire*, "wandering becomes a goal in itself," a goal that has the potential to reformulate how politics are to be thought.[23]

Their notion of constituent power relies upon an opposition of immanence to transcendence. The concept of immanence derives from the work of seventeenth-century philosopher Spinoza, and it is one that allows them to sidestep metaphysics. In its earlier formulations, the category of immanence dealt with human potential, the potential for existence or being in the world, and the existence of the godly within the human frame. Hardt and Negri suggest that the metaphysical category of transcendence has been set up against such immanence as a means of controlling society, that "the realm of potentiality ... is limited a priori by the imposition of transcendent rule and order."[24] Transcendence, in its invocation of a power that is larger than humanity, limits human potential. Setting up the divine as a category that is beyond the human allows practices such as sovereignty to be established. Transcendence is therefore to be challenged. Politics, Hardt and Negri suggest, should be conducted on an entirely human level, without reliance upon transcendent or sovereign structures. They state that "the plane of immanence is the one on which the powers of singularity are realized and the one on which the truth of the new humanity is determined historically, technically, and politically." This desire for an immanent politics leads them to call for a "materialist teleology."[25] Having brought politics down from a transcendental mode, they can claim a teleology once again, but this time position it on a materialist level.

Hardt and Negri have also been criticized for this argument. Timothy Brennan states that their conceptualization of immanence, like Spinoza's, "is oddly *transcendent*."[26] Human potential, as something that is never fully realized, exists outside of the material, and is therefore situated somewhere that is typically associated with transcendence. Immanence attempts to step in as a third term, but the negotiation is a difficult one, especially given the assertion in *Empire* that the arrival of the multitude is an inevitable process that is yet to come. There is an endpoint to the materialist teleology here, one that seems as transcendent as Fukuyama's claim. Hardt and Negri's endpoint is that of a communist utopia — *Empire* ends with an invocation of "the irrepressible lightness and joy of being communist"[27] — one in which the mechanisms of the state wither away under the influence of the constituent and immanent power of the people, who become self-organizing, nodal links in a decentred multitude. This teleology seems transcendent given the way in which it is imagined as an endpoint beyond human politics, and for the manner in which it seems to be an organizational power outside of control. The communist endpoint seems to be determined by what is finally a structuring power, one that determines the human relations to come and thus risks taking on the appearance of sovereignty.

This negotiation between transcendence and immanence is further related to the links between Hardt and Negri's work and that of Gilles Deleuze. Deleuze is one of the most discussed philosophers in the context of transnational studies. His work with Félix Guattari, in depicting a poststructural world, challenges readers to think a world of unpredictable shifts, of disrupted presence, of capitalism and schizophrenia in the same moment. A drive towards thinking the human as a unified whole through poststructural terms animates Deleuze's thinking; as Paul Passavant puts it, "for Deleuze there is a kind of unity to Being."[28] Such a drive towards unity propels *Empire* and *Multitude*. For Deleuze, totality remains a viable concept, and humanity retains a total character. This totality retains an openness, as it shifts and is unpredictable, disrupting its universality. While disavowing a totalizing project that would restrict human possibility, Deleuze creates a framework in which the total can still be conceptualized (while left open to modification). Bill Maurer finds that Empire is, ultimately, a "metaphysical utopia," a space that ends up transcending the human and immanent politics that Hardt and Negri construct through Spinoza and Deleuze.[29] The attempt to base constituent power on human immanence and on the Deleuzian smooth space of contemporary politics is difficult to maintain. Hardt and Negri slip, for many readers, towards transcendence even while claiming a materialist grounding and a theory of immanence. Keeping totality open challenges readers to think the whole in a way that is both complete and incomplete at once.

Hardt and Negri's attempts to sidestep idealist, Hegelian teleogies and a metaphysics of transcendence may not, ultimately, be entirely successful. Lee Quinby argues that

> while they assert that the multitude is or will be self-constituting, that stance is undercut throughout via conceptualizations that rely on a crude dialectical opposition that looks...like this: Empire (thesis) clashes with the counter-Empire of the multitude (antithesis) to produce a willed, creative telos (synthesis).[30]

The constituent power of the multitude reiterates universalizing structures of Eurocentric thought in this analysis. The multitude (itself a Spinozist concept) may not provide a universally valid means of thinking about resistance and the creation of alternatives in the contemporary world of late capitalism. The failure of any universal is inevitable, and Hardt and Negri know it; their work remains useful, as a result, for the arguments that they provoke, rather than only for the answers that they propose. Hardt and Negri's vision is not incomparable with those discussed in earlier chapters. Critics have noted similarities between their immanent vision and the messianic elements of *Specters of Marx*, for instance, and have proposed that the anti-nationalism of *Empire* and *Multitude* is consistent with Derrida's proposal for a new International.[31] There remains a messianic endpoint in Hardt and Negri's materialist teleology, one that Derrida shies away from in his attempt to disrupt linear history. Hardt and Negri's concept of the open-ended multitude as a manifestation of constituent power further parallels the Derridean refusal of closure or hegemony.

As perhaps the boldest attempt yet to formulate a global politics in response to transnational capitalism, then, *Empire* and *Multitude* present mixed results. There is shared terrain with previous theorizations of political struggle coming out of both Marxist and poststructural debates, and a broad recognition of the politics of decolonization, feminism, and anti-racism. However, the optimism of these books seems to erase differences between struggles. The idea that the multitude is creating a radical democracy without an agenda obscures political agendas on the left and the right, as there continue to be both dominant and marginalized discourses. It is in the interplay of competing "progressive" agendas that *Transnational Canadas* reads Canadian literature, arguing that the shift from high nationalism to multiculturalism is leading to new changes as discourses of both the nation-state and diversity become part of the totalizing, commodifying logic of Empire. Literature in Canada has begun to respond to capitalism in ways that both contest and comply with such commodification. Rey Chow, in concluding her survey of the contemporary scene of theory, area studies, and cultural studies, argues for the need to deconstruct "the ideological assumptions in discourses of 'opposition' and 'resistance' as well as in discourses of mainstream power."[32] It is too easy to read Canadian literature as an oppositional construct when, in fact, what constitutes opposition has changed—and much of this erstwhile oppositional discourse has become part of an institution that the machinery of capital is able to support.

Hardt and Negri's discourse of opposition should be read in this context because of its links to—and erasures of—indigeneity. These connect with discourses of Indigenous rejections of and resistance to Canada, and should again force consciousness of what it means to accept the nation-state as a site for resisting American imperialism. Empire emerges in Hardt and Negri's writing as maintaining an expansive frontier, one that derives from the original American conquest of its contemporary territory. The United States' constitution, they allege, enshrines a concept of liberated individualism that defines itself in the open-endedness of the at-the-time limitless geographical expansion of the frontier. This spirit of expansion in turn becomes foundational for Empire. It is also celebrated as a means for thinking about the potential of the multitude. This multitude is supposed to arrive through Empire, just as communism arrives via capitalism in Marx. This perspective has its source in Negri's *Insurgencies*, where he asserts that "space is the constitutive horizon of American freedom" and that this "freedom has at [the] moment [of independence] a frontier that is pure and simple opening."[33] The U.S. constitutional moment undoes the binary noted by Spinoza in his *Political Treatise* when he states that "freedom of spirit or strength of mind is the virtue of a private citizen: the virtue of a state is its security."[34] By enshrining the concept of freedom, associated with the frontier, in its foundation, the Unites States becomes a model for thinking past this binary: the security of the state is assured in its constitutionality, while individual freedom of spirit is affirmed as the primary value of that same state. The problem is that Indigenous people are completely erased. The same frontier of freedom necessarily inscribes the unfreedom of Indigenous peoples. Rather than merely consisting of open space, the American frontier consisted of the imposition of Eurocentric geographical demarcations upon an already-existing series of interconnected societies. Hardt and Negri's theory of the expansive multitude's birth on the American frontier reiterates the stereotype of the vanishing Native against which Slash and others fight. Paul Passavant makes this point in arguing that

> the coming to presence of the multitude occurred on the grounds of the continued repression and destruction of...indigenous peoples.... These tribes are necessarily outside the multitude's law of development [as] the negation of North America's tribes of indigenous peoples becomes constitutive of the multitude.[35]

The production of the multitude as an unmoored, volatile, and deterritorialized force of resistance means accepting the erasure of indigeneity and supporting the colonial processes of Empire. The openness of the multitude's foundational moment is one that is, however, demonstrably not part of a movement into limitless freedom, but is instead demarcated by genocide and repression.

Hardt and Negri's idea of the unmoored openness of the multitude seems to be complicit with ongoing processes of creating new colonial subjects. While they would not advocate the violence of imperialism—their project is specifically one of creating a counter-Empire—Empire remains, for them, part of the solution to transnational disparity. A certain and chilling colonization becomes acceptable as a result. The same can be said of Canada, of arguments in favour of the country as a way forward that is better than American imperialism. An adequate politics of the transnational in Canada, however, cannot advocate continuing the colonial project that has been reinvigorated by transnational corporatism and taken up with militaristic vigour by neo-liberal governments in the West, Canada's included. Theories of the global such as Hardt and Negri's, in their desire to come up with an adequate cognitive map through which to think resistance, become complicit in the colonial effects of capital.

Models of transnational feminism push this line of thought in more anti-colonial directions, looking towards change through messy processes of cultural work such as textual reading. Transnational feminism should be a project that, Caren Kaplan and Inderpal Grewal argue, brings Marxist, poststructural, and feminist perspectives to bear on one another. This work operates against masculinist Marxist theories that would continue to prioritize "traditional class analyses" and against those that recuperate "patriarchal representational practices within theorizations of contemporary transnational proletarian or subaltern movements."[36] Hardt and Negri may be bundled into this latter category. Lee Quinby, who has provided an excellent feminist critique of *Empire*, suggests that their perspective on the universalizing interconnectedness of the struggles of the multitudes is problematic, and that, ultimately, Hardt and Negri's "gender-blindness renders their concept of resistance to authority rhetorically engorged yet methodologically flaccid."[37] Quinby's own rhetorical flourish aside, what she argues is that the specificity of different ways of thinking towards social change needs to be more carefully articulated. This is at least in part because Hardt and Negri do not take full account of the problematics of cultural or political representation. Hardt and Negri choose to speak totalizingly on behalf of resistance movements, a practice that leads to many disagreements.

For Kaplan and Grewal, and for others in transnational feminism, "the situation today requires a feminist analysis that refuses to choose among economic, social, and political concerns."[38] This refusal to prioritize oppressions follows from the recognition of the interconnectedness between, for example, nationalism and gender, but it extends further in transnational feminist theory. Rather than being a refusal of strategy or tactics — as Hardt and Negri advocate — this refusal to prioritize is one that recognizes the contingency of such choices and that remains receptive to alternatives. Kaplan and Grewal suggest that "what we need are critical practices that link our understanding of postmodernity, global economic structures, problematics of nationalism, issues of race and imperialism, critiques of global feminism, and emergent patriarchies." For them, "theories of opposition that rely on unified subjects of difference and metaphysics of presence and voice cannot create alliances across differences and conflicts within a context of imperialism and decolonization."[39] The theory of the multitude falls within such a concept of a unified discourse of difference, failing to escape from a metaphysics of presence in the final analysis. Feminism has long maintained an engagement with discourses of globalization and has been investigating the ways in which they are gendered,[40] and it seems appropriate, as a result, to question Hardt and Negri's teleology in this light.

The progressive nature of Empire's endpoint in the multitude is, moreover, challenged when thinking about Canadian writing and shifts in the publishing industry under globalization. Canada never developed the same model of the frontier as the United States, nor the same ideologies of individualist freedom, though both are familiar here. While resistance in Canadian writing has shifted from an emphasis on a reified image of the nation as a means of opposition, and towards an approach that incorporates a critique of Canadian Eurocentrism and racism, politically engaged writing has not shifted towards a simply celebratory and decentred focus on the multitude. Canada, however, has become a representative for discourses of diversity: it regularly champions itself as a space of liberal tolerance and has proven readily able to absorb discourses of difference towards such ends. Critics, perhaps as a result, have been able to continue to speak in favour of a nationalist mode as though it were always, in the final analysis, necessary and good. Jonathan Kertzer, for example, asserts that we "are not free to reject [the nation] at will, since it has already helped to define the position from which we speak." While this may be true, it does not quite lead to his further assertion that "the nation will continue to be a prime forum for justice, because only a national setting can confer legitimacy on communities seeking to articulate their social distinctiveness and power."[41] Indigenous and transnational debates about sovereignty and nationhood suggest that, at the very least, the nation is a variable construct, and that it might be possible to do politics differently. At the same time, rejecting such a nationalism need not result in a merely celebratory postnational vision of the multitude. Where Canadian writing intersects most clearly with transnational lines of thinking, a substantial discomfort with such totalizing discourses is visible, challenging the drive towards total discourses of either the global or the national. The most challenging writing engages simultaneously in the contestation of the imperial nature of contemporary capitalism while unmooring the Canadian nation-state by recognizing that it, too, is an exclusionary and problematic construct, one whose interests tend to intersect neatly with capital. The nation versus the globe dichotomy is false in Canada, as both operate as interconnecting nodes of neo-liberal capitalism.

Notes to Chapter Nine

1. Michael Hardt and Antonio Negri, *Empire* (Cambridge: Harvard UP, 2000), xii.
2. Hardt and Negri, *Empire*, xiii–xiv.
3. Michael Hardt and Antonio Negri, *Multitude: War and Democracy in the Age of Empire* (New York: Penguin, 2004), xviii.
4. Timothy Brennan, "The Empire's New Clothes," *Critical Inquiry* 29.2 (2003): 351. Hardt and Negri respond to Brennan by arguing that Brennan's faith in the state is misplaced and renders him fearful of the apparent anarchism of Empire in their essay "The Rod of the Forest Warden: A Response to Timothy Brennan," *Critical Inquiry* 29.2 (2003): 368–73, and Brennan responds in turn in "The Magician's Wand: A Rejoinder to Hardt and Negri," *Critical Inquiry* 29.2 (2003): 374–78.
5. Hardt and Negri, *Empire*, 393.
6. Hardt and Negri, *Multitude*, xiii.
7. Gilles Deleuze and Félix Guattari, *A Thousand Plateaus: Capitalism and Schizophrenia*, trans. B. Massumi (Minneapolis: U of Minnesota P, 1987), 21.
8. Atilio Boron's *Empire and Imperialism: A Critical Reading of Michael Hardt and Antonio Negri*, trans. Jessica Casiro (London: Zed, 2005) summarizes many of the arguments. The essays of the volume *Debating Empire*, ed. Gopal Balakrishnan (London: Verso, 2003) give individual cases, as do those in *Empire's New Clothes: Reading Hardt and Negri*, ed. Paul Passavant and Jodi Dean (New York: Routledge, 2004). Some of these essays are discussed below. Scholarship on Hardt and Negri expanded exponentially during the writing of *Transnational Canadas*.
9. Timothy Brennan, "The Italian Ideology," *Debating Empire*, ed. Gopal Balakrishnan (London: Verso, 2003), 101.
10. Masao Miyoshi, "'Globalization,' Culture, and the University," *The Cultures of Globalization*, ed. Fredric Jameson and Masao Miyoshi (Durham, NC: Duke UP, 1998), 248.
11. Eric Hobsbawn, *Nations and Nationalism Since 1780: Programme, Myth, Reality*, 2nd ed. (Cambridge: Cambridge UP, 1992), 171.
12. Hardt and Negri, *Empire*, 274–75; *Multitude*, 199, 214, 224.
13. Fredric Jameson, *Postmodernism, or, The Cultural Logic of Late Capitalism* (Durham, NC: Duke UP, 1991), 326.
14. Hardt and Negri, *Empire*, 400, 403, 406.
15. Hardt and Negri, *Multitude*, xviii.
16. Hardt and Negri, *Multitude*, 347, 348.
17. Antonio Negri, *Insurgencies: Constituent Power and the Modern State*, trans. M. Boscagli (Minneapolis: Minnesota UP, 1999), 2.
18. Hardt and Negri, *Empire*, 358.
19. Negri, *Insurgencies*, 25, 22.
20. Hardt and Negri, *Empire*, 59.
21. Slavoj Žižek, "The Ideology of Empire and Its Traps," *Empire's New Clothes: Reading Hardt and Negri*, ed. Paul Passavant and Jodi Dean (New York: Routledge, 2004), 264.
22. Neil Smith, *The Endgame of Globalization* (New York: Routledge, 2005), 51.
23. Malcolm Bull, "Smooth Politics," *Empire's New Clothes: Reading Hardt and Negri*, ed. Paul Passavant and Jodi Dean (New York: Routledge, 2004), 220.
24. Hardt and Negri, *Empire*, 80.

25 Hardt and Negri, *Empire*, 73, 65.
26 Brennan, "The Italian Ideology," 112.
27 Hardt and Negri, *Empire*, 413.
28 Paul Passavant, "Postmodern Republicanism," *Empire's New Clothes: Reading Hardt and Negri*, ed. Paul Passavant and Jodi Dean (New York: Routledge, 2004), 11.
29 Bill Maurer, "On Divine Markets and the Problem of Justice: *Empire* as Theodicy," *Empire's New Clothes: Reading Hardt and Negri*, ed. Paul Passavant and Jodi Dean (New York: Routledge, 2004), 63.
30 Lee Quinby, "Taking the Millennialist Pulse of *Empire*'s Multitude: A Genealogical Feminist Diagnosis," *Empire's New Clothes: Reading Hardt and Negri*, ed. Paul Passavant and Jodi Dean (New York: Routledge, 2004), 243.
31 Kam Shapiro, "The Myth of the Multitude," *Empire's New Clothes: Reading Hardt and Negri*, ed. Paul Passavant and Jodi Dean (New York: Routledge, 2004), 289; Jeremy Gilbert, "Against the Empire: Thinking the Social and (Dis)Locating Agency 'Before, Across and Beyond Any National Determination,'" *Parallax* 7.3 (2001): 104.
32 Rey Chow, *Ethics After Idealism: Theory-Culture-Ethnicity-Reading* (Bloomington: Indiana UP, 1998), 13.
33 Negri, *Insurgencies*, 144.
34 Baruch Spinoza, "Political Treatise," *Complete Works*, ed. M. Morgan, trans. S. Shirley (Indianapolis: Hackett, 2002), 682.
35 Paul Passavant, "From Empire's Law to the Multitude's Rights: Law, Representation, Revolution," *Empire's New Clothes: Reading Hardt and Negri*, ed. Paul Passavant and Jodi Dean (New York: Routledge, 2004), 102–103.
36 Caren Kaplan and Inderpal Grewal, "Transnational Feminist Cultural Studies: Beyond the Marxism/Poststructuralism/Feminism Divides," *Between Woman and Nation: Nationalisms, Transnational Feminisms, and the State*, ed. Caren Kaplan et al. (Durham, NC: Duke UP, 1999), 349–50.
37 Quinby, "Taking the Millennialist Pulse of *Empire*'s Multitude," 240.
38 Kaplan and Grewal, "Transnational Feminist Cultural Studies," 358.
39 Kaplan and Grewal, "Transnational Feminist Cultural Studies," 358.
40 Many examples could be cited. Two useful ones on this note are Chandra Talpade Mohanty's "'Under Western Eyes' Revisited: Feminist Solidarity through Anticapitalist Struggles," *Feminism without Borders: Decolonizing Theory, Practicing Solidarity* (Durham, NC: Duke UP, 2003), esp. 247, and Carla Freeman, "Is Local : Global as Feminine : Masculine? Rethinking the Gender of Globalization," *Signs* 26.4 (2001): 1007–37.
41 Jonathan Kertzer, *Worrying the Nation: Imagining a National Literature in English Canada* (Toronto: U of Toronto P, 1998), 166, 176.

CHAPTER TEN

Mainstreaming Multiculturalism? The Giller Prize

The confluence of national and global forms of capital in Canada is visible in some of the directions taken by what can be thought of as a mainstreamed multicultural writing. While writing by racialized writers was implicitly political when Joy Kogawa and others of her generation picked up the pen, this is no longer necessarily the case. This is both a productive and an ambivalent development. Writing by racialized writers has been absorbed in large part in Canada through state discourses of official multiculturalism, as well as through the reception of such texts. This writing is still often critical and challenging, but it also is often easily integrated by the nation. When Roy Miki seeks to return a revolutionary, unresolved reading to *Obasan*, he does so against all the criticisms of that text that have sought to resolve it, to codify it into Canada in such a way that its critiques are historicized—and thereby nullified in the present. How texts written by racialized writers are produced and received in this country, in other words, has shifted. It should no longer be possible to assume that a text is implicitly progressive because it is somehow multicultural.

One of the most important things to acknowledge when thinking about Canadian writing in the era of globalization is how the publishing industry has shifted, how it has structured which writing is able to be published and disseminated. Reductions in government spending on publishing and promotions (programs that were often established or expanded in the 1960s and '70s) have affected the presses that learned how to structure their outputs in order to satisfy granting guidelines. Major changes in distribution have taken place in the last twenty years, especially with the rise of Chapters/Indigo. This rise has accompanied a collapse of small publishers and sellers (radical presses like Press Gang and Sister Vision, among others, folded during this period). A consolidation of the remaining publishing companies has led to the Bertelsmann corporation owning a vast share of Canada's major literary publishers.[1]

While the writing with which this book has been concerned is not marginal to Canadian literary reception, presses like Anansi, which published *Civil Elegies*, began as very small and ad hoc adventures. Authors like Michael Ondaatje and Margaret Atwood received a great deal of their early support from presses like Coach House Press and Anansi: Coach House published Ondaatje's *Dainty Monsters* in 1967, his book *the man with seven toes* in 1969, and *rat jelly* in 1973 (as well as later books of poetry), while Anansi published *The Collected Works of Billy the Kid* in 1970. Coach House published Atwood's *Murder in the Dark* in 1983 and *Good Bones* in 1992. Anansi published *The Circle Game* in 1964, *Power Politics* in 1971, and, significantly, *Survival* in 1972. These earlier publications led those publishing houses into larger ventures (with Coach House's up-and-down career), and those authors on to larger presses.

The consolidation of the publishing industry has radically affected how politically challenging discourse appears in books, but these changes are difficult to pin down. This difficulty results only in part because the industry controls what does and doesn't get into print. But what does get into print is indicative. The publishing industry seems, according to several critics, to have identified a rhetoric through which cultural difference can be enunciated in universalizing terms that sells well with both granting agencies and with the reading public. Some types of racially marked texts are more readily picked up, published, and sold in the transnational era than others. Graham Huggan's arguments about postcolonial literature are perhaps best known here, particularly his idea that "postcolonialism and its rhetoric of resistance have themselves become consumer products," which are pushed to stage their marginality in particular sociological, testimonial, and oppositional ways for their readers.[2] The goal of this analysis is not to blame the authors of such works, but rather to indicate how the machinery of the cultural industry functions in a transnational Canada vis-à-vis questions of racialization. Canada has moved towards marketing itself as one locus for cosmopolitan diversity in a globalized world. This process affects racially marked texts, which are appropriated to the project of constructing Canada in this light, a process with which many writers maintain an anxious relationship.

Perhaps these changes can best be approached through an extended example. The 2006 Scotiabank Giller Prize marked a moment of ambivalence for multicultural writing in Canada, one that received wide discussion. It was a huge success for first-time literary author Vincent Lam, whose *Bloodletting and Miraculous Cures* won the prize. *Bloodletting and Miraculous Cures* went on to sell about two hundred thousand copies, an enormous number for a book of short stories in Canada today. In an issue of Vancouver-based *Geist* magazine, however, Canadian writer and University of Guelph–based critic Stephen Henighan lambasted the Giller, accusing Margaret Atwood and those of her generation (including the award's judges for the year) of fixing the 2006 prize and demonstrating a Toronto-centric attitude that favours multinational publishing corporations (the remaining four shortlisted books were all published by small-to-medium-sized presses, a fact that had been celebrated when the shortlist was released; the large press book won). The fixing of the prize, moreover, Henighan alleged, was part of an attempt to lionize a new generation of writers in order to carry out the cultural projects of the earlier generation. Although this piece is consistent with Henighan's earlier attacks on Toronto and the Giller, it generated particular ire, especially for how Henighan handled questions of ethnicity and race. Ripostes to his screed appeared online and were printed in the following issues of *Geist*.

This debate is interesting because of what it suggests about the anxieties that surround ethnically and racially marked and marketed writing. Part Three argues that some examples of such writing in Canada, such as Lam's book, are received through a rhetoric that reinforces pre-existing ideas of Canadian diversity, those that privilege whiteness as a universal category and multicultural difference as precisely that — as difference. That is, *Bloodletting and Miraculous Cures* is being received as a work that demonstrates the already inclusive nature of the Canadian nation. This sort of reception, rather than challenging the real or imagined ethnicities of the nation through a reading of the book's representations of cultural difference, reinforces the idea that Canada is a nation-state that welcomes difference and is free of ethno-cultural strife. This form of multiculturalism obscures criticisms that Canada can, instead, accept only limited forms of difference, as critics of multiculturalism from Himani Bannerji to Sherene Razack have argued.[3] Canadian literature has sometimes been characterized in recent years as being synonymous with multiculturalism or postcolonialism. But what spaces might there be, today, for writers who are operating in a field that is saturated by the dictates of a marketplace that wishes to sell books, receive Canada Council grants, and other moneys, in order to maintain itself? This chapter re-examines ways in which the marketplace subsumes texts to a multiculturalism that is at times more interested in exploring the limits of acceptable difference than challenging the national imaginary. This is an opportunity to read against appropriation, to read against the commodification of diversity and to understand diversity as discursive and lived processes that have material outcomes.

This chapter is interested, therefore, in what everyday gestures about ethnicity, race, and multiculturalism in Canada mean. Critics of state multiculturalism such as Smaro Kamboureli have argued, for example, that Canada's Multiculturalism Act "recognizes the cultural diversity that constitutes Canada, but it does so by practicing a sedative politics, a politics that attempts to recognize ethnic differences, but only in a contained fashion," and that is used to manage Canada's differences. Kamboureli notes that the Act and its related policies try for "the impossible act of balancing differences," but the spectre of social management lurks behind the Act in her reading.[4] Eva Mackey, similarly, argues that "the state attempted" through multiculturalism "to institutionalise various forms of difference, thereby controlling access to power and simultaneously legitimating the power of the state." Multiculturalism, she observes, "was developed as a mode of managing internal differences."[5] It defines the limits of acceptable difference. Whether or how our readings should participate in this managerial function is a question with which Canadian critics should be very much concerned. It is crucial to identify the ways in which such a state multiculturalism becomes a strategy that determines that valence of literary texts.

The debate about Vincent Lam's book is a useful instance of public discussion of such issues. This is the case in part because literary awards such as the Giller have been questioned as a result of their increasing prominence. They have become central to the Canadian publishing industry, and the ceremonies for the Giller Prize for fiction and the Griffin Prize for poetry have become major media events. The ideologies informing these and other prizes have come under increasing scrutiny as critics and the media have noted their impact upon books' sales. Laura Moss begins her inquiry into the CBC's "literary survivor" program Canada Reads by noting the impact of the first competition in 2002 upon the reception and sales of Michael Ondaatje's winning novel, *In the Skin of a Lion*.[6] Danielle Fuller and DeNel Rehberg Sedo have suggested that Canada Reads is "conservative" according to a "bilingual and uncritically multicultural" model, although they hope for creative resistance.[7] The debate about the Giller, and specifically about *Bloodletting and Miraculous Cures*, has taken a similar but more vitriolic shape.

Henighan makes multiple allegations about the Giller in his piece in *Geist*, beginning with the assertion that "the Giller Prize is the most conspicuous example of corporate suffocation of the public institutions that built our literary culture.... Nothing signaled the collapse of the literary organism as vividly as the appearance of this glitzy chancre on the hide of our culture."[8] Henighan advances several pieces of evidence to support this assertion: up until 2004, he states, only one of the Giller winners lived more than two hours from downtown Toronto (Alice Munro would have to drive very, very fast for this to be true, but his point is taken); the awards ceremony has become a love-in among friends awarding one another prizes; and the shortlist is routinely made up of what he calls "the triumvirate of publishers owned by the Bertelsmann Group," namely Random House, Knopf Canada, and Doubleday Canada, with McClelland and Stewart acting as a sort of fourth musketeer, since it is 25 percent owned by Random House.[9] The 2006 Giller displayed, Henighan states, "the Canadian establishment at its most repellent," as Margaret Atwood installed Vincent Lam's book as the winner. Her sponsorship of Lam's book amounted, Henighan put it, to "*el dedazo*, the crook of the finger with which a Mexican president signals his successor."[10] The story was that Atwood met Lam on an Arctic cruise, where he was the ship's doctor, read his work, and then saw it to publication and the Giller. Her motivation, Henighan argues, is that sponsoring a previously unknown writer like Lam enables her and "the old Wasp establishment to claim parentage over the new multicultural establishment."[11] Vincent Lam's Vietnamese Canadian heritage, along with his wife's Anglo-Greek descent, Henighan suggests, makes him a perfect representative of the sort of multicultural Canada that Atwood and her friends would like to support (including the jury of the Giller that year—judges Adrienne Clarkson and Alice Munro have long been Atwood's friends, while the third, Michael Winter, is thanked by Lam in his book's acknowledgements).

Henighan's article is of a piece with his earlier writing about the Giller. In an essay called "Giller's Version" reprinted in his book *When Words Deny the World*, he notes the Toronto-centric nature of the Giller and bemoans its rise to prominence. He alleges that, unlike the more equitable Governor General's Literary Award, "the Giller has merely confirmed the status of writers already possessed of a wealthy publisher," and that "this is not a prize that is out to shake up our literary preconceptions."[12] The Giller is, he states, merely "commercial hype," an award that "has risen on the tide of a big-business dogma that reduces literature to a commodity and drowns a coast-to-coast Canadian culture in the local obsessions of one metropolitan centre."[13] Waxing poetic, Henighan states that "the Giller is the consummate expression" of right-wing Canada's "Hollywoodized, neo-conservative, market-driven, user-fee mentality."[14] This is at least in part, he adds, because the Giller has what amounts to an entry fee of $1500 per shortlisted book ($1250 when he was writing), which the Giller committee stipulates is for marketing. This cost precludes the shortlisting of books published by Canada's smaller presses, which operate on extremely thin margins, ensuring that the Bertelsmann Group will continue to reap the awards.

Although his argument in *Geist* is an updating and restating of this earlier argument, it drew a huge response. Henighan is, certainly, a rhetorician, one who designs to provoke. Supporters surface in the letters section of the next issues of *Geist*, declaring that Lam's book is "the worst-written book ever to win a major award in Canada,"[15] complaining of the failings of previous Giller-winning books, and voicing unease at the closeness of the writers within Toronto's gravitational field. Others disagreed, arguing, for example, that "the 2006 Giller Prize for fiction was something quite fantastic."[16] Opinions from Canada's literary figures, on the other hand, have tended to be strong in their defence of the Giller. While Toronto-based author Michael Redhill applauds Henighan's spirit, declaring it "open season on prizes and who gets 'em, juries and who serves on 'em, [and] what prizes mean to writers and books," he takes issue with most of Henighan's piece, particularly his comments about Lam's ethnicity, suggesting that they are founded in "racism and personal venom,"[17] a comment echoed by other readers. Elana Rabinovitch — one of the prize's organizers and sponsors, and the daughter of Jack Rabinovitch, who founded the prize for his late wife, Doris Giller, in 1994 — dismisses what she calls Henighan's "ravings about the treachery of jurors, conflicts of interest and other sinister goings-on" as poorly researched sour grapes.[18] And Newfoundland-based writer Lisa Moore alleges that Henighan's piece "is so way over the top it feels like the stuff of comic books," and that it "is ridiculous and paranoid," prior to dismissing his concerns about Lam's ethnicity.[19] In his response to her, Henighan suggests that she, in turn, is a "provincial" seeking the approval of Canada's metropolitan centres, but that she is "out of touch" with public sentiments. He suggests that her response is typical in Canada, where "we suffer from the illusion ... that the transition, over the last twenty years, from a literary culture developed by the public sector and small business to a corporate-dominated literary scene has made no impact on how books are selected, marketed, promoted, sold, recognized and canonized."[20] In a subsequent issue, he accuses Redhill, Moore, and his other critics of attempting to forestall a genuine debate about what he calls "interracial dynamics."[21]

What is lost in much of this debate is, perhaps surprisingly, Lam's book. The book itself is, ultimately, a fair first book. It is not, in this author's opinion, terribly good, but neither is it as inept as Stephen Henighan charges — although his target is the Giller itself. He merely alleges that some readers have found *Bloodletting and Miraculous Cures* to be "clichéd and sloppily written."[22] It is an account of students' progress through medical school and into various facets of the profession. In each story, more or less, doctors deal with a medical problem. The interest lies in the realism of those problems and their portrayal in print. The doctors themselves are imperfect on their way through medical school (one intern has been sleeping with his much younger cousin, for instance), but by the time their training is completed the characters have earned a sort of infallibility. Most complex is the character Fitzgerald, who drinks too much and may have been dismissed from a previous position. Later in the book, he appears to keep his habit mostly under control, and he suffers from SARS during that epidemic. Meanwhile, Chen's sleep deprivation does not severely impede his ability to administer care. Doctors are stressed and pushed to their limits, but, the book assures its readers, they are ultimately good people.

What seems more surprising about this book is that it was singled out to win the Giller. If there were a conspiracy to have it win — an over-the-top allegation, certainly — it could perhaps indeed be linked to how, as Henighan charges, it encapsulates the practices of multiculturalism in a politically neutral or even conservative manner, although this is far from necessarily the case. Henighan's assertion that Lam fulfills a role as the multicultural embodiment of the older WASP establishment may be overstated, but it is worth investigation at least in part because of the strong response that it drew. Henighan is particularly concerned with how the Giller and corporatism, through a cynical deployment of multiculturalism, derails a national project that is better, in his eyes, than the world under global capital (we saw a glimmer of this idea when his work was discussed in the introduction). While his critique of globalization is important, *Transnational Canadas* does not subscribe to his defence of the nation, which this book sees as complicit with the dictates of such corporatism. This book is aligned more with Jennifer Scott and Myka Tucker-Abramson when it comes to the Giller. Scott and Tucker-Abramson have observed that the Giller Prize systematically rewards commodified versions of ethnicity.[23] The multiple ethnicities of Lam's characters may be happenstance, given the book's setting in Toronto, but the cultural differences between its characters have given it a basic political value. Its demonstration of the fact that people of colour can exist on par with white people within the medical profession, in other words, has been enough to demonstrate that the text is progressive.

What needs investigation, however, is what this equality means. What Lam's doctors know, in essence, are cosmopolitan values and Western medicine. The ideals of cosmopolitanism that have governed Western, liberal notions of citizenship have been challenged of late, pushing towards a reconsideration of how people in cities might act. Benedict Anderson suggests that the cosmopolitan individual is likely "to insist on the near-pathological character of nationalism," pitting cosmopolitanism against the exclusions of the nation.[24] But the cosmopolitan ideal is also problematic. Examining the legacy of Immanuel Kant's search for a "universal cosmopolitan existence," Bruce Robbins finds that "cosmopolitanisms are now plural and particular."[25] The cosmopolitan ideal of the city has multiplied away from a universal and into a series of positions, but these may still be based on a mentality that fails to recognize difference beyond circumscribed limits — precisely the criticism that Anderson sees cosmopolitans levelling at nationalists. Robbins proposes the neologism of "cosmopolitics" as a way of indicating the contestations of politics in the contemporary city, a term that, Robbins argues, underlines "the need to introduce intellectual order and accountability" to celebratory gestures of cosmopolitanism, which otherwise present us with a self-congratulatory discourse based upon Eurocentric ideals.[26] Pheng Cheah, while questioning the ethos of cosmopolitanism, nevertheless avers that "cosmopolitanism is the obvious choice as an intellectual ethic or political project that can better express or embody genuine universalism" than nationalism.[27] It offers an image of tolerance for diversity and global cooperation, in contrast to the exclusions of racially organized nations. Kwame Anthony Appiah has recently defended the cosmopolitan along similar terms. However, in his critique of cosmopolitanism, Timothy Brennan asserts that "the discourse of cosmopolitanism is exceedingly narrow in what fascinates it, failing to link the market with the imagination, and then failing to link that nexus itself to the non-Western world."[28] Cosmopolitanism, in his analysis, is a style, a discourse of inclusion and tolerance that is interested only in itself and in replicating its values, failing to account for spaces that fall outside its reach. One is welcome to be different within a global city like Lam's Toronto, but only as long as those differences continue to make themselves recognizable and understood—only as long, that is, as they are consonant with the liberal-democratic values that Kant espoused in his original formulations of the term "cosmopolitan," modified by the vagaries of time. The cosmopolitan order may be tolerant, but it is not necessarily inclusive or accepting.

But this cosmopolitan base of knowledge certifies Lam's doctors to dispense a wide array of advice. Dr. Sri, for example, consults with an ambulance medic named Zoltan who has been having sexual difficulties. These began after he was called to a scene in which a man died of a heart attack after receiving a blow job. The medic is distracted by what he has seen and is unable to perform with his wife. Dr. Sri ends the story by dispensing the following remarkably banal advice:

> Why don't you go away for the weekend. Somewhere calm, where you will think differently. Don't let this pattern settle in, or it will become more of a problem. Think of a beautiful place, and go there with your wife. Have a good meal, a bottle of wine, and just let things happen naturally.[29]

This advice assumes that Zoltan has little imagination of his own, and, moreover, it has comparatively little to do with Sri's medical training. It is a normative gesture, one celebrating the "natural" nature of heterosexual coupling, and is consonant with the beliefs of the stories' characters. The progressive nature of the text's depictions of cultural difference is questioned by moments like these, in which the doctors display a vision of the world that is limited and normalizing, one that advocates a warm night with one's spouse in order to ward off soupçons of perversity, desire deemed to be a "problem," or threatening difference.

Vincent Lam's *Bloodletting and Miraculous Cures* may fit with the politics of the generation that Stephen Henighan accuses of fixing the Giller Prize. These may also be the politics of contemporary Canada's major publishing houses, which influence the outcomes of literary prizes by virtue of having the resources to promote their wares. But these bodies need not collude in the manner that Henighan alleges in order to maintain their influence. Margaret Atwood, Lam's booster, and the year's Giller judges are linked to a generation that has sought to understand Canada's multicultural mosaic as a point that differentiates the country from the American melting pot, and they have published with what have become the country's major publishers as well as its smaller presses. For this generation, which invested in the creation and stabilization of Canadian literature as an act of anti-colonial resistance in the first instance, such a working model of cultural difference may, indeed, represent a fulfillment of some of the shifts in the Canadian imaginary. The irritation of Henighan and others at the Giller Prize judges' decision to award Vincent Lam's book the top honour suggests, however, that these values may no longer be adequate in considering all that is being written in Canada today. The writers and presses of the past generation have now become the institution, and they will be questioned as they continue in this role.

Notes to Chapter Ten

1 These shifts are documented by Roy MacSkimming in *The Perilous Trade: Book Publishing in Canada 1946–2006* (Toronto: McClelland and Stewart, 2007).
2 Graham Huggan, *The Postcolonial Exotic: Marketing the Margins* (London: Routledge, 2001), 6.
3 For Bannerji, see *The Dark Side of the Nation: Essays on Multiculturalism, Nationalism and Gender* (Toronto: Canadian Scholars' P, 2000); for Razack, *Looking White*

People in the Eye: Gender, Race, and Culture in Courtrooms and Classrooms (Toronto: U of Toronto P, 1998).
4   Smaro Kamboureli, *Scandalous Bodies: Diasporic Literature in English Canada* (Toronto: Oxford UP, 2000), 82.
5   Eva Mackey, *The House of Difference: Cultural Politics and National Identity in Canada* (Toronto: U of Toronto P, 2002), 50.
6   Laura Moss, "Canada Reads," *Canadian Literature* 182 (2004): 6.
7   Danielle Fuller and DeNel Rehberg Sedo, "A Reading Spectacle for the Nation: The CBC and 'Canada Reads,'" *Journal of Canadian Studies* 40.1 (2006): 5.
8   Stephen Henighan, "Kingmakers," *Geist* 63 (2006): 61.
9   Henighan, "Kingmakers," 61.
10 Henighan, "Kingmakers," 61.
11 Henighan, "Kingmakers," 62.
12 Stephen Henighan, *When Words Deny the World: The Reshaping of Canadian Writing* (Erin, ON: Porcupine's Quill, 2002), 85.
13 Henighan, *When Words Deny the World*, 86.
14 Henighan, *When Words Deny the World*, 86.
15 Salvatore Difalco, "Letter to the Editor," *Geist* 64 (2007): 9.
16 Rowland Lorimer, "Letter to the Editor," *Geist* 65 (2007): 8.
17 Michael Redhill, "Letter to the Editor," *Geist* 65 (2007): 9, 10.
18 Elana Rabinovitch, "Letter to the Editor," *Geist* 64 (2007): 8.
19 Lisa Moore, "Letter to the Editor," *Geist* 64 (2007): 8–9.
20 Stephen Henighan, "Stephen Henighan Replies," *Geist* 65 (2007): 10, 9.
21 Stephen Henighan, "Witch Hunt," *Geist* 66 (2007): 74.
22 Henighan, "Kingmakers," 61.
23 Jennifer Scott and Myka Tucker-Abramson, "Banking on a Prize: Multicultural Capitalism and the Canadian Literary Prize Industry," *Studies in Canadian Literature* 31.2 (2007): 5–20.
24 Benedict Anderson, *Imagined Communities: Reflections on the Origin and Spread of Nationalism*, rev. ed. (London: Verso, 1991), 141.
25 Immanuel Kant, *Kant: Political Writings*, 2nd ed. (Cambridge: Cambridge UP, 1991), 51; Bruce Robbins, "Introduction Part I: Actually Existing Cosmopolitanism," *Cosmopolitics: Thinking and Feeling Beyond the Nation*, ed. Pheng Cheah and Bruce Robbins (Minneapolis: U of Minnesota P, 1998), 2.
26 Robbins, "Introduction Part I," 9.
27 Pheng Cheah, "Introduction Part II: The Cosmopolitical—Today," *Cosmopolitics: Thinking and Feeling Beyond the Nation*, ed. Pheng Cheah and Bruce Robbins (Minneapolis: U of Minnesota P, 1998), 21.
28 Timothy Brennan, "Cosmo-Theory," *The South Atlantic Quarterly* 100.3 (2001): 674.
29 Vincent Lam, *Bloodletting and Miraculous Cures* (Toronto: Doubleday Canada, 2005), 208.

CHAPTER ELEVEN

Global Subjectivities in Roy Miki's *Surrender*

Part Three continues by considering some of the further directions that are being taken in today's writing and by examining the spaces left for poetry through Roy Miki's 2001 book, *Surrender*. *Transnational Canadas* has focused upon poetry and fiction to the exclusion of other genres largely for reasons of space. But many writers of poetry are also novelists, and vice versa: Atwood, Cohen, Kogawa, Ondaatje, Armstrong, and Brand are all recognized in both genres. So these areas have developed considerable overlaps.[1]

But poetry may offer a different space for reflection. With *Surrender*, readers are pushed to examine notions of the self in responding to the conditions of global living. *Surrender* offers a way of thinking about difference and being that pushes against a reinscription of difference, and it gives its readers an opportunity to interrogate subjectivity. When the subject is asked to view her- or himself as an actor within a global system— and is no longer seen as imbued with agency within only a local or national setting—a series of questions arises, which Miki's text sets out to explore. These are questions not only about the subject, but also about how the global system is rewriting subjectivity, and about whose ends these rewritings serve. *Surrender* meshes with Roy Miki's broader project of questioning the legacies of national and state structures. The transnational dialogue focuses upon the differentiation between dominant American concepts of subjectivity and more mobile, transnational forms of subjectivity. For Miki, the latter, mobile form of the subject is aligned in part with Canada, but also with spaces that are depicted as escaping the hegemonic power of the United States. "The purpose," the poem "knocks at the door" states, "has always been / to restore the purchases beyond."[2] The "beyond" escapes the controls of the world system. This is a system evoked in the word "purchases," which not only connotes the world of consumerism, but is also spatially past the easy reach of those within this world. This out-of-reach "beyond," therefore, requires gaining the leverage that the word "purchase" also connotes.

The poems of *Surrender* suggest both formal and thematic ways of politicizing subjectivity as a strategy for dealing with the contemporary moment. The book rethinks the subject within globalizing spaces, asking its readers to query subjectivity in the context of the nation-state, all the while handling "the social," as the poem "speed bumps" states, "with kid gloves."[3] This image is one of care and delicacy, but it is complicated, in turn, by its associations with the luxury goods of the wealthy classes. These sorts of complications recur in *Surrender*, undermining simplistic or oppositional readings, pushing readers to engage with questions of control and domination.

This chapter queries how this text thinks subjectivity in the context of theorizations of globalization, examining the consequences of national citizenship and the problem of agency. *Surrender*, which won the 2002 Governor General's Award for English-language poetry—and thus has been incorporated, however broadly, into the discourse of the nation—provides a line into the difficulties of poetic disruption in a transnational setting. The book suggests that one important terrain for the counter-globalization debate has been cultural, and that questions of liberation continue to be situated at the level of language. While seeking liberation from systems that limit the subject to a static position, the multiple voices of *Surrender* find themselves running up against disciplinary forces that impose external order upon them. Agency remains, however provisional, in shuttling between positions of unhinged openness and a more material, perhaps necessary acknowledgement of the power of the regimes of Foucauldian biopower. Identity becomes "an island" in *Surrender*,[4] one that needs to be disrupted, while the transnational world that is depicted will not enable either an open-ended liberation or a disrupted selfhood. Finding spaces for agency remains an ongoing and complex negotiation.

Surrender, therefore, offers a rethinking of the subject within national and globalizing spaces. It is a tightly composed book that illustrates the ambivalence voiced above about the project of the multitude, just as it is a strong challenge to the history of Canadian racism and nationalism rather than a happenstance depiction of difference. Positioning itself transnationally, as a book written in and about many places, it contemplates how the subject might be conceptualized in the context of Empire. This is a space in which the subject is interpolated into a world system in which she or he may feel little agency, given the scale. Regaining agency becomes a problem, and its speakers project a number of possible positions from which to approach it. Pronouns vary radically in their presentation, most often appearing in the lower case, sometimes set off by quotation marks, sometimes without. These stylistic treatments challenge readers at a formal level and push them to consider the manner in which subjectivity is being deployed. This push emerges at the very opening of the book, in a poem entitled "make it new," where the speaker suggests that s/he has "altered" her or his "tactics to reflect the new era." This is an era in which "the earth is not heavy / with the weight of centuries" and in which "bodies / of multitudes" do not "tread muted on fleet denizens."[5] Instead, the poem suggests that this multitude is not silent, and that it responds to the Empire that is being created. This multitude emerges at the end of the volume, after the free play between subjects has been dismantled by regimes that reduce subjectivity to a single, stable meaning.

The text's shuttling strategy is connected to how concepts of subjectivity and being change under the transnational. A great deal is at stake in rethinking the subject either in the frameworks of (post-)postmodernity or according to Michael Hardt and Antonio Negri's immanent politics. Formerly stable concepts of identity and selfhood began to appear to be coercive in the analyses of deconstruction. As poststructural theorists of identity examined these concepts, they came to be seen as restricting how the body might exist and form allegiances with others, prompting the rise of, for instance, some of the strains of third-wave and transnational feminisms. The global era seems to magnify these issues. Concepts of identity-as-fixity limit the possibilities for social change. The expectation that the body will inhabit a single identity renders it individuated and isolated, left to fend for itself. In the place of identity—and the older restrictions of identity politics—Stuart Hall offers the concept of "identifications" as one way of thinking about how subjectivities might be reconceptualized.[6] Judith Butler, on a different tack, has queried the notion of "undoing gender" as a means of working towards liberation. Such acts of undoing, dissenting against the status quo and stable identities, have consequences when thought within a global framework. Regulatory institutions such as state-based citizenship work in opposition to these discourses, seeking to reinscribe difference and limit the play of bodies, while, on the flip side, international economic agreements dismantle the borders that prevent the free play of capital. Opening up the concept of the self offers one means of countering the deregulation of capitalism with human liberation. But this opening has a number of consequences, as *Surrender* makes clear.

It is necessary to return to Hardt and Negri's seizure of the Deleuzian concept of deterritorialization in order to make this argument. The expansive scope of global capitalism and its impact upon the individual are by no means assured. Theorizations of global capitalism have privileged ideas of deterritorialization, neglecting the reterritorialization that Deleuze and Guattari saw as accompanying any deterritorializing flow. Whether the subject is liberated through Hardt and Negri's deterritorializing model or simply opened up for recoding into a new system of control remains a very serious concern. If reterritorialization always accompanies deterritorialization, then it is necessary to pay attention to what sorts of reterritorializations take place in today's world after the liberation that the concept of deterritorialization has offered for so many theorists. This is an issue upon which *Surrender* focuses. The book's response challenges theorists who see deterritorialization as a promising event.

The deterritorialized global scene is one that is contested as forms of openness are shut down again and again through the legislative and disciplinary mechanisms that characterize the world under the so-called war against terror. For theorist of citizenship Saskia Sassen, subjectivity is shifting in new ways, being rescaled to the global, while remaining affected by state formations. For writers who are thinking about subjectivity, such as Miki, the deconstruction of fixed positions that accompanies the deterritorializing gestures of Empire, while promising, is nevertheless bounded by limits that illustrate whose interests these gestures serve. At present, the liberatory potential of deterritorialized bodies is limited by regimes that control them through an ever-increasing variety of surveillance and policing techniques. While the body has been extensively theorized in analyses that point towards the potential for social change through challenging categories of identity, these bodies are at the same time subjected to enormous repressive mechanisms, recognized in part by Foucault in his discussions of biopolitics and the incitement to discourse in the Christian West. These mechanisms are of direct concern to Miki, as the speaker of "knocks at the door" asks "what compelled the overture of disclosure?" in an almost direct allusion to Foucault.[7] Inasmuch as theorizing the body's potential unfixity is powerful, the disciplinary society in which the citizen exists makes global capitalism a difficult situation in which to transgress.

The resistant practices of minority poetic voices in Canada have, however, worked at times towards just such transgressions. This transgression can be witnessed in part through the poetic practices called for by Roy Miki, who states in the essay "Asiancy: Making Space for Asian Canadian Writing" that "formal disruptions...become strategies for resistance to norms" in minority writing.[8] Poetic practice, in other words, disrupts norms, creating a space for that which has been hitherto unrecognized. These disruptions become a way of creating political alliances in, for instance, the writing of M. NourbeSe Philip, who recognizes "the resistance of the people" in the poetic usage of what she terms racialized "badenglish."[9] Again this is the case with poet and critic Fred Wah, who argues for "racing the subjectified voice," the lyric "I," which has the effect of roughing up the certainties of the monological lyrical subject employed by Western poets.[10] These poets are focusing upon issues of race, which are crucial to a cultural project of dismantling the colonization of consciousness that accompanies late capitalism. This focus is pervasive throughout the work of Miki, Philip, and Wah, as Robert Budde argues:

> Even when their poetics do not address race issues directly,... [they] produce a critique of unitary identity construction, cultural naming, policing, identification strategies, hegemonic language practice, consumer referentiality, and monumental versions of the overly buttressed ego of the colonizer.[11]

It is productive to destabilize settled ideas of the nation-state through just such a focus on race in poetic practice, reading for places in which the subject might find connections to broader communities. This is not a search for an undifferentiated or universalized human condition, but rather a politics of alliance that remains open to difference. This is what is offered by the challenging writing of Miki and others. Questions of racialization are central to Miki's work, at critical, creative, and editorial levels.[12] His work consistently foregrounds the constructions of race in discussions of the national and transnational, pushing for accountable theorizations of globality. Critiquing the racialization of the national landscape is central, in Miki's work, to any liberatory transnational politics.

The speakers of *Surrender* are therefore important, given their disrupted and unsettling state. The early poem "attractive," for instance, makes the debate between subject positions clearer, as it stages a dialogue between two speakers. The speech of one of the speakers is set off through italics. In response to the primary speaker's unmoored and ungrammatical statement "raucous vibes in the sunder / down of lyric i am ambushed," a second, more forceful voice asserts "*let's get serious a poetic / text has to resonate*," calling for a more grounded, direct appeal to its readership.[13] The text maintains such an ambivalence through a disrupted lyrical "I" and a more fixed, dogmatic structure of subjectivity. It introduces multiple speakers and varies between capitalized and uncapitalized writing. While it strives for disruption, doubts emerge and push the text towards more stable concepts of selfhood. This doubting occurs particularly when the speaker of "speed bumps" notes that "identity is rife in the upper echelons," suggesting that the uncomplicated (self-) positioning of the dominant is, in part, what enables its dominance.[14] A deconstructive approach is sought, only to be challenged by situations in which "the colour of skin / obscures choices."[15] Simultaneously, however, the question of racialization contains productive potential. An italicized speaker in the poem "knocks at the door" states that "*each immigrant / moment is ape to undot the fault lines. falling between the seams / unbends the communication canal. Eruptions enter unannounced.*"[16] The uncoded status of the immigrant, falling between the seams, presents an opportunity for a seismic cultural shift. But this statement is closed down by an official discourse that asks that one "*sign on / the dotted line*," bringing the undotting immigrant moment back within the terrain of the dominant.[17]

While *Surrender* begins with a practice that highlights the disunity and hence the constructed nature of the lyrical "I," this position shifts. The unfixed dialogue between multiple voices is challenged by the surrounding space, which pushes the speakers into more and more stable identity formations. These shifts are part of the movement from classical metaphysics to poststructuralism and beyond, as "knocks on the door" suggests in a short series of statements: *"the subject stood still. then pirouetted. / then collapsed in a midden heap."*[18] The initial, static subject evokes the fixity of structuralism or classical metaphysics, with its confidence in master narratives, the underlying "deep structure" of the social, and the belief in a limited or knowable self. The pirouette evokes the radical free play of early poststructuralism and its celebration of the disrupted subject, as well as, in a Canadian setting, Pierre Trudeau's famous pirouette behind the Queen in 1977. The subject's final collapse into the midden heap, finally, suggests the disparity of global capitalism's so-called race to the bottom. But it also leaves open the question of what the subject does once collapsed into this position. No longer engaged in anxiously maintaining its stable ground or in free play, the subject's present and future become questions. What alternatives to the binary of stasis and play might be available? The answers may be found in the detritus of these momentarily polarized positions in Western thought—structuralism and poststructuralism—and rooting around in the trash becomes a means towards uncovering what those futures entail.

The thematics of this subject are highlighted in the poem "fool's scold, 1.4.97." This poem contains the most overt narrative thread in the volume. It is said to commemorate *"the last day of the restrictions / on freedom of movement"* imposed upon Japanese Canadians.[19] It thus reflects Miki's ongoing concern with the dispersal and imprisonment of Japanese Canadians during the Second World War and the redress movement in which he has been an important figure, a history that he details in the book *Redress: Inside the Japanese Canadian Call for Justice*. The poem connects to others in *Surrender* that quote RCMP and government sources, sources that limit the movement of Japanese Canadians. The poem itself focuses upon the experience of speaking about Japanese internment in California. It is about "the passage into empire,"[20] the American empire, and the disparity between the speaker's being allowed to cross the border because he possesses Canadian citizenship papers and then encountering immigration-related difficulties because of racism. The poem is an indictment of the United States and its shifting concept of national belonging. Central is the emergence of a first-person subject who is pushed into the certainties of immigration forms by U.S. officials. The following stanza exemplifies the fixity into which this speaker is pushed as he speaks with a border guard:

> new regulations, she continues, needed to deal with illegal
> aliens here. are there legal aliens here? i don't ask but at this
> interstice i imagine the border zone of "enemy alien,"
> thinking of the ja's [Japanese Americans] expelled from the coast in 42.[21]

The border guard demonstrates the continuity of racist policies within Empire. She also demonstrates the disparities of privilege, which are based upon citizenship in this instance. This privilege is, in turn, connected to the racial exclusions of nationalism. The speaker lives in an apparently contradictory position: he is Canadian, but not white. Yet he is able to escape from racial exclusions because of academic privilege, and because he holds the "right" passport. This fact is ironic given that the speaker is making the trip in order to speak about Japanese internment and the histories of racism.

The first-person voice, while undermining itself and seeking a liberating fragmentation, is unfree to do so within the spaces of the nation-state that the poem imagines. The crossing of borders—the progress of transgression, of ingressing into a space marked by its difference from Canada—denotes a site in which the body is interpolated into a sign system that forces a concretization of the first-person voice. The subject's unity returns at the point of control. The ruling powers reduce it to a single, mappable point that can be controlled, regulated, and processed. While the speaker thinks in terms of a disrupted presence, or rather a lack of presence, the regime in control of the means of representation at the border dictates a fall into limited modes. The border performs a violence, suturing an identity of individuated selfhood onto a body whose deterritorialized self might otherwise work towards broader politics and examine connections that disrupt the world into which it is thrust.

The remainder of *Surrender* consists of a voyage back out: after the sequence in "fool's scold" in which the speaker is pushed into a fixed subject position, the voice becomes less concrete. While there appears to be a single speaker on the border crossing, the remainder of the book is less certain. Poems on mobility and displacement dismantle the speaking subject and uncover political questions in ways that are connected to located subjects, but that are not limited to these positions. The short poem immediately following "fool's scold," entitled "on the sublime," deliberately hesitates "to use the first person," while the poem "surrender is a verbal sign," a few pages later, thematizes how "the i lower in case / balks at its own groan."²² Identity and stability become the tired signs of dogmatic structures that create individualism in the transnational capitalism in which the book's speakers unavoidably participate. The struggle to recover a flexible subjectivity is key to their resistant politics. After being thrust into metaphysical stasis by the regimes of imperial governance, the book becomes a process of recovering mobile subjectivity because, as the speaker of "surrender is a verbal sign" states, "my identity has worn out" and "all labels need to be licked."²³ By the text's end, the speaker of the poem "over heard" can state that "at the interval the sieve effect kicks in / all around 'us' the flow of capital."²⁴ But such an unfixed, open concept of the "we" in quotation marks re-emerges only in the very last line.

This shuttling between static and flexible structures points towards the ambivalence of theorizing a transnational politics of the subject. The constant motion in *Surrender* provides its speakers with a sense of agency, a movement in and out of the controlling interests of biopolitics, but at the same time illustrates the difficulties of operating in a deterritorialized mode. The deterritorializing process of the early poems of *Surrender*, moving from stasis to pirouette to midden heap, is followed by the reterritorialization of U.S. immigration forms and customs officers. Adopting an unfixed subjectivity leaves one open to a reterritorializing process that strips one of agency. This reterritorialization happens when dealing with the nation-state, the United States in "fool's scold," but countries from Canada to Australia in other poems. *Surrender* thus cautions against any simplistic theory of the multitude. It evokes an ambivalence for the resistance through deterritorialization that characterizes much of the thinking about the politics of counter-globalization: its disruptive poetic practices, both formal and thematic, highlight ways in which change might derive from thinking about the subject differently, understanding its locatedness as a node in a series of dissenting bodies. However, the process of being-subjected that *Surrender* narrates shows how Empire pushes the subject back into a rigid language of limited being. These limitations push the subject, in turn, towards a practice founded upon citizenship, as the speaker of "fool's scold" is forced to do, relying upon a Canadian passport in order to secure passage. *Surrender*'s closing attempts to recover the destabilized subject position of the book's opening highlight the struggles that one faces as a citizen of the globe: while unfixed subjectivities provide a new means of doing politics, these are at the same time limited by the imperial order. This is an order that subjects people—and some more than others, especially those who face racial discrimination, *Surrender* continually reminds its readers—to disciplinary regimes that force upon individuals the limited politics enabled by precisely such an individualized subject position. While these individualist politics might in themselves be sites of power, they may not allow communities to form, undermining attempts to rethink the subject as a means of breaking free.

Notes to Chapter Eleven

1. On this convergence, see Ian Rae's *From Cohen to Carson: The Poet's Novel in Canada* (Montreal and Kingston: McGill-Queen's UP, 2008).
2. Roy Miki, *Surrender* (Toronto: Mercury, 2001), 41.
3. Miki, *Surrender*, 21.
4. Miki, *Surrender*, 12.
5. Miki, *Surrender*, 9.
6. Stuart Hall, "Subjects in History: Making Diasporic Identities," *The House That Race Built*, ed. W. Lubiano (New York: Vintage, 1997), 292.
7. Miki, *Surrender*, 34.
8. Roy Miki, "Asiancy: Making Space for Asian Canadian Writing," *Broken Entries: Race, Subjectivity, Writing* (Toronto: Mercury, 1998), 117.
9. M. NourbeSe Philip, "A Genealogy of Resistance," *A Genealogy of Resistance and Other Essays* (Toronto: Mercury, 1997), 23.
10. Fred Wah, "Speak My Language: Racing the Lyric Poetic," *Faking It: Poetics and Hybridity: Critical Writing 1984–1999* (Edmonton: NeWest, 2000), 109.
11. Robert Budde, "After Postcolonialism: Migrant Lines and the Politics of Form in Fred Wah, M. NourbeSe Philip, and Roy Miki," *Is Canada Postcolonial? Unsettling Canadian Literature*, ed. Laura Moss (Waterloo: Wilfrid Laurier UP, 2003), 285.
12. Pauline Butling, writing alongside Susan Rudy, has described Miki's "editorial activism" in *Writing in Our Time: Canada's Radical Poetries in English (1957–2003)* (Waterloo: Wilfrid Laurier UP, 2005), 240–41.
13. Miki, *Surrender*, 12.
14. Miki, *Surrender*, 21.
15. Miki, *Surrender*, 25.
16. Miki, *Surrender*, 33.
17. Miki, *Surrender*, 33.
18. Miki, *Surrender*, 43.
19. Miki, *Surrender*, 70.
20. Miki, *Surrender*, 71.
21. Miki, *Surrender*, 76.
22. Miki, *Surrender*, 78, 81.
23. Miki, *Surrender*, 90.
24. Miki, *Surrender*, 131.

CHAPTER TWELVE

Writing Past Belonging in Dionne Brand's *What We All Long For*

Dionne Brand's 2005 novel *What We All Long For* represents a generational shift in the politics of being in Canadian space, one that builds upon Roy Miki's destabilized sense of subjectivity in *Surrender* but pushes the notions of community and belonging in different directions. In it, young, poor, and racialized characters navigate their lives and loves within the Greater Toronto Area, from College Street to the suburb of Richmond Hill. Being non-white within Canada has given them strong anti-national consciousnesses. Their parents, conversely, try to belong to a nation-state that refuses to recognize them because of their ancestry. They are paralyzed, striving for an impossible acceptance by the nation alongside a nostalgic longing for a lost past. The younger generation, however, feels little belonging to either the Canadian nation or to their ancestral homes; for them, finding community is an urban project, one engaged in the active social construction of space, and they fracture notions of belonging through a focus upon the component parts of that very word: being and longing.[1] Instead of the concept of belonging, which Brand herself eschews, her characters engage in the mixed forms of "struggle work" that she has discussed in an interview.[2] In the place of finding belonging, the young character Tuyen, for instance, spends her time creating a piece of installation art whose goal is to capture all of the longings of the city. These represent the collective aspirations of the chaotic, displaced, and dispersed urban community. The work remains unfinished at the novel's end, because it cannot be completed: the city itself is the expression of its own desires—it is the installation, in other words—and it remains an unfinished space, one that crosses the geographies inhabited by the book's protagonists' parents and recombines in new and unexpected ways. The protagonists, recognizing the city's incomplete nature, see it as a battleground, as a space for action and for the creation of a viable sense of self—a space for building culture from below. This final chapter argues that *What We All Long For* represents some of the ways in which communities are being articulated in the global city, and how these, in turn, relate to a notion of Canada as a transnational space. Such cities are (although not exclusively) providing alternative grounds for thinking through concepts of subjectivity and being, against earlier models of belonging. In this sense, Brand's focus on the city and belonging is similar to Miki's focus on migration and subjectivity in *Surrender*, and her characters' urbanity can also be compared with Lam's characters' cosmopolitanism in *Bloodletting and Miraculous Cures*. Brand's urban space is but one of any number of grounds upon which understandings of selfhood are being articulated as the nation-state is rethought in the context of global capitalism. The goal is to show how Brand's protagonists—Tuyen, Carla, Jackie, and Oku—think themselves into being within Toronto and the world. This chapter explores how their self-imaginings contrast with their parents', and how these protagonists suggest some of the politics of forming communities across borders.

This discussion of *What We All Long For* also furthers analyses of Brand's writing by pushing a step further Marlene Goldman's suggestion that Brand pursues a "politics of drifting" in her writing. Goldman suggests that, in reading Brand, examinations of belonging are insufficient, bounded by the limits of a politics of identity that relies on static modes of being. Instead, the notion of drifting, which Goldman derives from Brand's *At the Full and Change of the Moon*, is used to show how Brand "offers an alternative to the boundedness of home and the nation-state." Drifting, Goldman states, becomes a "legitimate resistant practice" against "both the model of the Euro-American modernist exile, whose desires for belonging are typically nostalgic and directed toward a lost origin—and the model of the immigrant—whose desires are reoriented toward a new home and a new national community."³ Instead of pledging allegiance to the nation-state or longing for a lost home, drifting offers a possibility for creating new and liberating politics, Goldman suggests. Brand pursues a rhizomatic form of resistance, in which one point or subject can connect to any other in order to form community across borders. Ellen Quigley has made this point, arguing that, for Brand, the project of decolonizing the self involves the negation of "legitimate subjects, objects, communities, and origins."⁴ Grounded notions of selfhood and belonging are disrupted in order to uncover a site for being that is open, neither nostalgic nor caught within the politics of inclusion/exclusion or an inside/outside dichotomy. This desire for openness begins with the self, who is disrupted into multiplicity, allowing for communities based on such ideas of selfhood to themselves become open, inclusive, and disruptive of the staid social, political, and cultural borders of the world.

This chapter pushes these formulations further by looking at how, in Deleuzian terms (which both Goldman and Quigley pursue), the drifting or deterritorialization that they examine functions. As in Miki's *Surrender*, the self needs to remain in motion, pursuing a Deleuzian line of flight in order to escape the domination of contemporary biopolitics, the process through which the body itself becomes subject to legislation and surveillance. The intention here, as before, is to pursue reterritorialization, the second half of the Deleuzian equation. This remains a key point when examining the question of belonging in Brand's writing, because her liberated notion of selfhood risks becoming reinscribed by a placid sense of globalism if analysis fails to note that deterritorialization and drifting need to be ongoing processes. Deterritorialization is a continual project, particularly in the case of Brand, whose project is focused upon modes of being that constantly work to elude the dominant. *What We All Long For* demonstrates this point in focusing upon protagonists who work to construct a new Toronto from below, but whose relatives and friends are caught within a racist system that limits how their bodies and beings function. Characters are physically imprisoned or socio-economically restricted. The system seeks to reterritorialize drifting bodies; ensuring their ongoing motion becomes a concern as Brand's characters mix and merge. The drifting bodies that face reinscription should keep readers from maintaining any simplistic celebration of motion, however; for many, such as those facing exile, movement is neither desired nor empowering. Yet for some, critically considered movement becomes a way of forming community.

The transnational subjects of the novel can be situated within broader discussions about the purpose and possibility of citizenship. Canadian philosopher Mark Kingwell, in *The World We Want*, suggests that citizenship continues to be a forum for achieving a just world, one in which suffering is minimized and happiness (however one defines it) can be pursued. He argues, echoing a number of commentators on citizenship, that citizenship needs to be rethought, made to fit our globalizing, "shape-shifting world."[5] The globally minded citizen that Kingwell proposes begins within the Athenian polis. Kingwell notes the ways in which democratic polities have been tied to capitalism, and provides a reminder that this original conceptualization of the citizen is grounded in the city-state. The urban foundation of politics is preserved in the etymology of the term itself, founded in the Greek *polis*, just as it is in the concept of citizenship, rooted in the Latin term *civis* (citizen) and linked to the *civitas* (city). The role of the city might be brought out in accounts of contemporary citizenship. The city is not the sole venue for doing politics—indeed, *Transnational Canadas* has been concerned since its discussion of bpNichol in the introduction with ways in which Canadian literature moves back and forth from the rural to the urban (and in between)—but it is one of the grounds that is contested under global capitalism, and that requires new thinking about how citizenship might operate in spaces where people live while holding passports to countries from all around the world. Such a city provides a challenge to concepts of belonging and citizenship. The contemporary global city looms large, pushing for recognition as one space in which issues of citizenship are contested and reconfigured.

Brand's politics are a far cry from Kingwell's; his ideas are included in part to discuss the surprising "we" of Brand's title, which suggests something of the politics of motion or drifting that she pursues. Kingwell writes in universal terms in order to make his claims for citizenship, a claim that is consciously constructed in the light of deconstruction. Rather than Kingwell's neo-universalism, Brand's "we" is a term that remains in flux, a term whose referent is unclear and in the process of being constructed. Similar to Tuyen's project of encoding the longings of the city into an art installation, the "we" of the title suggestively refers to all of those living in Toronto and the world, an open-ended polity that is ever shifting. But this is equally a "we" that might divide itself further and further—or that might be built into a new form of community, one based upon alliances. Quigley suggests that, in the case of Brand's 1996 novel, *In Another Place, Not Here*, "Brand interpellates readers in a culturally hybrid, rhizomatic coalition."[6] This same statement holds true for *What We All Long For*, which invites readers into a coalition through its title and by prompting them to consider their position vis-à-vis this gesture of inclusive, first-person pluralism. The characters of the novel, by participating in the incremental construction of the city and the world through their actions, suggest possibilities for an open-ended politics that might include the reader as well.

There are good reasons for Brand to focus on the role of cities in the globalizing world. Granted, a certain amount of Toronto-centrism is likely involved. But there is more. Saskia Sassen suggests that the internationalization of financial systems and the dissolution of manufacturing in the West have led to cities being interconnected in broad, transnational systems that exceed the connections between nation-states. For her, "the transformation in the composition of the global economy accompanying the shift to services and finance brings about a renewed importance of major cities."[7] Whether these nodal cities are taken as rhizomatic sites within Empire, or whether they are seen simply as shifting sites of political and commercial congress, it is clear that the actions of city-dwellers change under continual and increasing migrations. Such movements create communities that live in diaspora or exile, as do the focal characters in Brand's novel. These racialized communities, in Sassen's analysis of Tokyo, London, and New York, have been subjected to increasing segregation and economic stratification under the shifts associated with globalization. Increasingly large gaps between the richest and poorest segments of urban society coincide with white and non-white racial demarcations in the West, making the global city a site of renewed tension.

What citizenship or political action might mean is contested in such a space. Living within a global city requires an assessment of what is included or permitted in official urban (or urbane) discourse, and requires admitting a wider range of alternatives than has hitherto been allowed. The problematic is one that extends to—and beyond—questions of Canadian multiculturalism. When thinking about questions of mobility in this context, it is no longer adequate to celebrate only the ways in which the cosmopolitan world allows for movement across borders. For some, especially the privileged, increased mobility is liberating, as it enables new forms of travel and ways of experiencing the world. Privileged cosmopolitans tend to celebrate their mobility; Aihwa Ong, for example, examines ways in which the "flexible citizenship" that comes with a rising global order allows the wealthy "to both circumvent *and* benefit from different nation-state regimes by selecting different sites for investments, work, and family relocation."[8] For others, however, mobility is forced, a result of displacement due to war or poverty. Those who are excluded from the transnational cosmopolitan ideal by virtue of racialization, gendering, or lack of economic privilege may experience mobility as an enforced mark of their marginalization. It seems therefore pertinent to focus upon ways in which the city becomes one site for challenging the status quo and for reimagining how communities can function in ways that exceed normalizing logics. How, in other words, can mobility be conceptualized and used by both the privileged and the impoverished as an expression of politics? *What We All Long For*, by focusing on nomadic communities formed between diasporic subjects, pushes readers to recognize ways in which the city presents both an opportunity and a risk. Sassen suggests the need for a concept of global citizenship in cities where both the elites of corporate capitalism and the tiers of impoverished and displaced populations come together.[9] While the notion of global citizenship remains questionable, that she can make such a claim suggests something of the open-ended modes of belonging that contestations of citizenship present.

Such open conceptualizations of citizenship, refracted through global routes of migration, are active in Toronto, whether or not it is thought of as a global city in Sassen's terms (terms that she suggests are not empirical or definable). Pico Iyer, writing in *The Global Soul*, names Toronto as a global city, but it need not be formally named as such in order to read the ways in which its citizens and denizens are affected by global flows.[10] The editors of the volume *uTOpia: Towards a New Toronto* aver that "a city, by its very nature, is not owned; it is shared."[11] A city is constructed, like a nation or a nation-state, at a social level, from below, contested and reformed at every instant. Toronto's shifting demographics, connected to the flows of transnational migration, present continual and massive generational shifts that change the sensibilities of the place, even while its formal political structures remain in place. The city drifts, in other words; what is key is to see how this mobility, the politics of drifting, opens up to the transnational. The goal here is to look for ways in which the city, in its continual motion, might escape the limited narratives of the nation discussed in Part One of this book and enable the creation of alternative spaces, for both the elites who traditionally revel in cosmopolitanism and those for whom mobility is more difficult.

Concerns with migration and displacement are crucial to Dionne Brand's writing. In her earlier book *In Another Place, Not Here*, Brand tracks the lives of women who arrive in Toronto and pursue relationships with one another that are divided by the routes of migration. When the character Elizete leaves the Caribbean plantation on which she has worked and comes to Toronto after her lover Verlia's death, she finds that she has become "a woman from nowhere," a displaced person who is overlooked. The city, it turns out, is "imaginary," a space that is collectively constructed by those who already belong; this belonging excludes the women in the novel, who are caught between love and death.[12] They pursue anti-racist and anti-sexist activism in Toronto and resist the American attack in Grenada, an act that claims Verlia's life, but none of these acts enable them to take up citizenship. Their struggles are transnational, moving across space; the narrator suggests that, for Elizete, "no country will do."[13] This rootlessness is even larger; it is conceptual, breaking the bounds of identity, encompassing the question of belonging itself. The narrator states the following of the book's characters:

> And belonging? They were past it. It was not wide enough, not gap enough, not distance enough. Not rip enough, belonging. Belonging was too small, too small for their magnificent rage. They had surpassed the pettiness of their oppressors who measured origins speaking of a great patriarch and property marked out by violence, a rope, some iron; who measured time in the future only and who discarded memory like useless news.[14]

What does it mean to reject the concept of belonging? This is the moment at which Brand's writing takes a radical step. This passage suggests, in its rejection of belonging, that while oppressors cling to beliefs in origins and static models of being, these are insufficient to the women of the text. The women transgress borders and seek, when encountering the same, familiar exclusions upon arriving in Toronto, to form their own links in resistance. But these links remain tenuous. Elizete moves into temporary refuges, staying with women who hope to find men whose citizenship will ensure their legitimacy. Citizenship is a passport to belonging, with its fixing stamp of approval. It is denied to the women of the text, and they are pushed to the margins, hopeful in their shared spaces of love, but excluded by the white majority. The title of the book, taken from Brand's earlier book of poetry *No Language Is Neutral*, is instructive. The line that becomes the title of the book is incomplete, fragmented in its later form; in its fuller version, it reads "In another place, not here, a woman might touch / something between beauty and nowhere, back there / and here, might pass hand over hand her own / trembling life."[15] The sense of crossing, of revelling in drifting, is couched within the title of the novel, but the city that Brand depicts never allows such revelling to develop.

It is tempting to attempt to find spaces of belonging in Brand's writing. While this focus is not necessarily misplaced, it might represent an earlier phrase of Brand's thinking, and as a result this present analysis is interested more in how belonging is deferred. She is explicit in her recent writing, stating in *A Map to the Door of No Return* that "belonging does not interest" her.[16] In an interview, she suggests that a desire for belonging, expressed through the notion of home, is a form of nostalgia that feminists of colour need to reject, because it is "really not something that [they] have experienced."[17] That is, given histories and lives of displacement, the idea of a homeplace is always denied or deferred to women of colour. By extension, so too is a sense of belonging. Searching for it is, Brand suggests, a form of nostalgia that prevents action.[18] Instead, Joanne Saul has recently suggested that Brand has begun to shape "a potentially new way of envisioning citizenry, both national and global, within a world order dominated by the expansion of global capital."[19] That envisioning looks for modes of being and longing that do not rely upon belonging, pushing towards an open, mobile politics of coalition-making.

In *What We All Long For*, the generation of newcomers to Toronto is frustrated in their attempts at belonging in a racist space; their children, instead, become the focus when they contest the exclusions that they face more effectively than their parents. These children live in a space between the nation and a universalizing cosmopolitanism. Their site of struggle is the city, but Brand's urban youths are far from Benjaminian *flâneurs*, going about the city with "amamnestic intoxication."[20] Instead, the city is an invigorating and troubling site for struggle work. The Toronto of *What We All Long For* is caught in a complex web of migrations, colonial and postcolonial, intra- and international. It is instructive to examine the genealogies of resistance here, to borrow a phrase from M. NourbeSe Philip, in order to witness ways in which the webs of displacement that condition urban life lead to a mobile and political sense of the self. Iyer suggests that "how much you imported from your previous life, how much you left behind" is the main concern of Torontonians, and this dialogue becomes a crisis for Brand's immigrant generation.[21] The parents in the novel leave their cognitive schemata behind when they face exile or displacement, and attempt to work with the schema handed to them by their adoptive nation, pushed into communities divided upon ethno-cultural lines while longing for national acceptance. The results are painful for them, given the ethos of the nation and the limitations of its multiculturalism, which knows only how to accept difference when it appears in recognizable (stereotypical) forms. The schema for belonging in Canada assumes that one is white; attempting to fit into such a model when one is not white tends to have negative consequences.

Tuyen's parents, Cam and Tuan, are the most important example of this process. Their route to Toronto is one of exile from Asia during the Vietnam War: they leave their home in favour of a refugee camp in Hong Kong and later depart for Canada. The novel focuses upon these travels because Tuan and Cam are separated from their eldest son, Quy, as they leave Vietnam. He ends up in Pulau Bidong, Malaysia, a place where, he states in his portion of the narrative, "identity was watery, up for grabs" as people attempted to escape to somewhere better.[22] His parents arrive in Toronto devastated by their loss, and spend their energies searching for Quy, leaving their remaining children—sisters Ai and Lam, both born in Vietnam, and Binh, brother to Tuyen, both born in Canada—acutely aware of their parents' loss. Quy, in turn, becomes a hard-headed monk involved in illegal human trafficking prior to discovering his family through his mother's efforts, leading to his eventual travel to Toronto to reunite with his family.

Cam and Tuan, caught in their nostalgia for their missing son and the past, struggle in Canada. They are insomniac, and Cam becomes fixated upon "birth certificates, identity cards, immigration papers, and citizenship papers and cards," laminating and copying them so that her earlier mistake of misplacing her son has no chance of being repeated.[23] They strive to get along in Canada, but they cannot achieve their goals. Cam's medical accreditation is not recognized and she is unable to retrain because of her struggles with English, while Tuan's hopes of regaining his engineering career fade. Tuan's dream is retained only in his hobby of "drawing all the buildings of the city as if he had built them."[24] Instead, the couple opens a Vietnamese restaurant—the Saigon Pearl—in downtown Toronto, giving in to the stereotypical view of ethnicity that the city foists upon them. They are, the narrator suggests, "being defined by the city" rather than constructing its definition.[25] They hope for better for their children, bidding them to fit into the society around them as best they can, and accepting the discourses of national belonging that are given to them upon their arrival. They find relative comfort in their eventual achievement of suburban living, but continue to be plagued by the loss of Quy. They are split between feelings of limited belonging to the nation-state and intense nostalgia, caught sleepless between the two.

The other parents, while less crucial to the text, display similar patterns. Oku's parents, while not obviously in exile—the novel does not describe their diasporic movements precisely—nevertheless rely upon hard work as a means of gaining acceptance. Oku's father, Fitz, suggests that life was better back home, evoking a similar—but less pointed—nostalgia to Tuan and Cam's. He tells Oku that he will be able to succeed in Canada through perseverance and hard work, something that he attempts himself, though with middling results. Oku's mother, Clare, seems less convinced of this ability to fit in, but is quieter, telling Oku that his father is "not a bad man," just one who has been denied the chance to succeed. The narrator, speaking for her, states that if he were "a different man in this country, he could be further ahead." Both parents seem to Oku to be "people who somehow lived in the near past and were unable or unwilling to step into the present."[26] Their feelings of belonging are uncertain, and they prevaricate, longing simultaneously for the past and for inclusion in the present.

Carla's family is complex, as her Italian mother, Angie, and her Jamaican father, Derek, never develop a secure relationship; Derek remains married to another woman, named Nadine. Derek struggles for power over women and is caught in the web of his philandering after Angie kills herself, leaving Carla and her younger brother, Jamal, in his and Nadine's care. Their transnational movements evoke the fears of miscegenation felt by Angie's family, and theirs becomes a transcultural romance with a tragic ending, illustrating limits of the society's acceptance of difference.

Jackie's parents, however, represent a noteworthy case. For the Bernards, the routes of migration remain within Canada, but are pointedly racialized. They migrate to Toronto from Halifax, following the movements of other family members. Once there, they try to fit in within black communities as young, hip, and dangerous people. Her father is a barber, and both parents devote their time to the Paramount nightclub—a place populated by "black people and a few, very few, hip whites"—until it goes under.[27] At this point their lives take turns for the worse. They struggle with alcoholism, and Jackie's father does stints in jail in Guelph after their community collapses. Theirs is a community that the narrator states is extremely "tight," to the point that it relies upon the physicality of nightclubs to sustain itself.[28] The disappearance of these structures prompts the narrative to query who controls the city, noting that while people are at times able to build it from the ground up, these constructs are threatened by development, by "the constant construction of this and that" by the city's elites.[29] Jackie's parents' community positions itself beyond the bounds of the law, seeing the police as being of "another race altogether," as well as beyond the capitalist movements of development, but this avoidance, set within the racially determined structures of society, positions the community as a focus for policing.[30] The novel, as a result, suggests several things via the generation of immigrant parents: first, that the scripts of national belonging with which they are provided never fit in a racist country and, second, that communities formed through racial demarcations are fragile, given the power, both economic and social, of the wealthy and white. The multicultural theory of the nation, in this depiction, is shown to be remarkably limited.

The parents' children, however, present an alternative by seeing the city as the grounds for their being, enacting different modes of citizenship and conceptualizations of subjectivity. They find home across borders and in the spaces resulting from displacement. In depicting their lives, Brand seems far more optimistic than in her earlier writing. With the parents' generation, Brand sets out a number of difficulties faced by racialized immigrants. With the children, however, possibilities are expressed, even as they face the recriminations of the reterritorializing and disciplinary system. Brand refuses in *What We All Long For* to sentimentalize the struggles of the city, unlike, for example, Dennis Lee, whose *Civil Elegies*, as discussed in Chapter Three, laments the failure of Toronto and, by extension, the nation. Brand's focus is, instead, more comparable to that of Michael Ondaatje's *In the Skin of a Lion*, as discussed in Chapter Seven, in which Toronto is a dizzying place for newly arrived immigrants, whose struggles construct the city. The ways in which the immigrants in Ondaatje's novel are "sewn into history"—transforming it through their labour — are important not only for them, but for the city itself, even when these are ambivalent processes tied to capitalism and ownership. Rather than despairing at the external forms of the city and accepting them as loss, the ugliness of the urban is contested and altered through both political and artistic action, as well as through simple acts of inhabitation. Existence is a means of expressing politics, as it is also in *Slash*.

The children born to the city's immigrants define its being. They are Torontonian above all else, and they drift in the city, chasing their desires. Brand states elsewhere that she observes "a becoming" when she rides the streetcar in Toronto, watching the diasporic bodies ride and collide, and she begins *What We All Long For* similarly.[31] The novel opens by zooming in from a discussion of the city and the way that it smells, "most of all, [of] longing," to a description of three of her protagonists riding the subway. Taking the perspective of a subway rider, the narrator describes Oku, Tuyen, and Carla tumbling onto the subway after a night out on the city. They are described as, respectively, "a young black man...carrying a drum in a duffel bag," "Asian [and] beautiful in a strange way," and, finally, as possibly "Italian, southern."[32] These descriptions point towards the uncertainties of their ancestries and, importantly, refuse strict national identifications. The narrator returns to their physicality, observing later that Carla is "not phenotypically black," just as she cannot be easily labelled as Italian either.[33] The narrator refuses to construct absolute ethno-national borders in their lives. The narrative voice suggests, moreover, that their mirth derives in part from their freedom to transgress differences such as those between the segregated communities that characterize the city. The protagonists' hope is infectious, but the narrative voice, reflecting the thoughts of other passengers in the subway, is aware of the risks of their self-proclaimed freedom, casting doubts on their futures. Their laughter leads to jealousy in other passengers as they think back to their own youths and to privileges that they have lacked. The narrator imagines another rider thinking of these characters as "free loaders"; this rider is reassured by thinking that "life will get them hard some time."[34] Such doubts resurface continually in the novel, again and again representing the risks of reterritorialization and the need for these bodies to remain in motion so that their politics of drifting can remain effective. The divided neighbourhoods of the city are full of "people who are used to the earth beneath them shifting, and they all want it to stop," states the narrator, but this very motion is liberating for the protagonists.[35] What remains to be seen is the extent to which this might remain so.[36]

Transformative, open modes of being seem to be available to this generation. Carla, Tuyen, and Oku, as well as Jackie, who have been friends since high school at Harbord Collegiate Institute, recognize their diasporic ancestries, but are not in search of either a lost origin or an adoptive nationalism. They are aware that they are connected to their ancestral homeplaces, but, rather than becoming stuck somewhere between an impossible longing for that past home and the reality of the present one, the children recognize this bifurcation as the site, as Brand elsewhere puts it, that "opens all nationalisms to their imaginative void."[37] Instead of becoming a fixing, limiting space that frames the past, present, and future, this site becomes one that bridges between times and places. The parents ask that their children "fit in and stop making trouble," but Canada is not a suitable nation for such an assimilative stance, in that it requires, Tuyen states, "a blonde wig [to] fit right in."[38] The narrator states that the children had "never been able to join in what their parents called 'regular Canadian life'" because "they weren't the required race."[39] Oku is warned by his Rastafarian acquaintance on the street that if he were to follow the "white man ways" he would be "doomed," like the homeless musician Clifford Hall, whom he sees around the city.[40] The novel's protagonists do not see being Canadian "as a possible way of being in the world," and they are frightened by their parents' instructions to "join up and get along."[41] Nor are their ancestral homes sites for national belonging. Tuyen states that she has "some ancient Chinese-Vietnamese shit" to work through, but refuses to name her national affinity when Carla asks for it.[42] The narrator states, with a note of ambivalence, that Tuyen and her brother Binh are "not Vietnamese but that desired ineffable nationality: Western," while her culture is "North American."[43] Their parents' "past had never been their past."[44] Instead of seeing themselves as mere national subjects, then, the children view the city as the site of their being: they are, readers are told, "born in the city from people born elsewhere."[45] Theirs is an urban space that is connected to global modes of living before it is connected to discourses of the nation, and their parents' attempts to fit into national modes strike them as risible. They thus feel split between what the narrator terms "two countries—their parents' and their own," that of their parents' nostalgia and their own, open sense of themselves.[46] They focus their struggle work on building and creating transnational ways of being in the city, ways of constructing communities through longing and loving.

Tuyen, in creating her installation art, is perhaps the best illustration of the process of pursuing longings in order to create the city. Having fled from Cam and Tuan's pained nostalgia, she lives downtown on College Street, above a store, and next door to Carla. Her apartment is an assemblage, "a mess of wood rails and tree stumps, twigs and rope, debris, really," which she works into her art. Her early experiences with her family's isolation prompt her, as a child, to insist upon assimilating by demanding that everyone speak English, that they eat "like normal people," and that her parents forget the past.[47] As a result, "her own understanding of Vietnamese [is] deliberately minimal" as she grows up "translating the city's culture to her parents."[48] She loathes "the sense of sameness or ease" that she is "supposed to feel" with other Asian people, preferring a more diverse but undifferentiated world.[49] Her insistence upon such an even globe is renounced, however, as an adult, when she demands that her brother Binh's girlfriend refer to herself by her given name of Hue rather than her anglicized name of Ashley. She comes to see the city as beautiful because it is "polyphonic, murmuring," filling Tuyen with hope at the "gathering of voices and longings that subsumed themselves up into a kind of language, yet indescribably."[50] Her installation similarly changes in the novel, while she ponders "how she [is] going to execute the collection of longings" that she plans.[51] It is, initially, envisioned as a *lubaio*, a traditional post on which people leave notes, in this case "messages to the city."[52] The installation then shifts to a more contemporary mode in which she muses about capturing "the characteristics of her family," and, later still, becomes a larger, three-room installation whose parameters she is unable to fully imagine.[53] It is designed to capture "every longing in the city."[54] The longings of the city are expansive, breaking beyond the confined spaces that Tuyen might create for them, given that the city itself represents the sum of its people's desires. She is engaged in the process of creating this piece throughout the novel, and it remains necessarily incomplete as it concludes.

Tuyen is motivated in part by her unrequited love for Carla, which she has harboured since high school. Carla struggles throughout the novel to reconcile herself to the earlier suicide of her mother. Carla also spends the novel struggling with her younger brother, Jamal, who has ended up in the Mimico Correctional Institute for carjacking.[55] Jamal's criminality displays the danger of the society of surveillance, in which his drifting body is disciplined and recoded by a legal system that looks down on him for being black. Carla, who is not as clearly racially marked as Jamal, feels free in the city, and works as a bicycle courier, racing along its streets entranced by "the minutiae of transient wants and needs" — the daily struggles of living.[56] This job allows her to "ignore the world where you had to fit."[57] She sees "the city as a set of obstacles to be crossed and circled, avoided and let pass," rather than to get caught up in.[58] The narrator describes Carla as being "light," unable to stop her restless movement because "light moves."[59] She sees the risks that Jamal faces in his own restlessness, and attempts to help him despite her knowledge that it is difficult to remain free as a person of colour. She tells Jamal that he "can't be at the wrong place at the wrong time" because he is black.[60] Her response is to insist on motion; the narrator states that it is Jamal who sends "her speeding through the city with the random logic of an element."[61] This insistence, though, becomes a risk; Carla claims that she has "no desire" as one means of keeping the future open so that she can honour the memory of her mother and tend to her brother.[62] At the end of the novel, however, she manages to let go of both Jamal and the memory of her mother after confronting her wayward father. She embraces instead an open-ended future, grasping the drifting politics that her friends embody and desire for her, one that is based not on fear but on possibility.

Oku is also painfully aware of the dangers facing men like himself and Jamal. Imprisonment is always a risk, even without contravention of the law. Oku states that being imprisoned is a "rite of passage for a young black man."[63] Oku experiences arrest at the age of eighteen, caught alone on the street at night, but is never charged. He struggles to free himself from his father's dictates that he should work hard in order to be accepted, knowing the futility of this attempt, while concealing the fact that he has dropped out of a master's program in English at the University of Toronto. Feeling that the future's openness presents a threat, and afraid because he does not "know where to go from here," Oku wanders the city.[64] He is at risk of being pulled into a life of petty criminality with his friend Kwesi, a small-time operator of a mobile shop who lives by his intelligence, always one step ahead of the law.[65] Oku's desires are not limited to finding community in this space; he desires, instead, to experience the world. He is searching for a life that lies between those choices that he sees available to him: either being "bled out in a parking lot outside a club," floating "out of his body" like the homeless and mentally ill Rasta and musician he sees on the streets, or else ending up with "the hard-headed bitterness of his father, living in the fantasies of *if only*."[66] He decides to shun Kwesi and criminality, worried that a life of oppression at the hands of the police will lead only to ending "up in the system fighting to get out." In this life he would be pushed into a reactionary mode and, never being able to construct a life for himself, always be imprisoned, even when "the bars were invisible."[67] Instead, he masters a broad culinary repertoire in distinction to his father's preference of "the mono-culture of Jamaican food," opening boundaries where his father prefers the comfort of the known.[68] His unfulfilled desire for Jackie fills him with hope, and the novel concludes by pushing him towards a future in which he will remain in motion, not falling prey to the life offered by Kwesi. He also eschews the pragmatic but impossible choice offered by his father of working according to other people's standards in order to gain acceptance. Instead, his hopes lie with his formed community of diasporic friends, who support him and offer him the potential for fulfillment.

Jackie is similarly escaping the confines of her parents' communities. Raised in Alexandra Park, a largely segregated community, she sees her parents' slow collapse after the Paramount nightclub closes, and vows to live her life differently, never longing for the Halifax to which her parents wish to return. Although Oku is in love with her, she denies him, having sex with him but never committing to him in any other way because, as Oku reckons, she sees in him the return to her parents' way of living; he seems to her "like so many burned-out guys in Vanauley Way," the street on which her parents live.[69] She opts for a German boyfriend named Reiner, who is peripheral to the novel and offers her a different life than the one she has known, one of industrial music, moving "around the city from one ubiquitous dungeon-like club to another."[70] She runs a small used clothing store on Queen Street called Ab und Zu, which sells "post-bourgeois clothing," and she is content with a life of border crossings.[71] Oku, the narrator states, leaves her feeling "liquid and jittery and out of control," while Reiner leaves her feeling "separate and apart, in command of self."[72] Both present her with ways of maintaining her movement in the city, but Oku leaves her uncertain and does not allow her to maintain her sense of self.

This younger generation lives lives that do not adhere to national distinctions, just as they eschew a simplistic cosmopolitan ideal. The novel spends much of its energy setting up these distinctions. The Canadian nation is void to its protagonists, but a cosmopolitan celebration of the global coming together of ethno-cultural groups is not satisfying as long as oppression persists. Tuyen — taking photographs in Koreatown as people celebrate South Korea's surprising defeat of Italy in the 2002 World Cup — is struck by the national lines that demarcate the city, the "small neighbourhoods that seemed at least slightly reconciled" prior to breaking "into sovereign bodies" during the World Cup, and is prompted by the sight to recall her and Oku's participation in the 2001 protests in Quebec City against the Summit of the Americas.[73] Their participation in the protest suggests their denial of a celebratory cosmopolitanism, but this participation is two-sided: the protest excites them, especially Oku, who joins the black bloc anarchists and is arrested after climbing the notorious security fence that confronted residents of Quebec throughout the summit. At the same time, the divisive, us-versus-them mentality of the protest lingers with Tuyen, who sees parallels between such confrontations and the exclusions of nationalism. Carla takes this sentiment further, as she feels disturbed by the art show that Tuyen mounts of her protest photos in their apartment building. To her, the photos and the protest recall her mother's suicide, an act that signifies the ultimate border crossing.[74] The exclusions of the city and global capitalism are not to be reversed through the formation of merely oppositional counter-movements or a reliance upon narrow conceptions of community. Instead, hope lies, for them, in the opportunities that they create to reconstruct urban space. They build their communities across borders, rhizomatically connecting to each other without a predetermined logic. They are linked by their desire for inclusivity, and not limited by the discourses that are handed to them.

What We All Long For, then, proposes through these characters that communities existing in resistance to racism, nationalism, and oppression need not be formed on a strictly oppositional basis or seek acknowledgement and inclusion. Instead, the lives of Tuyen, Carla, Oku, and Jackie suggest in various ways that transgressing against borders, while maintaining an openness towards difference and the future, might enable new webs of social relations. The novel, in this sense, seems extremely hopeful. Its protagonists see "the street outside, its chaos, as their only hope," and they feel "the city's violence and its ardour in one emotion." They are all "trying to step across the borders of who they were" because they are, "in fact, borderless."[75] But the novel recognizes the difficulty of pursuing such deterritorializing lines of flight. These characters are engaged in struggle work, and those around them highlight the risks that they face, be it through their parents' unhappiness — Oku's father, Fitz, refuses to answer when his son asks him if he is happy — or through the criminalization and discipline faced by Jamal.

The novel ends by further questioning its optimism. After arriving in Toronto, Quy is reunited to Binh and Tuyen, and they take him to meet his parents. At the same time, Carla gets her father to bail Jamal out of prison. Jamal promptly steals his father's car and picks up a friend; they head north, looking to steal another car, and happen upon Quy, who is sitting in the back of Binh's BMW outside his parents' home in Richmond Hill. Jamal forces him from the car and he and his friend beat Quy nearly to death. The outcome of this event is left undetermined, and the novel ends with Tuan and Cam coming to see their long-lost son most likely die. Jamal will probably be caught, as he has not been careful to conceal his theft of Derek's car, while Tuyen's parents will be devastated, with repercussions for the whole family. But the *significance* of this event is also undetermined. Quy is an ambivalent figure, one who exploits the rootlessness of the contemporary world towards his own ends, in a manner that is similar to that of Brand's Toronto-based protagonists, but with a selfish purpose. His likely death suggests an inability to be reintegrated into life in the city, but it is, of course, also an act of chance. This questioning of the novel's earlier optimism, however, does not entirely erase the sense of possibility that the novel contains: Carla has relinquished her younger brother's difficulties so that he can learn to care for himself and is moving towards a future in which she will be free to create sustaining communities, and her friends are discovering ways in which they can remain mobile. Not everyone will escape from the reterritorializing gaze of the society of racialized surveillance, but it remains possible that the freedom these characters all long for might be realized. There is optimism to be found, but a great deal is left to chance; the geography of the city returns again and again in mentions of snowstorms and traffic flows, which disturb "the pretence of order and civilization," leaving people "bewildered as they should be, aimless and directionless as they really are," caught in their unending struggle work.[76]

Notes to Chapter Twelve

1. Such a splitting of the term also occurs in Bina Toledo Freiwald's analysis of "the complex relations between being, longing, and belonging" in her essay "Cartographies of Be/longing: Dionne Brand's *In Another Place, Not Here*," *Mapping Canadian Cultural Space: Essays on Canadian Literature*, ed. Danielle Schaub (Jerusalem: Hebrew U Magnes P, 2000), 38.
2. Pauline Butling, "Dionne Brand on Struggle and Community, Possibility and Poetry," *Poets Talk: Conversations with Robert Kroetsch, Daphne Marlatt, Erin Mouré, Dionne Brand, Marie Annharte Baker, Jeff Derksen and Fred Wah* (Edmonton: U of Alberta P, 2005), 70.
3. Marlene Goldman, "Mapping the Door of No Return: Deterritorialization and the Work of Dionne Brand," *Canadian Literature* 182 (2004): 22, 13, 26.
4. Ellen Quigley, "Picking the Deadlock of Legitimacy: Dionne Brand's 'noise like the world cracking,'" *Canadian Literature* 186 (2005): 64.
5. Mark Kingwell, *The World We Want* (Toronto: Penguin, 2000), 2.
6. Quigley, "Picking the Deadlock of Legitimacy," 65.
7. Saskia Sassen, *The Global City: New York, London, Tokyo*, 2nd ed. (Princeton: Princeton UP, 2001), 87.
8. Aihwa Ong, "Flexible Citizenship among Chinese Cosmopolitans," *Cosmopolitics: Thinking and Feeling Beyond the Nation*, ed. Pheng Cheah and Bruce Robbins (Minneapolis: U of Minnesota P, 1998), 136.
9. Saskia Sassen, "The Repositioning of Citizenship: Emergent Subjects and Spaces for Politics," *Empire's New Clothes: Reading Hardt and Negri*, ed. Jodi Dean and Paul Passavant (New York: Routledge, 2004), 175–98.
10. Pico Iyer, *The Global Soul: Jet-Lag, Shopping Malls and the Search for Home* (London: Bloomsbury, 2000), 121.
11. Jason McBride and Alana Wilcox, eds., *uTOpia: Towards a New Toronto* (Toronto: Coach House, 2005), 11.
12. Dionne Brand, *In Another Place, Not Here* (Toronto: Vintage, 1996), 49, 70. Similarly, in *thirsty*, Brand suggests that "a city is all interpolation" (Toronto: McClelland and Stewart, 2002), 37. It is created, in this sense, by being read, by being imagined and then retold by the viewer with details added to it. This provocative phrase in *thirsty* suggests the power that drifting appraisals of space might have.
13. Brand, *In Another Place, Not Here*, 110.
14. Brand, *In Another Place, Not Here*, 42–43.
15. Dionne Brand, *No Language Is Neutral* (Toronto: McClelland and Stewart, 1990), 31.
16. Dionne Brand, *A Map to the Door of No Return* (Toronto: Vintage, 2001), 85.
17. Butling, "Dionne Brand on Struggle and Community, Possibility and Poetry," 84.
18. Many critics have searched for belonging in Brand's writing. Heather Smyth seizes on questions of "who belongs and who does not" in her analysis of *In Another Place, Not Here*, looking for ways of achieving the "full cultural citizenship of Caribbean lesbians in Canada and the Caribbean," in "Sexual Citizenship and Caribbean-Canadian Fiction: Dionne Brand's 'In Another Place, Not Here' and Shani Mootoo's 'Cereus Blooms at Night,'" *Ariel* 30.2 (1999): 143–44. Smyth is aware of ways in which belonging is always deferred in the novel, but she searches for a utopian space that Brand seems less interested in finding. Bina Toledo

Freiwald similarly focuses on issues of the home and finding places of "be/longing" in "Cartographies of Be/longing," 37–53.
19 Joanne Saul, "'In the Middle of Becoming': Dionne Brand's Historical Vision," *Canadian Woman Studies / Cahiers de la femme* 23.2 (2004): 60.
20 Walter Benjamin, *The Arcades Project*, trans. H. Eiland and K. McLaughlin (Cambridge: Harvard UP, 1999), 417.
21 Iyer, *The Global Soul*, 137.
22 Dionne Brand, *What We All Long For* (Toronto: Vintage, 2005), 9.
23 Brand, *What We All Long For*, 63.
24 Brand, *What We All Long For*, 113.
25 Brand, *What We All Long For*, 66.
26 Brand, *What We All Long For*, 187, 86, 190.
27 Brand, *What We All Long For*, 95.
28 Brand, *What We All Long For*, 98.
29 Brand, *What We All Long For*, 183.
30 Brand, *What We All Long For*, 99.
31 Dionne Brand, *Bread Out of Stone* (Toronto: Vintage, 1994), 142.
32 Brand, *What We All Long For*, 1, 2, 3.
33 Brand, *What We All Long For*, 106.
34 Brand, *What We All Long For*, 4.
35 Brand, *What We All Long For*, 4.
36 Jody Mason pointed out a parallel line in Brand's *thirsty*, in which the narrator speaks of a longing for "a waiting peace, for life, for just halting" (Toronto: McClelland and Stewart, 2002), 22. While movement remains an asset for Brand's protagonists in *What We All Long For*, it is important to note the ways in which it is a motion that they largely control and elect, not one that derives from enforced migrations or otherwise. While the politics of motion are key in this narrative, readers might observe a contrasting pattern in, for example, Indigenous writing, in which motion—for example Tommy Kelasket's in *Slash*, as discussed in Chapter Eight—is threatening rather than liberating. That said, the notion of Indigenous community in *Slash* and elsewhere suggests a concept of subjectivity and alliance-making that remains flexible and open to differences, providing common ground with Brand's thinking.
37 Brand, *A Map to the Door of No Return*, 49.
38 Brand, *What We All Long For*, 19.
39 Brand, *What We All Long For*, 47.
40 Brand, *What We All Long For*, 173.
41 Brand, *What We All Long For*, 47, 48.
42 Brand, *What We All Long For*, 16.
43 Brand, *What We All Long For*, 67, 125.
44 Brand, *What We All Long For*, 47.
45 Brand, *What We All Long For*, 20.
46 Brand, *What We All Long For*, 20.
47 Brand, *What We All Long For*, 129.
48 Brand, *What We All Long For*, 65, 120.
49 Brand, *What We All Long For*, 130.
50 Brand, *What We All Long For*, 149.
51 Brand, *What We All Long For*, 155.

52 Brand, *What We All Long For*, 17.
53 Brand, *What We All Long For*, 126.
54 Brand, *What We All Long For*, 158.
55 As such, Jamal's experiences parallel Brand's description of her visit to Mimico in *A Map to the Door of No Return*, 107 and following.
56 Brand, *What We All Long For*, 28.
57 Brand, *What We All Long For*, 106.
58 Brand, *What We All Long For*, 32.
59 Brand, *What We All Long For*, 29.
60 Brand, *What We All Long For*, 35.
61 Brand, *What We All Long For*, 41.
62 Brand, *What We All Long For*, 52.
63 Brand, *What We All Long For*, 46.
64 Brand, *What We All Long For*, 88.
65 Brand, *What We All Long For*, 45.
66 Brand, *What We All Long For*, 175.
67 Brand, *What We All Long For*, 165, 166.
68 Brand, *What We All Long For*, 132.
69 Brand, *What We All Long For*, 266.
70 Brand, *What We All Long For*, 45.
71 Brand, *What We All Long For*, 99.
72 Brand, *What We All Long For*, 101.
73 Brand, *What We All Long For*, 203.
74 Brand, *What We All Long For*, 206.
75 Brand, *What We All Long For*, 212, 213.
76 Brand, *What We All Long For*, 105.

CONCLUSION TO PART THREE

Literature in Canada is and has been intensely interested in issues of belonging and subjectivity alongside questions of racialization and ethnicity. In some instances, difference arguably has been deployed in order to buttress the nation and has at times implicitly demonstrated the seeming virtue of (ongoing) European colonization in creating a space for multicultural difference. These issues underlie the arguments that have been taking place about Vincent Lam's *Bloodletting and Miraculous Cures*, and the book itself displays an acceptance of the cosmopolitan mores that may play a role in allowing this reification to take place. But difference is not necessarily deployed in such a manner. In the work of Roy Miki and Dionne Brand, difference functions as a marker of the nation's reinscription of bodies within limited borders. Thinking about Canada and the transnational simultaneously, their works push readers to consider a world of global flows in which bodies variously resist and are circumscribed by regimes of dominance and commodification, the nation prominent among these regimes. At this point, it is possible to begin to talk about transnational Canadas.

CONCLUSION

Transnational Canadas

The flows of transnational life confront writers in Canada at any number of levels, from the material level of dealing with the publishing industry to the intricacies of composing cultural works in a globalizing milieu. Vancouver-based poet and critic Jeff Derksen evokes some of these challenges in the poem "Jerk" from *Transnational Muscle Cars*:

> I want to see
> the real relations
> but you've got Nikes on and I like you
> so I have to try and understand. And if
> that shirt's from The Gap, then one arm was sewn
> in Malaysia, the other in Sri Lanka. Why then
> is it hard to "see" ideology when you're
> wearing it? Is it "out there"? Or deeper inside
> than even desire could get?[1]

The speaker demonstrates confusion at liking a person but simultaneously disdaining the statement that her or his clothing makes, given its sweatshop manufacture. People are "sewn" into global capitalism in every way (much like Ondaatje's characters' relationship to history). The speaker of Derksen's poem goes on to recognize that the ideologies of capital are pervasive in society, penetrating to the level of consciousness and branding all spaces, from the urban to the rugged and rural: even "the mountain," the speaker notes, "is named / after a commodity."[2] Derksen is very much concerned with the various "scales" of capitalism. Projects of articulating what it might mean to write in Canada today have become plural in this environment—hence *Transnational Canadas*. From nationalism to multiculturalism to articulating shifting senses of subjectivity and the self in the contemporary world, cultural work takes on a diversity of tactics in an environment saturated by capital. Arundhati Roy, in her well-known speech from the World Social Forum in Porto Alegre, Brazil, suggests that responses to Empire need to operate through such a diversity. "Our strategy," she writes, speaking of the political left,

> should be not only to confront empire, but to lay siege to it. To deprive it of oxygen. To shame it. To mock it. With our art, our music, our literature, our stubbornness, our joy, our brilliance, our sheer relentlessness—and our ability to tell our own stories. Stories that are different from the one we're being brainwashed to believe. The corporate revolution will collapse if we refuse to buy what they are selling—their ideas, their version of history, their wars, their weapons, their notion of inevitability.[3]

Central among her ideas is that art, literature, and storytelling might allow the multitudes of people in the world to seize the means of representation in order to shift the discursive terrain and create an alternative future, one in which global capitalism is not an inevitable outcome for all people.

Telling alternative stories, however, is complex because this process can be easily subsumed to the marketplace that surrounds and penetrates everyone's lives, as Derksen's "Jerk" reminds its readers. Spivak maintains that the subaltern, as soon as her speech is heard, becomes implicated in the structures of domination. At an individual level, this is a desirable effect, one that empowers. At the same time, writings that get classified as multicultural, composed by previously subaltern voices, are also appropriated to dominant structures in Canada and used at times in order to illustrate the benevolence of the nation-state in tolerating a diversity of voices. Whether it is able to recognize all voices will suggest the limits of this discourse, and patterns of inclusion and exclusion are very revealing as a result. This very useful display of tolerance is also a display of the inclusivity of the marketplace, of capital's construction of subjects to participate in the circulation of goods and commodities. *Transnational Canadas* hopes to upset any lingering romanticism that readers have about texts by making this argument. Books are cultural commodities that participate in the logic of capital. Their literary contents may resist processes of appropriation in a variety of ways—this book has argued that *Slash* continues to offer a strong example of resistance from an Indigenous-centred perspective and that *Surrender* and *What We All Long For* query subjectivity as a means of recognizing and undoing processes of reterritorialization under Empire—but the market in which texts circulate remains. There is no need to lament the fact, but there is still a tendency to privilege cultural products as being "outside" the market. Instead, books participate in it, and, at a textual level, the freedoms that individual characters search out, by being subsumed to national discourses, can be used to sustain the state as well as capitalism.

In Canadian literature, texts marked by difference are becoming a major part of national discourse. In Spivakian terms, this is probably a good thing, although it is also ambivalent. Some of these texts are, indeed, postnational in the sense that Davey argued, but they might still be recuperated by the nation. Texts that seek to avoid such appropriations seem to be effective when they maintain their mobility, when they link themselves to texts, values, and ideals that create literary communities that push against readers' assumptions. This can be a process of finding sustained notions of flexibility that might be analogous to Hardt and Negri's multitude, but the diversity of struggles in Derksen's poem, for example, suggests a less optimistic world. Such skeptical understandings of the world alongside a notion of flexibility can be important also to Indigenous writers who resist colonization such as Jeannette Armstrong. Seeking to avoid being rendered into the white cultural imaginary as a static and primitive people, writers such as Armstrong and Métis poet Gregory Scofield focus upon the need to evade being defined by the state. Scofield, in his work, does so in order to retain a flexible sense of Indigenous selfhood that can shift in order to reflect so-called traditional knowledges in the present and future. The need to portray queer Indigenous life in a contemporary world that is also rooted in traditional ways of living animates Scofield's *Love Medicine and One Song* and other books. This is not only an act of making space for another category of difference within

Canadian discourse, but also one of finding flexibility in order to evade such containment. He queries how such a contemporary Indigenous self might be expressed in his poem "Mixed Breed Act," from the 1996 book *Native Canadiana*:

> How do I act I act without an Indian act
> Fact is I'm so exact about the facts
> I act up when I get told I don't count
> Because my act's not written
>
> So I don't get told who I am or where to go
> If I want to hang solo with my tribe
> Check out other rezless Indians
> No DIA director can pop me on a bus
>
> Send me home homeless as I am
> I'm exact about my rights.[4]

The poem expresses anger at the government's failure to recognize Métis rights, rendering the speaker homeless, but it also suggests that this failure leaves room to create the self and to move in the world. The poem continues to express this sentiment in stating "Truth is my treaty number's not listed / So I don't get obscene phone calls / From politicians breathing heavy in my ear."[5] Evading the politicians allows for the flexibility necessary to determine the self and to create community with "other rezless Indians." This spirit of rezless/restless and resistant flexibility animates the writing of writers who position themselves in a complex relationship with the nation-state, its funding bodies, and its literary marketplace, all of which entail compromise and negotiation.[6]

This ambivalence and compromise is visible in writers' self-conscious assessments of writing in the globalizing world. In 2000, the poet Di Brandt was able to write effusively about the survival of CanLit through the 1990s, despite predictions of its death at the hands of the Free Trade Agreement with the United States and NAFTA, as well as the processes of market liberalization under global capitalism. Brandt argues that the '90s inaugurated the "greatest flowering, the coming of age, the very golden age of Canadian literature, both at home and abroad."[7] Canadian literature has been successfully exported as a cultural commodity in this period, while consolidating its market share within the nation-state. The downside to this flowering, Brandt states, is "commercialism," but this, she suggests, is the price that is to be paid in the contemporary world.[8] It is useful to think about this point: Brandt's acceptance of global capitalism is unromantic (while she is being laudatory and romantic about CanLit itself), and her means of assessing the success of CanLit is based upon market indicators rather than political or literary worth. While questions of aesthetics have not been foregrounded in *Transnational Canadas*, the political valence of writing is important for this book's analysis and is seen, as a result, as being a more important marker for textual importance. At the same time, Brandt seems to be right in her assessment, and the consequence of this commercial success may be a voiding of the political. By always already existing within a literary marketplace, Canadian literature is implicated in its processes even when it challenges them. Writing that makes productive use of this tension, like Derksen's, pushes literature to consider itself and its role as a cultural commodity that works to create a different world, but is also asked to do the work of capital.

Transnational Canadas has been interested in how literary writing has become both a part of the construct of the nation and a commodity for exchange in a time when international trade agreements have become interested in including culture within their scope. As Derksen reminds readers, a politics of purity is not only unlikely; it is, rather, likely to separate people from one another, from those who might be important allies, colleagues, and friends. Pursuing such a politics of purity, of belief in culture as a space outside of capital, is a romantic ideal that privileges art without recognizing the myriad struggles of writers and creators of cultural content. Language retains transformative potential, just as it did a decade or more ago when the postcolonial was celebrated for the liberatory potential of hybridity and cultural politics were seen as being immanent in texts, which, at that time, had no outside to them. As much, then, as language delights, and in so doing sells products, it also continues to instruct, to use the old Horatian paradigm, or else works to reformulate the terrain of official discourse through dialogism, to be more Bakhtinian. Global capital poses a series of questions for literary writing, ones that also abut with the forces of the nation. The answers that have been offered show how, to a large extent, engaging in literary work that challenges the values of global capital also implicates such work in its structures. Writing that stays sharp, on its toes, or electrically in motion, as

CONCLUSION

Carla does in *What We All Long For*, challenges the thought processes and imaginative worlds that are available in today's multiply thought and lived Canadas.

There remain substantial incoherences in today's world and its state of ongoing warfare—Marx's internal contradictions?—which allow for critical reworkings of how politics take place. The shifts in Canadian writing in English since the centennial period show those politics in action. Literature in Canada has changed since the period of cultural nationalism that produced—and was produced by—writers such as Atwood and Lee. This book has argued that the rise of globalization as a dominant structure of feeling has pushed writers to look towards transnational flows. Doing so has not meant that localities have been eschewed, but rather that the subjective project of mapping oneself into the world requires a search beyond the borders of Canada or of individuals' already-known communities. This movement into the transnational is not, either, to capitulate to global capital by rejecting the nation. The nation/globe dichotomy, this book has argued, is a false one. It relies upon a static, European model of nationhood in most instances, one that is used in contrast to the perceived anarchism of the global. *Transnational Canadas* counters that nation-states such as Canada have become active participants in the neo-liberal processes of market restructuring that characterize economic globalization, and should not, therefore, be seen as bastions against such globality.

Towards this end, this book has examined the field of transnationalism alongside its Canadian texts, looking for a genealogy that traces through Marxist, poststructural, Indigenous, and postcolonial studies. These lenses have been useful for examining writers from Leonard Cohen to Dionne Brand, and they allow for reading shifts in Canadian literature from cultural nationalism through the culture wars and identity politics up to the present day. Changes in writing are influenced by the changes in thinking in this country, but are also related to shifting concepts of the self and other in Western, postcolonial, and Indigenous thought, looking towards ways that alternative models of belonging might be conceived. As the processes of global capital move inwards, colonizing new reaches of the body, and outwards, threatening an environmental apocalypse that might do the planet in before too long, thinking about subjectivity and the processes that govern people as subjects seems key. Writers discussed throughout *Transnational Canadas* have offered different ways in which the body might retain its ability to express its politics and alliances, be it through expressing a national affinity or through maintaining a sense of movement. Such shifting expressions of possibility in English Canadian writing should be witnessed and considered in light of the global era as literature moves into ever-more interrogative and self-aware negotiations with the market within which it is now situated.

Notes to Conclusion

1 Jeff Derksen, "Jerk," *Transnational Muscle Cars* (Vancouver: Talonbooks, 2003), 10.
2 Derksen, "Jerk," 10.
3 Arundhati Roy, "Confronting Empire," World Social Forum, Porto Alegre, Brazil, January 27, 2003.
4 Gregory Scofield, "Mixed Breed Act," *Native Canadiana: Songs from the Urban Rez* (Victoria: Polestar, 1996), 56.
5 Scofield, "Mixed Breed Act," 56.
6 Scofield's *Native Canadiana*, for instance, is published by Polestar, which receives Canada Council and other funding—a fact that should surprise no one, as government funding is an important part of doing business in the Canadian publishing industry. In this case, such funding means that resistance to one branch of the government—the Department of Indian Affairs—is funded by another.
7 Di Brandt, "Going Global," *Essays on Canadian Writing* 71 (2000): 106.
8 Brandt, "Going Global," 107.

BIBLIOGRAPHY

Adams, Howard. *Prison of Grass: Canada from a Native Point of View*. Rev. ed. Saskatoon: Fifth House, 1989.

Agamben, Giorgio. *Homo Sacer: Sovereign Power and Bare Life*. Trans. D. Heller-Roazen. Stanford: Stanford UP, 1998.

Ahmad, Aijaz. *In Theory: Classes, Nations, Literatures*. London: Verso, 1992.

Alfred, Taiaiake. *Peace, Power, Righteousness: An Indigenous Manifesto*. Don Mills, ON: Oxford UP, 1999.

Anderson, Benedict. *Imagined Communities: Reflections on the Origin and Spread of Nationalism*. Rev. ed. London: Verso, 1991.

Appiah, Kwame Anthony. *Cosmopolitanism: Ethics in a World of Strangers*. New York: Norton, 2006.

Arendt, Hannah. *Eichmann in Jerusalem: A Report on the Banality of Evil*. New York: Viking, 1964.

Armstrong, Jeannette. "Land Speaking." *Speaking for the Generations: Native Writers on Writing*. Ed. Simon J. Ortiz. Tucson: U of Arizona P, 1998. 174–94.

———. *Slash*. Penticton, BC: Theytus, 1985.

Atwood, Margaret. *The Handmaid's Tale*. Toronto: McClelland and Stewart, 1985.

———. *Oryx and Crake*. Toronto: McClelland and Stewart, 2003.

———. *Surfacing*. Toronto: McClelland and Stewart, 1972.

———. *Survival: A Thematic Guide to Canadian Literature*. Toronto: Anansi, 1972.

Balakrishnan, Gopal, ed. *Debating Empire*. London: Verso, 2003.

Bannerji, Himani. *The Dark Side of the Nation: Essays on Multiculturalism, Nationalism and Gender*. Toronto: Canadian Scholars' P, 2000.

Barbour, Douglas. "Down with History: Some Notes Towards an Understanding of *Beautiful Losers*." *Open Letter*, Second Series 8 (1974): 48–60.

Beauregard, Guy. "After *Obasan*: Kogawa Criticism and Its Futures." *Studies in Canadian Literature* 26.2 (2001): 5–22.

Beddoes, Julia. "Which Side Is It On? Form, Class, and Politics in *In the Skin of a Lion*." *Essays on Canadian Writing* 53 (1994): 204–15.

Beedham, Matthew. "*Obasan* and Hybridity: Necessary Cultural Strategies." *The Immigrant Experience in North American Literature: Carving Out a Niche*. Ed. K. Payant and T. Rose. Westport: Greenwood, 1999. 139–49.

Benjamin, Walter. *The Arcades Project*. Trans. H. Eiland and K. McLaughlin. Cambridge: Harvard UP, 1999.

Bennett, Donna. "English Canada's Postcolonial Complexities." *Essays on Canadian Writing* 51–52 (1993–94): 164–210.

Blodgett, E.D. "Reflections on the Prose of Dennis Lee." *Tasks of Passion: Dennis Lee at Mid-Career*. Ed. Karen Mulhallen et al. Toronto: Descant Editions, 1982. 103–17.

Bök, Christian. "The Secular Opiate: Marxism as an Ersatz Religion in Three Canadian Texts." *Canadian Literature* 147 (1995): 11–22.

Boron, Atilio A. *Empire and Imperialism: A Critical Reading of Michael Hardt and Antonio Negri*. Trans. Jessica Casiro. London: Zed, 2005.

Bradley, Nicholas. "'Green of the Earth and Civil Grey': Nature and the City in Dennis Lee's *Civil Elegies*." *Canadian Poetry* 55 (2004): 15–33.

Brand, Dionne. *Bread Out of Stone: Recollections on Sex, Recognitions, Race, Dreaming and Politics*. Toronto: Vintage, 1994.

———. *In Another Place, Not Here*. Toronto: Vintage, 1996.

———. *A Map to the Door of No Return*. Toronto: Vintage, 2001.

———. *No Language Is Neutral*. Toronto: McClelland and Stewart, 1990.

———. *thirsty*. Toronto: McClelland and Stewart, 2002.

———. *What We All Long For*. Toronto: Knopf, 2005.

Brandt, Di. "Going Global." *Essays on Canadian Writing* 71 (2000): 106–13.

Brennan, Timothy. "Cosmo-Theory." *The South Atlantic Quarterly* 100.3 (2001): 659–91.

———. "The Empire's New Clothes." *Critical Inquiry* 29.2 (2003): 337–67.

———. "The Italian Ideology." *Debating Empire*. Ed. G. Balakrishnan. London: Verso, 2003. 97–120.

———. "The Magician's Wand: A Rejoinder to Hardt and Negri." *Critical Inquiry* 29.2 (2003): 374–78.

Budde, Robert. "After Postcolonialism: Migrant Lines and the Politics of Form in Fred Wah, M. NourbeSe Philip, and Roy Miki." *Is Canada Postcolonial? Unsettling Canadian Literature*. Ed. Laura Moss. Waterloo: Wilfrid Laurier UP, 2003. 282–94.

Bull, Malcolm. "Smooth Politics." *Empire's New Clothes: Reading Hardt and Negri*. Ed. P. Passavant and J. Dean. New York: Routledge, 2004. 217–30.

Butling, Pauline. "Dionne Brand on Struggle and Community, Possibility and Poetry." *Poets Talk: Conversations with Robert Kroetsch, Daphne Marlatt, Erin Mouré, Dionne Brand, Marie Annharte Baker, Jeff Derksen and Fred Wah*. Edmonton: U of Alberta P, 2005. 63–87.

Butling, Pauline, and Susan Rudy. *Writing in Our Time: Canada's Radical Poetries in English (1957–2003)*. Waterloo: Wilfrid Laurier UP, 2005.

Canada, Government of. *Report of the Royal Commission on National Development in the Arts, Letters, and Sciences, 1949–1951*. Ottawa: King's Printer, 1951.

Chariandy, David. *Soucouyant*. Vancouver: Arsenal Pulp, 2007.

Chariandy, David, and Kit Dobson. "Spirits of Elsewhere Past: A Dialogue on *Soucouyant*." *Callaloo* 30.3 (2007): 808–17.

Cheah, Pheng. "Introduction Part II: The Cosmopolitical — Today." *Cosmopolitics: Thinking and Feeling Beyond the Nation*. Ed. Pheng Cheah and Bruce Robbins. Minneapolis: U of Minnesota P, 1998. 20–41.

———. "Spectral Nationality: The Living On [*sur-vie*] of the Postcolonial Nation in Neocolonial Globalization." *Boundary 2* 26.3 (1999): 225–52.

Chow, Rey. *Ethics After Idealism: Theory-Culture-Ethnicity-Reading*. Bloomington: Indiana UP, 1998.

Cohen, Leonard. *Beautiful Losers*. Toronto: McClelland and Stewart, 1966.

———. *The Favourite Game*. Toronto: McClelland and Stewart, 1963.

Coleman, Daniel. *White Civility: The Literary Project of English Canada*. Toronto: U of Toronto P, 2006.

Criglington, Meredith. "The City as a Site of Counter-Memory in Anne Michaels's *Fugitive Pieces* and Michael Ondaatje's *In the Skin of a Lion*." *Essays on Canadian Writing* 81 (2004): 129–53.

Currie, Noel Elizabeth. "Jeannette Armstrong and the Colonial Legacy." *Canadian Literature* 124–125 (1990): 138–52.

Davey, Frank. "*Beautiful Losers*: Leonard Cohen's Postcolonial Novel." *Intricate Preparations: Writing Leonard Cohen*. Ed. Stephen Scobie. Toronto: ECW, 2000. 12–23.

———. "Canadian Canons." *Critical Inquiry* 16.3 (1990): 672–81.

———. *Margaret Atwood: A Feminist Poetics*. Vancouver: Talonbooks, 1984.

———. *Post-national Arguments: The Politics of the Anglophone-Canadian Novel since 1967*. Toronto: U of Toronto P, 1993.

———. *Surviving the Paraphrase: Eleven Essays on Canadian Literature*. Winnipeg: Turnstone, 1983.

Davidson, Arnold. *Writing Against the Silence: Joy Kogawa's Obasan*. Toronto: ECW P, 1993.

Deleuze, Gilles, and Félix Guattari. *A Thousand Plateaus: Capitalism and Schizophrenia*. Trans. B. Massumi. Minneapolis: U of Minnesota P, 1987.

Derksen, Jeff. *Transnational Muscle Cars*. Vancouver: Talonbooks, 2003.

Derrida, Jacques. "Force of Law: The 'Mystical Foundation of Authority.'" *Deconstruction and the Possibility of Justice*. Ed. D. Cornell et al. New York: Routledge, 1992. 3–67.

———. "Marx and Sons." *Ghostly Demarcations: A Symposium on Jacques Derrida's* Specters of Marx. Ed. Michael Sprinker. London: Verso, 1999. 213–69.

———. *The Other Heading: Reflections on Today's Europe*. Trans. P. Brault and M. Naas. Bloomington: Indiana UP, 1992.

———. *Specters of Marx: The State of the Debt, the Work of Mourning, and the New International*. Trans. Peggy Kamuf. New York: Routledge, 1994.

Difalco, Salvatore. Letter to the Editor. *Geist* 64 (2007): 9.

Djwa, Sandra. "'Here I am': Atwood, Paper Houses, and a Parodic Tradition." *Essays on Canadian Writing* 71 (2000): 169–85.

———. "The Where of Here: Margaret Atwood and a Canadian Tradition." *The Art of Margaret Atwood: Essays in Criticism*. Ed. A. Davidson and C. Davidson. Toronto: Anansi, 1981. 15–34.

Dragland, Stan. "On Civil Elegies." *Tasks of Passion: Dennis Lee at Mid-Career*. Ed. Karen Mulhallen et al. Toronto: Descant Editions, 1982. 170–88.

Duffy, Dennis. *Gardens, Covenants, Exiles: Loyalism in the Literature of Upper Canada / Ontario*. Toronto: U of Toronto P, 1982.

Eagleton, Terry. *After Theory*. London: Allen Lane, 2003.

———. *The Illusions of Postmodernism*. Oxford: Blackwell, 1996.

———. *Literary Theory: An Introduction*. Oxford: Blackwell, 1983.

———. "Marxism Without Marxism: Jacques Derrida and *Specters of Marx*." *The Eagleton Reader*. Oxford: Blackwell, 1998. 260–64.

———. *Walter Benjamin, or, Towards a Revolutionary Criticism*. London: NLB, 1981.

Emberley, Julia. *Thresholds of Difference: Feminist Critique, Native Women's Writings, Postcolonial Theory*. Toronto: U of Toronto P, 1993.

Embry, Carlos. *America's Concentration Camps: The Facts about Our Indian Reservations Today*. New York: David McKay, 1956.

Fagan, Kristina. "Tewatatha:wi: Aboriginal Nationalism in Taiaiake Alfred's *Peace, Power, Righteousness: An Indigenous Manifesto*." *American Indian Quarterly* 28.1–2 (2004): 12–29.

Fanon, Frantz. *The Wretched of the Earth*. Trans. C. Farrington. New York: Grove, 1963.

Fee, Margery. "Upsetting Fake Ideas: Jeannette Armstrong's 'Slash' and Beatrice Culleton's 'April Raintree.'" *Canadian Literature* 124–125 (1990): 168–80.

Fiamengo, Janice. "Postcolonial Guilt in Margaret Atwood's *Surfacing*." *American Review of Canadian Studies* 29 (1999): 141–63.

Findlay, Len. "Always Indigenize! The Radical Humanities in the Postcolonial Canadian University." *Ariel: A Review of International English Literature* 31.1–2 (2000): 307–26.

Freeman, Carla. "Is Local : Global as Feminine : Masculine? Rethinking the Gender of Globalization." *Signs* 26.4 (2001): 1007–37.

Freiwald, Bina Toledo. "Cartographies of Be/longing: Dionne Brand's *In Another Place, Not Here*." *Mapping Canadian Cultural Space: Essays on Canadian Literature*. Ed. Danielle Schaub. Jerusalem: Hebrew U Magnes P, 2000. 37–53.

Frye, Northrop. *The Bush Garden: Essays on the Canadian Imagination*. 2nd ed. Concord, ON: Anansi, 1995.

———. Conclusion to *Literary History of Canada: Canadian Literature in English*. Ed. Carl F. Klinck. Toronto: U of Toronto P, 1965. 821–49.

Fuller, Danielle, and DeNel Rehberg Sedo. "A Reading Spectacle for the Nation: The CBC and 'Canada Reads.'" *Journal of Canadian Studies* 40.1 (2006): 5–36.

Gilbert, Jeremy. "Against the Empire: Thinking the Social and (Dis)Locating Agency 'Before, Across and Beyond Any National Determination.'" *Parallax* 7.3 (2001): 96–113.

Goldie, Terry. *Pink Snow: Homotextual Possibilities in Canadian Fiction*. Peterborough, ON: Broadview, 2003.

Goldman, Marlene. "Mapping the Door of No Return: Deterritorialization and the Work of Dionne Brand." *Canadian Literature* 182 (2004): 13–28.

Gramsci, Antonio. *Selections from the Prison Notebooks*. Ed. and Trans. Q. Hoare and G. Smith. London: Lawrence and Wishart, 1971.

Grant, George. "Canadian Fate and Imperialism." *Technology and Empire: Perspectives on North America*. Toronto: Anansi, 1969. 63–78.

———. *Lament for a Nation: The Defeat of Canadian Nationalism*. Toronto: McClelland and Stewart, 1965.

Green, Matthew. "A Hard Day's Knight: A Discursive Analysis of Jeannette Armstrong's *Slash*." *The Canadian Journal of Native Studies* 19.1 (1999): 51–67.

Guédon, Marie-Françoise. "*Surfacing*: Amerindian Themes and Shamanism." *Margaret Atwood: Language, Text, and System*. Ed. S. Grace and L. Weir. Vancouver: U of British Columbia P, 1983. 91–111.

Guha, Ranajit. "On Some Aspects of the Historiography of Colonial India." *Selected Subaltern Studies*. Ed. R. Guha and G. Spivak. New York: Oxford UP, 1988. 37–44.

———. Preface to *Selected Subaltern Studies*. Ed. R. Guha and G. Spivak. New York: Oxford UP, 1988. 35–36.

Hall, Stuart. "Subjects in History: Making Diasporic Identities." *The House That Race Built*. Ed. W. Lubiano. New York: Vintage, 1997. 289–99.

Hardt, Michael, and Thomas Dumm. "Sovereignty, Multitudes, Absolute Democracy: A Discussion between Michael Hardt and Thomas L. Dumm about Hardt and Negri's *Empire*." *Empire's New Clothes: Reading Hardt and Negri*. Ed. P. Passavant and J. Dean. New York: Routledge, 2004. 163–73.

Hardt, Michael, and Antonio Negri. *Empire*. Cambridge: Harvard UP, 2000.

———. *Labor of Dionysus: A Critique of the State-Form*. Minneapolis: U of Minnesota P, 1994.

———. *Multitude: War and Democracy in the Age of Empire*. New York: Penguin, 2004.

———. "The Rod of the Forest Warden: A Response to Timothy Brennan." *Critical Inquiry* 29.2 (2003): 368–73.

Harrison, James. "The 20,000,000 Solitudes of *Surfacing*." *Dalhousie Review* 59 (1979): 74–81.

Helms, Gabriele. *Challenging Canada: Dialogism and Narrative Techniques in Canadian Novels*. Montreal and Kingston: McGill-Queen's UP, 2003.

Henighan, Stephen. "Kingmakers." *Geist* 63 (2006): 61–62.

———. "Stephen Henighan Replies." *Geist* 64 (2007): 9–10.

———. *When Words Deny the World: The Reshaping of Canadian Writing*. Erin, ON: Porcupine's Quill, 2002.

———. "Witch Hunt." *Geist* 66 (2007): 74–75.

Henry, Michelle. "Canonizing Craig Womack: Finding Native Literature's Place in Indian Country." *American Indian Quarterly* 28.1–2 (2004): 30–51.

Highway, Tomson. *Kiss of the Fur Queen*. Toronto: Doubleday, 1998.

Hobsbawn, Eric. *Nations and Nationalism since 1780: Programme, Myth, Reality*. 2nd ed. Cambridge: Cambridge UP, 1992.

Hodne, Barbara, and Helen Hoy. "Reading from the Inside Out: Jeannette Armstrong's *Slash*." *World Literature Written in English* 32.1 (1992): 66–87.

Huggan, Graham. *The Postcolonial Exotic: Marketing the Margins*. London: Routledge, 2001.

Hutcheon, Linda. "*Beautiful Losers*: All the Polarities." *Canadian Literature* 59 (1974): 42–56.

———. *The Canadian Postmodern: A Study of Contemporary English-Canadian Fiction*. Toronto: Oxford UP, 1988.

———. *Narcissistic Narrative: The Metafictional Paradox*. Waterloo: Wilfrid Laurier UP, 1980.

———. *A Poetics of Postmodernism: History, Theory, Fiction*. New York: Routledge, 1988.

———. *The Politics of Postmodernism*. 2nd ed. London: Routledge, 2002.

Isernhagen, Hartwig. *Momaday, Vizenor, Armstrong: Conversations on American Indian Writing*. Norman: U of Oklahoma P, 1999.

Iyer, Pico. *The Global Soul: Jet-Lag, Shopping Malls and the Search for Home*. London: Bloomsbury, 2000.

Jameson, Fredric. "Marx's Purloined Letter." *New Left Review* 209 (1995): 75–109.

———. *The Political Unconscious: Narrative as a Socially Symbolic Act.* Ithaca, NY: Cornell UP, 1981.

———. *Postmodernism, Or, The Cultural Logic of Late Capitalism.* Durham, NC: Duke UP, 1991.

———. *A Singular Modernity: Essay on the Ontology of the Present.* London: Verso, 2002.

Jani, Pranav. "Karl Marx, Eurocentrism, and the 1857 Revolt in British India." *Marxism, Modernity and Postcolonial Studies.* Ed. C. Bartolovich and N. Lazarus. Cambridge: Cambridge UP, 2002. 81–97.

Jones, D.G. *Butterfly on Rock: A Study of Themes and Images in Canadian Literature.* Toronto: U of Toronto P, 1970.

Jones, Manina. "Slash Marks the Spot: 'Critical Embarrassment' and Activist Aesthetics in Jeannette Armstrong's *Slash*." *West Coast Line* 33.3 (2000): 48–62.

Kamboureli, Smaro. *Scandalous Bodies: Diasporic Literature in English Canada.* Don Mills, ON: Oxford UP, 2000.

Kant, Immanuel. *Kant: Political Writings.* 2nd ed. Cambridge: Cambridge UP, 1991.

Kaplan, Caren, and Inderpal Grewal. "Transnational Feminist Cultural Studies: Beyond the Marxism/Poststructuralism/Feminism Divides." *Between Woman and Nation: Nationalisms, Transnational Feminisms, and the State.* Ed. C. Kaplan et al. Durham, NC: Duke UP, 1999. 349–63.

Kertzer, Jonathan. *Worrying the Nation: Imagining a National Literature in English Canada.* Toronto: U of Toronto P, 1998.

King, Thomas. "Godzilla vs. Postcolonial." *Unhomely States: Theorizing English-Canadian Postcolonialism.* Ed. Cynthia Sugars. Peterborough, ON: Broadview, 2004. 183–90.

———. *The Truth about Stories: A Native Narrative.* Toronto: Anansi, 2003.

Kingwell, Mark. *The World We Want.* Toronto: Penguin, 2000.

Klooß, Wolfgang. "From Colonial Madness to Postcolonial Ex Centricity: A Story about Stories of Identity Construction in Canadian Historiographic (Meta-) Fiction." *Historiographic Metafiction in Modern American and Canadian Literature.* Ed. Bernd Engler and Kurt Müller. Paderborn, Germany: Ferdinand Schöningh, 1994. 53–79.

Kogawa, Joy. *Emily Kato.* Toronto: Penguin, 2005.

———. *Itsuka.* Toronto: Viking, 1992.

———. *Obasan.* Toronto: Penguin, 1981.

Kroetsch, Robert. "On Being an Alberta Writer." *Open Letter* Fifth Series 4 (1983): 69–80.

Kymlicka, Will. *Multicultural Citizenship: A Liberal Theory of Minority Rights.* Oxford: Clarendon, 1995.
Laclau, Ernesto. "'The Time is Out of Joint.'" *Diacritics* 25.2 (1995): 86–96.
Laing, R.D. *The Divided Self.* New York: Pantheon, 1969.
Lam, Vincent. *Bloodletting and Miraculous Cures.* Toronto: Doubleday Canada, 2005.
Larsen, Neil. "Marxism, Postcolonialism, and *the Eighteenth Brumaire.*" *Marxism, Modernity and Postcolonial Studies.* Ed. C. Bartolovich and N. Lazarus. Cambridge: Cambridge UP, 2002. 204–20.
Lawrence, Bonita. *"Real" Indians and Others: Mixed-Blooded Urban Native Peoples and Indigenous Nationhood.* Vancouver: UBC P, 2004.
Leahy, David. "Re-Reading Linda Hutcheon on *Beautiful Losers, Prochain épisode* and *Trou de mémoire.*" *Studies in Canadian Literature* 18.2 (1993): 27–42.
Lecker, Robert. *The Cadence of* Civil Elegies. Toronto: Cormorant, 2006.
———. "The Canonization of Canadian Literature: An Inquiry into Value." *Critical Inquiry* 16.3 (199): 656–71.
———. *Making It Real: The Canonization of English-Canadian Literature.* Toronto: Anansi, 1995.
———. "Response to Frank Davey." *Critical Inquiry* 16.3 (1990): 682–89.
Lee, Dennis. "Cadence, Country, Silence: Writing in Colonial Space." *Boundary 2* 3.1 (1974): 151–68.
———. *Civil Elegies and Other Poems.* Don Mills, ON: Anansi, 1972.
———. "Grant's Impasse: Beholdenness and the Silence of Reason." *Body Music.* Toronto: Anansi, 1998. 129–59.
———. *Kingdom of Absence.* Toronto: Anansi, 1967.
———. *Savage Fields: An Essay in Literature and Cosmology.* Toronto: Anansi, 1977.
Lee, SKY. *Disappearing Moon Café.* Vancouver: Douglas and McIntyre, 1990.
Lesk, Andrew. "Leonard Cohen's Traffic in Alterity in *Beautiful Losers.*" *Studies in Canadian Literature* 22.2 (1997): 56–65.
Lorimer, Rowland. Letter to the Editor. *Geist* 65 (2007): 8–9.
Lowry, Glen. "The Representation of 'Race' in Ondaatje's *In the Skin of a Lion.*" *CLCWeb: Comparative Literature and Culture* 6.3 (2004). http://clcwebjournal.lib.purdue.edu/clcweb04-3/lowry04.html.
Lundgren, Jodi. "'Colour Disrobed Itself from the Body': The Racialized Aesthetics of Liberation in Michael Ondaatje's *In the Skin of a Lion.*" *Canadian Literature* 190 (2006): 15–29.
Lunson, Lian, dir. *Leonard Cohen: I'm Your Man.* Con Artists Productions, 2005.
MacDonald, R.D. "Lee's 'Civil Elegies' in Relation to Grant's 'Lament for a Nation.'" *Canadian Literature* 98 (1983): 10–30.

Mackey, Eva. *The House of Difference: Cultural Politics and National Identity in Canada*. Toronto: U of Toronto P, 2002.

Macri, F.M. "*Beautiful Losers* and the Canadian Experience." *Journal of Commonwealth Literature* 8.1 (1973): 88–96.

MacSkimming, Roy. *The Perilous Trade: Book Publishing in Canada 1946–2006*. Toronto: McClelland and Stewart, 2007.

Mani, Lata. *Contentious Traditions: The Debate on Sati in Colonial India*. Berkeley: U of California P, 1998.

Maracle, Lee. *I Am Woman: A Native Perspective on Sociology and Feminism*. Vancouver: Press Gang, 1996.

Marx, Karl. *Capital*. Vol. 1. Trans. B. Fowkes. London: Penguin, 1976.

———. *Capital*. Vol. 3. Trans. D. Fernbach. London: Penguin, 1981.

———. *A Contribution to the Critique of Political Economy*. Trans. S. Ryazanskaya. New York: International, 1970.

———. "The Eighteenth Brumaire of Louis Napoleon." *Later Political Writings*. Ed. and Trans. T. Carver. Cambridge: Cambridge UP, 1996. 31–127.

———. *The German Ideology*. Amherst, MA: Prometheus, 1998.

———. *Surveys from Exile*. Ed. D. Fernbach. London: Pelican, 1973.

Marx, Karl, and Friedrich Engels. *The Communist Manifesto*. London: Penguin, 1967.

———. *Selected Correspondence, 1846–1895: Karl Marx and Friedrich Engels*. Trans. D. Torr. New York: International, 1942.

Mason, Jody. "'The animal Out of the Desert': The Nomadic Metaphysics of Michael Ondaatje's *In the Skin of a Lion*." *Studies in Canadian Literature* 31.2 (2006): 66–87.

Mathur, Ashok. "Abstract." TransCanada One: Literature, Institutions, Citizenship Conference Website. 2005. http://www.transcanadas.ca/transcanada1/mathur.shtml.

———. "Transubracination: How Writers of Colour Became CanLit." *Trans. Can.Lit: Resituating the Study of Canadian Literature*. Ed. Smaro Kamboureli and Roy Miki. Waterloo: Wilfrid Laurier UP, 2007. 141–51.

Maurer, Bill. "On Divine Markets and the Problem of Justice: Empire as Theodicy." *Empire's New Clothes: Reading Hardt and Negri*. Ed. P. Passavant and J. Dean. New York: Routledge, 2004. 57–72.

McBride, Jason, and Alana Wilcox. *uTOpia: Towards a New Toronto*. Toronto: Coach House, 2005.

Miki, Roy. *Broken Entries: Race, Subjectivity, Writing*. Toronto: Mercury, 1998.

———. *Surrender*. Toronto: Mercury, 2001.

Miyoshi, Masao. "'Globalization,' Culture, and the University." *The Cultures of Globalization*. Eds. F. Jameson and M. Miyoshi. Durham, NC: Duke UP, 1998. 247–70.

Mohanty, Chandra Talpade. "'Under Western Eyes' Revisited: Feminist Solidarity through Anticapitalist Struggles." *Feminism without Borders: Decolonizing Theory, Practicing Solidarity*. Durham, NC: Duke UP, 2003. 221–51.
Moodie, Susanna. *Roughing It in the Bush*. 1852. Ed. Michael A. Peterman. New York: Norton, 2007.
Moore, Lisa. Letter to the Editor. *Geist* 64 (2007): 8–9.
Morley, Patricia. *The Immoral Moralists*. Toronto: Clarke, Irwin and Co., 1972.
Moss, Laura. "Canada Reads." *Canadian Literature* 182 (2004): 6–10.
———, ed. *Is Canada Postcolonial? Unsettling Canadian Literature*. Waterloo: Wilfred Laurier UP, 2003.
Mukherjee, Arun. "The Vocabulary of the 'Universal': The Cultural Imperialism of the Universalist Criteria of Western Literary Criticism." *Oppositional Aesthetics: Readings from a Hyphenated Space*. Toronto: TSAR, 1994. 17–29.
Mulvey, Laura. "Visual Pleasure and Narrative Cinema." *Feminism and Film Theory*. Ed. C. Penley. New York: Routledge, 1988. 57–79.
Munton, Ann. "Simultaneity in the Writings of Dennis Lee." *Tasks of Passion: Dennis Lee at Mid-Career*. Ed. Karen Mulhallen et al. Toronto: Descant Editions, 1982. 143–69.
Naranjo, Isaías. "Visions of Heidegger in Dennis Lee and Robert Kroetsch." *University of Toronto Quarterly* 70.4 (2001): 869–80.
Negri, Antonio. *Insurgencies: Constituent Power and the Modern State*. Trans. M. Boscagli. Minneapolis: Minnesota UP, 1999.
Nichol, bp. "A / LAKE / A / LANE / A / LINE / A / LONE." Toronto: bpNichol lane, n.d.
Ondaatje, Michael. *Divisadero*. Toronto: McClelland and Stewart, 2007.
———. *In the Skin of a Lion*. Toronto: Vintage, 1987.
———. *Leonard Cohen*. Toronto: McClelland and Stewart, 1970.
Ong, Aihwa. "Flexible Citizenship among Chinese Cosmopolitans." *Cosmopolitics: Thinking and Feeling Beyond the Nation*. Ed. Pheng Cheah and Bruce Robbins. Minneapolis: U of Minnesota P, 1998. 134–62.
Onley, Gloria. "Margaret Atwood: Surfacing in the Interests of Survival." *West Coast Review* 7.3 (1973): 51–54.
Passavant, Paul. "From Empire's Law to the Multitude's Rights: Law, Representation, Revolution." *Empire's New Clothes: Reading Hardt and Negri*. Ed. P. Passavant and J. Dean. New York: Routledge, 2004. 95–120.
———. "Postmodern Republicanism." *Empire's New Clothes: Reading Hardt and Negri*. Ed. P. Passavant and J. Dean. New York: Routledge, 2004. 1–20.
Passavant, Paul, and Jodi Dean, eds. *Empire's New Clothes: Reading Hardt and Negri*. New York: Routledge, 2004.
Philip, M. NourbeSe. "A Genealogy of Resistance." *A Genealogy of Resistance and Other Essays*. Toronto: Mercury, 1997. 9–30.

Prakash, Gyan. "Postcolonial Criticism and Indian Historiography." *Dangerous Liaisons: Gender, Nation, and Postcolonial Perspectives.* Ed. A. McClintock et al. Minneapolis: Minnesota UP, 1997. 491–500.

Prasad, Madhava. "On the Question of a Theory of (Third) World Literature." *Dangerous Liaisons: Gender, Nation, and Postcolonial Perspectives.* Ed. A. McClintock et al. Minneapolis: Minnesota UP, 1997. 141–62.

Quigley, Ellen. "Picking the Deadlock of Legitimacy: Dionne Brand's 'noise like the world cracking.'" *Canadian Literature* 186 (2005): 48–67.

Quinby, Lee. "Taking the Millennialist Pulse of *Empire*'s Multitude: A Genealogical Feminist Diagnosis." *Empire's New Clothes: Reading Hardt and Negri.* Ed. P. Passavant and J. Dean. New York: Routledge, 2004. 231–51.

Rabinovitch, Elana. Letter to the Editor. *Geist* 64 (2007): 8.

Rae, Ian. *From Cohen to Carson: The Poet's Novel in Canada.* Montreal and Kingston: McGill-Queen's UP, 2008.

Razack, Sherene. *Looking White People in the Eye: Gender, Race, and Culture in Courtrooms and Classrooms.* Toronto: U of Toronto P, 1998.

Redhill, Michael. Letter to the Editor. *Geist* 65 (2007): 9–10.

Richler, Noah. *This Is My Country, What's Yours? A Literary Atlas of Canada.* Toronto: McClelland and Stewart, 2006.

Robbins, Bruce. "Introduction Part I: Actually Existing Cosmopolitanism." *Cosmopolitics: Thinking and Feeling Beyond the Nation.* Ed. Pheng Cheah and Bruce Robbins. Minneapolis: U of Minnesota P, 1998. 1–19.

Rose, Marilyn. "Politics into Art: Kogawa's *Obasan* and the Rhetoric of Fiction." *Mosaic* 21 (1998): 215–26.

Roy, Arundhati. "Confronting Empire." *World Social Forum.* Porto Alegre, Brazil. January 27, 2003. http://www.zmag.org/content/showarticle.cfm?ItemID=2919.

Ryan, Michael. *Marxism and Deconstruction: A Critical Articulation.* Baltimore: Johns Hopkins UP, 1982.

Ryga, George. Forward to *Slash.* By Jeannette Armstrong. Penticton, BC: Theytus, 1985.

Said, Edward. *Orientalism.* New York: Vintage, 1978.

Sarkowsky, Katja. "A Decolonial (Rite of) Passage: Decolonization, Migration and Gender Construction in Jeannette Armstrong's *Slash.*" *Zeitschrift für Anglistik und Amerikanistik* 49.3 (2001): 233–43.

Sassen, Saskia. *The Global City: New York, London, Tokyo.* 2nd ed. Princeton: Princeton UP, 2001.

———. "The Repositioning of Citizenship: Emergent Subjects and Spaces for Politics." *Empire's New Clothes: Reading Hardt and Negri.* Ed. P. Passavant and J. Dean. New York: Routledge, 2004. 175–98.

Saul, Joanne. "'In the Middle of Becoming': Dionne Brand's Historical Vision." *Canadian Woman Studies / Cahiers de la femme* 23.2 (2004): 59–63.

Scobie, Stephen. *Leonard Cohen*. Vancouver: Douglas and McIntyre, 1978.

Scofield, Gregory. *Love Medicine and One Song*. Victoria: Polestar, 1997.

———. *Native Canadiana: Songs from the Urban Rez*. Victoria: Polestar, 1996.

Scott, Jennifer, and Myka Tucker-Abramson. "Banking on a Prize: Multicultural Capitalism and the Canadian Literary Prize Industry." *Studies in Canadian Literature* 31.2 (2007): 5–20.

Shapiro, Kam. "The Myth of the Multitude." *Empire's New Clothes: Reading Hardt and Negri*. Ed. P. Passavant and J. Dean. New York: Routledge, 2004. 289–314.

Siemerling, Winfried. "Oral History and Writing of the Other in Ondaatje's *In the Skin of a Lion*." *CLCWeb: Comparative Literature and Culture* 6.3 (2004). http://clcwebjournal.lib.purdue.edu/clcweb04-3/siemerling.html.

Shetty, Sandhya, and Elizabeth Jane Bellamy. "Postcolonialism's Archive Fever." *Diacritics* 30.1 (2000): 25–48.

Smith, Linda Tuhiwai. *Decolonizing Methodologies: Research and Indigenous Peoples*. London: Zed, 1999.

Smith, Neil. *The Endgame of Globalization*. New York: Routledge, 2005.

Smyth, Heather. "Sexual Citizenship and Caribbean-Canadian Fiction: Dionne Brand's 'In Another Place, Not Here' and Shani Mootoo's 'Cereus Blooms at Night.'" *Ariel* 30.2 (1999): 141–60.

Spinoza, Baruch. "Political Treatise." *Complete Works*. Ed. M. Morgan. Trans. S. Shirley. Indianapolis: Hackett, 2002. 676–754.

Spivak, Gayatri Chakravorty. "Can the Subaltern Speak?" *Marxism and the Interpretation of Culture*. Ed. C. Nelson and L. Grossberg. Urbana: U of Illinois P, 1988. 271–313.

———. *A Critique of Postcolonial Reason*. Cambridge: Harvard UP, 1999.

———. "Diasporas Old and New: Women in the Transnational World." *Textual Practice* 10.2 (1996): 245–69.

———. "Ghostwriting." *Diacritics* 25.2 (1995): 65–84.

———. "Scattered Speculations on the Question of Value." *In Other Worlds: Essays in Cultural Politics*. New York: Routledge, 1988. 154–75.

———. "Subaltern Studies: Deconstructing Historiography." *Selected Subaltern Studies*. Ed. R. Guha and G. Spivak. New York: Oxford UP, 1988. 3–32.

———. "Subaltern Talk: Interview with the Editors." *The Spivak Reader*. Ed. D. Landry and G. MacLean. New York: Routledge, 1996. 287–308.

Sprinker, Michael, ed. *Ghostly Demarcations: A Symposium on Jacques Derrida's Specters of Marx*. London: Verso, 1999.

Stacey, Robert. "A Political Aesthetic: Michael Ondaatje's *In the Skin of a Lion* as 'Covert Pastoral.'" *Contemporary Literature* 49.3 (2008): 439–69.

Szeman, Imre. *Zones of Instability: Literature, Postcolonialism, and the Nation.* Baltimore: Johns Hopkins, 2003.

Taylor, Charles. *Multiculturalism and "The Politics of Recognition."* Princeton: Princeton UP, 1992.

Wah, Fred. "Speak My Language: Racing the Lyric Poetic." *Faking It: Poetics and Hybridity: Critical Writing 1984–1999.* Edmonton: NeWest, 2000. 109–26.

Warrior, Robert. *Tribal Secrets: Recovering American Indian Intellectual Traditions.* Minneapolis: U of Minnesota P, 1995.

Weisman, Adam Paul. "Reading Multiculturalism in the United States and Canada: The Anthological vs. the Cognitive." *University of Toronto Quarterly* 69.3 (2000): 689–715.

Wilkins, Peter. "'Nightmares of Identity': Nationalism and Loss in *Beautiful Losers.*" *Intricate Preparations: Writing Leonard Cohen.* Ed. Stephen Scobie. Toronto: ECW, 2000. 24–50.

———. "Defense of the Realm: Canada's Relationship to the United States in Margaret Atwood's *Surfacing.*" *Yearbook of Research in English and American Literature* 14 (1998): 205–22.

Williamson, Janice. "Jeannette Armstrong: 'what I intended was to connect... and it's happened.'" *Tessera* 12 (1992): 111–29.

Womack, Craig. *Red on Red: Native American Literary Separatism.* Minneapolis: U of Minnesota P, 1999.

Woodcock, George. "Surfacing to Survive: Notes on the Recent Atwood." *Ariel* 4.3 (1973): 16–28.

Zieroth, Dale. "Reclaiming the Body / Reclaiming the Nation: A Process of Surviving Colonization in Dennis Lee's *Civil Elegies and Other Poems.*" *Canadian Literature* 98 (1983): 35–43.

Žižek, Slavoj. "Have Michael Hardt and Antonio Negri Rewritten the Communist Manifesto for the Twenty-First Century?" *Rethinking Marxism* 13.3–4 (2001): 190–98.

———. "The Ideology of Empire and Its Traps." *Empire's New Clothes: Reading Hardt and Negri.* Ed. P. Passavant and J. Dean. New York: Routledge, 2004. 253–64.

———. *Welcome to the Desert of the Real! Five Essays on September 11 and Related Dates.* London: Verso, 2002.

INDEX

A
Agamben, Giorgio, 15, 119–20, 122
Alfred, Taiaiake: colonial inheritance and nationhood, 119; Indigenous autonomy, 119; pan-Native concept, 139. *See also Peace, Power, Righteousness: An Indigenous Manifesto*
American Indian Movement, 123
Anderson, Benedict, 115, 164
anti: capitalist resistance, 145; capitalist work, 6, 11; colonial nationalism, 120; nationalism, 150; racist work, 96, 100
Appiah, Kwame Anthony, 165
Aquin, Hubert, 56
Armstrong, Jeannette, 205; English language, 128. *See also Slash*
Asian Canadian writers, 92
"Asiancy: Making Space for Asian Canadian Writing" (Miki), 173
At the Full and Change of the Moon (Brand), 180
Atwood, Margaret: ambivalence with Canada, 67; Canadian identity and belonging, 28; *The Circle Game*, 158; comments by Djwa, 30–31; comments by Woodcock, 30; dystopic look at global corporatism, 36; Frye's "garrison mentality," 33; *Good Bones*, 158; *The Handmaid's Tale*, 27–28; limits of Canadian nationalism, 23; *Murder in the Dark*, 158; nationalism, claim for, 68; nationalism as defence against international imperialism, 68; national space to resist American imperialism, 55; *Oryx and Crake*, 36–37; *Power Politics*, 158; sponsorship of Lam's book, 161, 166. *See also Surfacing; Survival*

B
Bannerji, Himani, 73, 160
Baudrillard, Jean, 20
Beauregard, Guy, 93, 97
Beautiful Losers (Cohen), 6, 55; alienation of the self, soul, or mind, 59; centennial construction of the nation, 56; comments by Goldie, 64; comments by Hutcheon, 60, 65; comments by Lee, 58–59; comments by Ondaatje, 56, 58; complicity with past, 60–61; fractures within Canada, 56; French domination of Indigenous peoples, 61; history, 68; homoeroticism, 64; metaphysics, 57; as moral fable, 59; nationalism and perversion, 65; nationalism and proto-postmodernism, 55; national politics, problems with, 57; national rhetoric, inability to embrace, 61; 1960s ethos, 55; ontology of

modernity, 59; politics, complex vision of, 56; proto-postmodern novel, 6; Quebec nationalism, 61–63; Quebec possibilities for liberation, 57; search for meaning in history, 60; separation, false promise of, 62; sex/gender dualisms, 64; sexual emancipation *vs.* jealousy, 64; sexually explicit text, 56; sexual politics of the text, 62–64; summary of book, 56–57; void in the world, 61–62. *See also* Cohen, Leonard
Beddoes, Julia, 107
Beedham, Matthew, 95
Bennett, Donna, 73
Bertelsmann Corporation, 158, 161
Bhabha, Homi, 93
Bloodletting and Miraculous Cures (Lam): cosmopolitanism, 180, 201; Scotiabank Giller Prize, 140–41, 159, 163, 166. *See also* Lam, Vincent
Body Music (Lee), 45
Bök, Christian, 107
"Borders" (King), 121–22
Brand, Dionne: *At the Full and Change of the Moon,* 180; belonging excludes women, 185; citizenship as passport to belonging, 185; city and belonging, 180; comments by Goldman, 180–81; comments by Quigley, 181, 183; comments by Saul, 186; compared to *In the Skin of a Lion,* 189; compared to Kingwell, 182; compared to *Slash,* 190; deterritorialization, 181; home and nation-state, 180; *In Another Place, Not Here,* 183, 185; *A Map to the Door of No Return,* 186; migration and displacement, 184; *No Language Is Neutral,* 186; nomadic communities, 184; politics of drifting, 180; question of being, 181; reinscription of bodies within limited borders, 201. *See also What We All Long For*
Brandt, Di, 206–7
Brennan, Timothy, 145, 148–49
Budde, Robert, 173
The Bush Garden (Frye), 42
Butler, Judith, 172

C

"Cadence, Country, Silence: Writing in Colonial Space" (Lee), 45
Canada Council for the Arts, 3, 160
Canada Reads competition [CBC], 106, 161
Canadian diversity, xiii, 73, 159
Canadian Literature, 124
Canadian multiculturalism, 73, 75
Canadian nationalism, 73, 115–16
The Canadian Postmodern (Hutcheon), 67
"Can the Subaltern Speak?" (Spivak), 79, 82, 84, 86
Capital (Marx), 80
CBC (Canadian Broadcasting Corporation), 4; Canada Reads competition, 106, 161
Chapters/Indigo, 158
Chariandy, David, ix
Cheah, Pheng, 165
Chow, Rey, 151
The Circle Game (Atwood), 158
Civil Elegies (Lee), 6, 41; absence as structure for being, 48–49; belief in transcendence, 45; belonging and subjectivity, 51; colonization of Canadian spaces, 44; comments by MacDonald, 44; comments by Naranjo, 45; comments by Zieroth, 44; critique by Lecker, 43, 45; cultural

castration and stunting of vision, 41; deconstruction *vs.* Marxism, 51; "despotic land" of the Canadian Shield, 48; erasure of Indigenous concerns, 51; extraction of Canada's natural resources, 46; gendered perspectives, 51; Governor General's Award, 43; mapping of poem by Kertzer, 45; mobile conceptions of subjectivity, 52; moral determinations for defending Canada, 49; nationalist longing or nostalgia, 6; nationalist politics of the centennial period, 41; nation and space, problems of, 42–43; nations in a global era, 42; objection to ecological destruction, 51; poststructural workings of Canadian–American dialectic, 6; potential for culture in Canada, 42; reference to Frye, 42; reference to Grant, 42; "the void," 44; void, mobile subjectivities in, 52; void, popular embrace of, 50; void, rejection of the, 51; void in the world, 61. See also Lee, Dennis
Clarkson, Adrienne, 162
Coach House Press, 158
Cohen, Leonard: *The Favourite Game*, 56 57; *I'm Your Man* (film), 55; metafictive historiographic consciousness, 67; proto-postmodern discourse, 23. See also *Beautiful Losers*
The Collected Works of Billy the Kid (Ondaatje), 158
The Communist Manifesto (Marx and Engels), 10–11, 14, 16, 80
Conclusion to *Literary History of Canada* (Frye), 32–33, 67
A Critique of Postcolonial Reason (Spivak), 76, 79, 110

D
Dainty Monsters (Ondaatje), 158
Davey, Frank: comments on *Slash*, 115, 125–27; *Post-national Arguments*, 77, 115, 125; post-national state is invisible to citizens, 125; sovereignty and political representation, 77
Deleuze, Gilles: comparison to *Empire*, 145, 149; poststructural thinking, 145; poststructural world, 149; reterritorialization, 172; transnational studies, 149
Derksen, Jeff, 203–5, 207
Derrida, Jacques, 9; comments by Fukuyama, 11–12, 20; comments by Jameson, 21; comments by Spivak, 79–80; concept of history, 21; contemporary biopolitics, analysis of, 15; decentred nature of human society, 19; emancipation in justice, 16; end of Cold War, 12–13; on Marx, 14, 15, 18; nationalism sows hatred, 17–18; new International, 17, 21; *The Other Heading*, 19; techno-economics, 15; undeconstructible messianism, 16. See also *Specters of Marx*
Djwa, Sandra, 30–31
Docherty, Thomas, 5
Doubleday Canada, 161

E
Eagleton, Terry, 6, 19–20
The Eighteenth Brumaire of Louis Napoleon (Marx), 81
Empire (Hardt and Negri), 120, 140, 143; anti-nationalism, 150; Canadian Eurocentrism and racism, 154; comments by Bull, 148; comments by Jameson, 148;

comments by Maurer, 148; communist utopia, 149; comparison to Deleuze, 145, 149; comparison to Guattari, 145; comparison to Shelley, 147; contingent list of demands, 146; endpoint in the multitude, 154; globalization of political and social problems, 143–44; multitude as alternative to imperial rule, 144; multitude lacks tactics, 148; multitude's arrival is inevitable, 149; new *Communist Manifesto* for 21st century, 140; obsolescence of the state, 144; power centre without borders, 144; power of cultural interpretation, 147; power of nation-states, 147; transnational capitalism, 150. *See also* Hardt, Michael, and Antonio Negri

The End of History and the Last Man (Fukuyama), 11

Engels, Friedrich, 10–11. *See also The Communist Manifesto*

F

Fanon, Franz, 115

The Favourite Game (Cohen), 56–57

Fee, Margery, 124

Findlay, Len, 75

First Nations, 4

Foucault, Michel, 15, 20, 119, 173

Frye, Northrop: Atwood *vs.*, 33; *The Bush Garden*, 42; comments on *Surfacing*, 27–28, 32; "garrison mentality," 33; *Literary History of Canada*, 32–33; literature of protest is unhinged, 67; "Where is here?", 32–33; writers and globalization, 71

Fukuyama, Francis: comments by Derrida, 11–12, 20; dialectical materialism and neo-Hegelianism, 14; *The End of History and the Last Man*, 11

Fuller, Danielle, 161

G

Geist magazine, 159, 162

Giller, Doris, 163

Giller Prize: *Bloodletting and Miraculous Cures* (Lam), 140–41; criticism by Henighan, 159, 161–64, 166; for fiction, 161–62; politics of, 141

globalization, 9–10, 75, 157, 208

The Global Soul (Iyer), 184

Goldie, Terry, 64

Good Bones (Atwood), 158

Goto, Hiromi, 92

Governor General's Award: *Civil Elegies* (Lee), 43; *Surrender* (Miki), 170

Gramsci, Antonio, 85

Grant, George: Canada as branch plant of American capitalism, 46; Canada's relationship to modernity, 47; *Lament for a Nation*, 6, 42, 46; modernity as "universal and homogenous state," 47

Grewal, Inderpal, 153

Guattari, Félix: poststructural thinking, 145; poststructural world, 149; reterritorialization, 172

Guha, Ranajit, 85

H

Hall, Stuart, 172

The Handmaid's Tale (Atwood), 27–28

Hardt, Michael, and Antonio Negri: anti-capitalist resistance, 145; anti-colonial nationalism, 120; colonial effects of capital, 152; comments by

Brennan, 145, 148–49; comment by Jameson, 145–46; comments by Miyoshi, 145; comments by Quinby, 150; communal utopia, 149; communist end point, 149; contingent list of demands, 146; deterritorializing model, 172; discourse of opposition, 151; expansive frontier, 151; gender-blindness, 153; immanent politics, 171; *Insurgencies*, 147, 151; materialist teleology, 148, 150; metaphysical category of transcendence, 148; multitude, democracy of the, 144–45; multitude and diversity of struggles, 205; multitude as weapon for undermining capitalism, 146; patriarchal representational practices, 153; political agency and counter-Empire, 121; political struggles and Western sovereign nationalisms, 121; postcolonialism, 75; racial segregation, 115; "refusal of strategy or tactics," 153; rejection of nationalism as structure of sovereignty, 120; resistance movements, 153; socialist strategy *vs.* contingent tactics, 146; social movement struggles, 145; socio-economic transformations, 145; sovereignty and nationhood, 128; theological tone, 144; transnational feminism, 152–53; universalism, 150. *See also* Empire; Multitude
Harper government, 75
Heidegger, Martin, 47
Henighan, Stephen, 159, 161–64, 166
Henry, Michelle, 117
Highway, Tomson, 101
Hobsbawn, Eric, 115, 145
Hoy, Helen, 124

Huggan, Graham, 158
Hutcheon, Linda: *The Canadian Postmodern*, 67; comments on *Beautiful Losers*, 60, 65; historiographic metafiction, 22; models of history, 20; postmodernism, Canadian, 67; postmodernism and Marxism, 9; revelling in the ex-centric, 71

I
Imagined Communities (Anderson), 115
In Another Place, Not Here (Brand), 183, 185
Indigenous peoples, 75
Insurgencies (Negri): comments by Smith, 147; comparison to Žižek, 147; constituent power, 147; new constitutional model, 147; provisional tactics, 147; space and American freedom, 151. *See also* Hardt, Michael, and Antonio Negri
In the Skin of a Lion (Ondaatje), 76, 102, 105; capitalist models of history and knowledge, 108–9; class practices and multiculturalism, 109; comments by Beddoes, 107; comments by Bök, 107; comments by Lundgren, 109; comments by Mackey, 105; comments by Mason, 108; comments by Siemerling, 107; comments by Stacey, 108; comments by Spivak, 110; comments on *Beautiful Losers*, 56, 58; comparison to *Obasan*, 108; cosmopolitan citizenship, undercutting of, 108; cultural politics of class and ethnicity, 107; ethnicity and racialization, 135; history of workers, restoring, 106; insider-and-outsider perspective, 135; politicization of history,

107; politics, surface-level, 106; politics of ethnicity and multiculturalism, 102; revolutionary politics, 76–77; summary of, 106–7. *See also* Ondaatje, Michael

Itsuka (Kogawa), 92; assimilation and norms, 101; being defined from outside, 92; blind faith in democracy, 96; nationalistic ideologies, inadequacy of, 96; notions of tolerance and difference, 96. *See also* Kogawa, Joy

Iyer, Pico, 184

J

Jameson, Fredric: cognitive mapping, 4, 20; comments on Derrida, 21; comments on *Empire*, 148; comments on Hardt and Negri, 145–46; comments on *Specters of Marx*, 20; Marxist insistence on revolution, 21; Marx's legacy, 21; *The Political Unconscious*, 21; on the postmodern, 22; *Postmodernism, or, The Cultural Logic of Late Capitalism*, 20; postmodern / poststructural nexus, 6; psychic life of postmodern world, 21; questions of history, 21; *A Singular Modernity*, 22; social movements and capitalism, 145; weakening of historicity, 20

Japanese-Canadian: internment, 98–99; label, 94, 100; redress movement, 100

"Jerk" (Derksen), 203–5

Justice, Daniel Heath, 116

K

Kamboureli, Smaro, 73, 95, 160
Kant, Immanuel, 164–65
Kaplan, Caren, 153

Kertzer, Jonathan, 45, 154
King, Thomas: "Borders," 121–22; Native literature and colonial encounter, 124; postcolonialism and Native literature, 125
Kingdom of Absence (Lee), 45
Kingwell, Mark, 182
Kiss of the Fur Queen (Highway), 101
Kiyooka, Roy, 92
Klooß, Wolfgang, 72
Knopf Canada, 161
Kogawa, Joy: Canadian nation-state has history of racism, 129; Japanese redress movement, 91. *See also Itsuka*; *Obasan*
Kroetsch, Robert, 56, 71–72
Kymlicka, Will, 73

L

Laclau, Ernesto, 114
Lam, Vincent: sponsored by Atwood, 161, 166. *See also Bloodletting and Miraculous Cures*
Lament for a Nation (Grant), 6, 42, 46
Landry, Donna, 84
Lawrence, Bonita, 119
Lawrence, Margaret, 72
Lecker, Robert, 43, 45, 47
Lee, Dennis, 189; ambivalence with Canada, 67; *Body Music*, 45; "Cadence, Country, Silence: Writing in Colonial Space," 45; comments on *Beautiful Losers*, 58–59; dialectical vision, 44; Governor General's Award, 43; influence of Grant, 46–47; *Kingdom of Absence*, 45; laments history, 68; limits of Canadian nationalism, 23; national space to resist American imperialism, 55; poststructural ethos, 42; *Savage Fields*, 58. *See also Civil Elegies*

Location of Culture (Bhabha), 93
Love Medicine and One Song (Scofield), 205
Lundgren, Jodi, 109

M
MacDonald, R.D., 44
Mackey, Eva, 73, 88, 160; and *In the Skin of a Lion*, 105; and *Obasan*, 95
MacLean, Gerald, 84
MacLennan, Hugh, 31
the man with seven toes (Ondaatje), 158
A Map to the Door of No Return (Brand), 186
Maracle, Lee, 119
Marx, Karl, 10; "Asiatic Mode of Production," 81; *Capital*, 80; *The Eighteenth Brumaire of Louis Napoleon*, 81; legacy of, 14, 21; "The Modern Theory of Colonization," 80–81; small holding peasants, 81–82; *Surveys in Exile*, 81; and the world outside the West, 81
Marxism, 10; deconstruction *vs.*, 51; postmodernism and, 9; poststructuralism, 4, 76, 139
Marxism and Deconstruction (Ryan), 5
Marxist: discourse, poststructural and, 74; insistence on revolution, 21; joke, 18; models of value and capitalist colonization, xiv; traditions in the Third World, 76
Mason, Jody, 108
Massey Commission, 3–4, 31
Massey, Vincent, 3
Mathur, Ashok, 129
Maurer, Bill, 149
Mbembe, Achile, 15
McClelland and Stewart, 4, 161
McLuhan, Marshall, 47

Miki, Roy, 92; "Asiancy: Making Space for Asian Canadian Writing," 173; comments on *Obasan*, 94, 97–98; deconstruction of fixed positions, 172; Governor General's Award, 170; questions of radicalism, 174; racialization of the national landscape, 174; reinscription of bodies within limited borders, 201; "resolutionary" *vs.* "revolutionary" reading, 157; tensions of state multiculturalism, 76. *See also* Surrender
"Mixed Breed Act" (Scofield), 206
Miyoshi, Masao, 145
Moodie, Susanna, ix
Moore, Henry, 43
Moore, Lisa, 163
Mouffe, Chantal, 114
Mukherjee, Arun, 97
Mulroney government, 91
multiculturalism: Canada's state vision of, 88; Canadian, 73, 75; complicity with state, 95; nation-state, diversity and, 151; as partial challenge to structures in Canada, 113; politics of ethnicity and, 102; politics of state, 93; racism and, 76; state discourse and, 94; tensions of state, 76
Multiculturalism Act, 72–73, 91, 94, 160
multicultural literature, 74, 87
multicultural policy, 105
Multitude (Hardt and Negri), 120, 140–41; anti-nationalism, 150; contingent list of demands, 146; globalization of political and social problems, 143–44; transnational capitalism, 150. *See also* Hardt, Michael, and Antonio Negri
Munro, Alice, 161–62
Murder in the Dark (Atwood), 158

N

Naranjo, Isaías, 45
nationalism: anti-, 150; anti-colonial, 120; Canadian, 73, 115–16; Canadian, and racial exclusion, 115; Canadian, limits to, 23; claim for, 68; communities resist racism, oppression and, 195; as defence against international imperialism, 68; globalization and, x; Native, 116; non-Western, 116; perversion and, 65; proto-postmodern opportunities and, 55; Quebec, 61–63; sows hatred, 17–18; as structure of sovereignty, rejection of, 120; tied to sovereignty, 117; trans-, 9, 208; Western sovereign, political struggles and, 121
National Library of Canada, 3
Nazi Germany concentration camps, 120
Negri, Antonio, 15
neo-imperialism, 9, 75
neo-liberalism, 13, 52, 101, 116, 139
Nichol, bp, xiii, 182
No Language Is Neutral (Brand), 186
non-Western nationalism, 116

O

Obasan (Kogawa), 76, 91; anti-racist work, 96, 100; assimilation and politics of recognition, 101; belief in Canadian democracy, 99; Canadian practices of labelling and prejudice, 93; comments by Beauregard, 93, 99; comments by Beedham, 95; comments by Kamboureli, 95; comments by Mackey, 95; comments by Miki, 94, 97–98; comments by Mukherjee, 97; cultural politics, 93; ethnicity and racialization, 135; histories of violence and racism, 92; inclusion, desire for, 100; Japanese Canadian internment, 98–99; Japanese Canadian label, 94, 100; Japanese Canadian redress movement, 100; marginalization, 98; multiculturalism and state discourse, 94; national recuperation, attempts at, 98; oppression of Japanese Canadians, 94; past and its brutal consequences, 99; politics of inclusion, 91; racism and multiculturalism, 76; reconciliation with past, 99, 101; reconfiguration of state, 76; and state multiculturalism, 95; summary of book, 92–93. *See also* Kogawa, Joy
Official Languages Act, 73
Ondaatje, Michael: *The Collected Works of Billy the Kid*, 158; comments on *Beautiful Losers*, 56, 58; *Dainty Monsters*, 158; *the man with seven toes*, 158; *rat jelly*, 158. *See also In the Skin of a Lion*
Ong, Aihwa, 184
Oryx and Crake (Atwood), 36–37
The Other Heading (Derrida), 19

P

Passavant, Paul, 149
Peace, Power, Righteousness: An Indigenous Manifesto (Alfred), 77, 114–16; comparison to *Slash*, 114, 117; genocide of Indigenous people, 118; Indigenous autonomy, 118–19; self-representation and unfixed political body, 119; sovereignty and Indigenous struggles, 117; sovereignty as coercive Western notion, 118. *See also* Alfred, Taiaiake

Philip, M. NourbeSe, 173
Political Treatise (Spinoza), 151
The Political Unconscious (Jameson), 21
postcolonialism, 76, 125, 139
postcolonial studies, xiv, 75–76, 208
Postmodernism, or, The Cultural Logic of Late Capitalism (Jameson), 20
Post-national Arguments (Davey), 77, 115, 125
poststructural: discourse, 74; ethos, 42; Marxist discourse and, 74; nexus, postmodern, 6; questions, 76; thinking, nomadic, 145; workings of Canadian–American dialectic, 6
poststructuralism, 4, 76, 139; postcolonialism, Indigenous thinking and Marxism, 139; postmodern tensions and Marxism, 4
Power Politics (Atwood), 158
Prakash, Gyan, 83
Prasad, Madhava, 3
Press Gang, 158
Prison Notebooks (Gramsci), 85

Q
Quigley, Ellen, 181, 183
Quinby, Lee, 150

R
Rabinovitch, Elana, 163
Rabinovitch, Jack, 163
radical democracy, 143
Random House, 161
rat jelly (Ondaatje), 158
Razack, Sherene, 160
Redhill, Michael, 162
Red on Red: Native American Literary Separatism (Womack), 77, 114–16
Robbins, Bruce, 164–65
Roughing It in the Bush (Moodie), ix
Roy, Arundhati, 204
Royal Commission on National Arts, Letters and Sciences, 3
Ryan, Michael, 5
Ryga, George, 123

S
Sassen, Saskia, 172, 183
Saul, Joanne, 186
Savage Fields (Lee), 58
"Scattered Speculations on the Question of Value" (Spivak), 87–88
Scofield, Gregory: *Love Medicine and One Song,* 205; "Mixed Breed Act," 206
Scotiabank Giller Prize, 141, 159, 163, 166
Scott, Jennifer, 164
Sedo, DeNel Rehberg, 161
Shelley, Percy, 147
Siemerling, Winfried, 107
A Singular Modernity (Jameson), 22
Sister Vision, 158
Slash (Armstrong), 77, 113; activism of Indigenous people, 123; activist movements, 139; borders not recognized by Indians, 122; Canada has questionable right of existence, 129; not a Canadian novel, 129; and Canadian policy, 125; colonial belonging, 131; comments by Davey, 115, 125–27; comments by Fee, 124; comments by Hoy, 124; comments by King, 124–25; compared to comments by Laclau and Mouffe, 114; comments by Ryga, 123; community revitalization and growth, 77; comparison to "Borders," 121–22; comparison to *Imagined Communities,* 115; comparison to *Peace, Power, Righteousness,* 114, 117; comparison to *Red on Red,*

114; configuration of the dominant, 114; critique of colonial governments in North America, 113; existence as a means of expressing politics, 190; fictionalized history of Indigenous protest movement, 130; Indigenous assimilation, 123; Indigenous-centred worldview, 129; Indigenous knowledges, 77; Indigenous struggles of self-determination, 114; insider-and-outsider perspective, 136; limitations of the Canadian label, 131; pan-Native consciousness, 131; pan-Native sense of self, 130; power and legacy of colonialism, 135; racial segregation, 115; residential schools, 124; resistance from Indigenous-centred perspective, 205; self-determination and self-representation, 114; sovereignty and nationhood, 113; state's relationship to cultural diversity, 123; Western notions of sovereignty, 121; white settler-invader populations, 77; women, deep appreciation of, 130. *See also* Armstrong, Jeannette
Smith, Linda Tuhiwai, 77
Smith, Neil, 147
Social Sciences and Humanities Research Council of Canada, 4
Soucouyant (Chariandy), ix
Specters of Marx: The State of the Debt, The Work of Mourning, and the New International (Derrida): anti-capitalist work, 6, 11; comments by Baudrillard, 20; comments by Eagleton, 19–20; comments by Jameson, 20; Marxism's demise, 10; Marxist joke, 18; messianic elements, 150; rejects Marxist dialectic, 13.

See also Derrida, Jacques
Spinoza, Benedict de, 148, 151
Spivak, Gayatri Chakravorty: "Can the Subaltern Speak?", 79, 82, 84, 86; comments by Landry, 84; comments by MacLean, 84; comments by Prakash, 83; comments on Derrida, 79–80; comments on Gramsci, 85; comments compared to *In the Skin of a Lion,* 110; critique of Marx's *Contribution,* 81; *A Critique of Postcolonial Reason,* 76, 79, 110; hegemony, 139; historical record of women, 110; Marxist traditions in the Third World, 76; Marx and the world outside the West, 81; openness of identity, 87; oppressions of capitalism, 80; postcolonial cultural critic, 79; poststructural questions, 76; "Scattered Speculations on the Question of Value," 87–88; struggles with subaltern speech, 84; subaltern insurgency, 85; subaltern woman cannot speak, 84–85; universal equivalents, 87; "white men saving brown women from brown men," 81; women and the global South, 76
The Spivak Reader (Spivak), 84
Stacey, Robert, 108
Subaltern Studies Group, 85
Surfacing (Atwood), 6, 27, 158; American corruption in the Canadian sphere, 30; American-free margins of society, 32; American *vs.* Canadian values, 34–35; Canada–US split, 33; Canadian community, ideal of unified, 36; Canadian identity and belonging, 28; Canadian resistance needs untangling, 37; cognitive map of

Canada–US divisions, 37; cognitive mapping of transnational world, 29; comments by Frye, 27–28, 32; comments by Woodcock, 30; erasure of French and Indigenous perspectives, 35; Hugh MacLennan's two solitudes *vs.*, 31; man's hold on power, 37; national body for collective empowerment, 35; nationalist longing or nostalgia, 6; national resistance to imperialism, 41; recap of book, 28; re-creation of stereotypical images, 34; stark naturalism, 36; survival as dominant theme, 31; United States as a colonizing nation, 33; US–Canadian cross-border tension, 29; victimhood, 31–32, 34; "Where is here?" (Frye), 32–33. *See also* Atwood, Margaret

Surrender (Miki), 140, 169, 179; classical metaphysics and, 175; control and domination, 170; deterritorialization, 172, 177; disciplinary forces imposing external order, 170; disunity and the lyrical "I," 174; first-person voice, 176; Governor General's Award, 170; identity and stability, 177; identity as an island, 170; Japanese Canadian, dispersal and imprisonment of, 175; legacies of national and state structures, 170; notions of the self, 169; reterritorialization under Empire, 205; subjectivity, 169–70, 179; subjectivity under globalization, 141; subject position, destabilized, 177; subject within national and globalizing spaces, 171; transnational politics, 140. *See also* Miki, Roy

Surveys in Exile (Marx), 81

Survival (Atwood), xii, xiii; Atwood's argument, 6; cognitive map, 37; comments by Frye, 31, 33; creative nonvictimization, 36; national discussion of Canada, 27; national sado-masochism, 31; as "propaganda for Canadian literature," 30; surviving against nature, Americans, and oneself, 31; victimhood, 31. *See also* Atwood, Margaret

T
Taylor, Charles, 72
Thomson, Tom, 48
transnational capitalism, 10, 12, 22, 71, 80, 115, 150, 177
transnationalism, 5, 9, 114, 116, 141, 208
Transnational Muscle Cars, 203
Trudeau, Pierre, 175
Tucker-Abramson, Myka, 164

U
uTOpia: Towards a New Toronto (McBride and Wilcox), 184

W
Wah, Fred, 173
Weaver, Jace, 116
Weisman, Adam Paul, 73
What We All Long For (Brand), 140, 179, 181, 183, 189; belonging in a racist space, 186; communities divided by ethno-cultural lines, 187; communities resist racism, nationalism, and oppression, 195; cosmopolitan celebration, 195; cosmopolitan ideal, 194; desire for inclusivity, 195; ethno-cultural groups, 195; ethno-national borders in lives, 190; fears of miscegenation,

188; imperial forms of capitalism, 142; migrations, complex web of, 186; nomadic communities, 184; racially determined structures of society, 189; resistance politics, 142; reterritorialization under Empire, 205; reterritorializing gaze, 196; transnational politics, 140. *See also* Brand, Dionne

Wiebe, Rudy, 72

Winter, Michael, 162

Womack, Craig: colonial inheritance and nationhood, 119; comments by Henry, 117; comments by Lawrence, 119; Indigenous autonomy, 119; Indigenous nationalists, 116–17; Indigenous national resistance, 77; nationalism tied to sovereignty, 117; Native nationalism, 116; pan-Native concept, 139; *Red on Red: Native American Literary Separatism,* 77, 114–16; sense of national continuity, 116; tribal specific concerns, 116

Woodcock, George, 30, 33

World Social Forum, 204

The World We Want (Kingwell), 182

Writing Thru Race conference, 82

Z

Zieroth, Dale, 44

Žižek, Slavoj, 22–23, 147–48

Books in the TransCanada Series
Published by Wilfrid Laurier University Press

Smaro Kamboureli and Roy Miki, editors
Trans.Can.Lit: Resituating the Study of Canadian Literature / 2007 / xviii + 234 pp. / ISBN 978-0-88920-513-0

Smaro Kamboureli
Scandalous Bodies: Diasporic Literature in English Canada / 2009 / xviii + 270 pp. / ISBN 978-1-55458-064-4

Kit Dobson
Transnational Canadas: Anglo-Canadian Literature and Globalization / 2009 / xviii + 240 pp. / ISBN 978-1-55458-063-7

www.ingramcontent.com/pod-product-compliance
Lightning Source LLC
Chambersburg PA
CBHW071154070526
44584CB00019B/2792